GOD IN FRANCE

STUDIES IN PHILOSOPHICAL THEOLOGY, 28

Editorial Profile:
Philosophical theology is the study of philosophical problems which arise in
reflection upon religion, religious beliefs and theological doctrines.

1   H. de Vries, *Theologie im Pianissimo & zwischen Rationalität und
    Dekonstruktion*, Kampen, 1989
2   S. Breton, *La pensée du rien*, Kampen, 1992
3   Ch. Schwöbel, *God: Action and Revelation*, Kampen, 1992
4   V. Brümmer (ed.), *Interpreting the Universe as Creation*, Kampen, 1991
5   L.J. van den Brom, *Divine Presence in the World*, Kampen, 1993
6   M. Sarot, *God, Passibility and Corporeality*, Kampen, 1992
7   G. van den Brink, *Almighty God*, Kampen 1993
8   P.-C. Lai, *Towards a Trinitarian Theology of Religions: A Study of Paul
    Tillich's Thought*, Kampen, 1994
9   L. Velecky, *Aquinas' Five Arguments in the* Summa Theologiae *Ia 2, 3*, Kampen,
    1994
10 W. Dupré, *Patterns in Meaning. Reflections on Meaning and Truth in Cultural
    Reality, Religious Traditions, and Dialogical Encounters*, Kampen, 1994
11 P.T. Erne, *Lebenskunst. Aneignung ästhetischer Erfahrung*, Kampen, 1994
12 U. Perone, *Trotz/dem Subjekt*, Leuven, 1998
13 H.J. Adriaanse, *Vom Christentum aus: Aufsätze und Vorträge zur Religions-
    philosophie*, Kampen, 1995
14 D.A. Pailin, *Probing the Foundations: A Study in Theistic Reconstruction*,
    Kampen, 1994
15 M. Potepa, *Schleiermachers hermeneutische Dialektik*, Kampen, 1996
16 E. Herrmann, *Scientific Theory and Religious Belief. An Essay on the
    Rationality of Views of Life*, Kampen, 1995
17 V. Brümmer & M. Sarot (eds.), *Happiness, Well-Being and the Meaning of Life.
    A Dialogue of Social Science and Religion*, Kampen, 1996
18 T.L. Hettema, *Reading for Good. Narrative Theology and Ethics in the Joseph
    Story from the Perspective of Ricoeur's Hermeneutics*, Kampen, 1996
19 H. Düringer, *Universale Vernunft und partikularer Glaube. Eine theologische
    Auswertung des Werkes von Jürgen Habermas*, Leuven, 1999
20 E. Dekker, *Middle Knowledge*, Leuven, 2000
21 T. Ekstrand, *Max Weber in a Theological Perspective*, Leuven, 2000
22 C. Helmer & K. De Troyer (eds.), *Truth: Interdisciplinary Dialogues in a
    Pluralist Age*, Leuven, 2003
23 L. Boeve & L.P. Hemming (eds.), *Divinising Experience. Essays in the History
    of Religious Experience from Origen to Ricœur*, Leuven, 2004
24 P.D. Murray, *Reason, Truth and Theology in Pragmatist Perspective*, Leuven,
    2004
25 S. van Erp, *The Art of Theology. Hans Urs von Balthasar's Theological Aes-
    thetics and the Foundations of Faith*, Leuven, 2004
26 T.A. Smedes, *Chaos, Complexity, and God. Divine Action and Scientism*,
    Leuven, 2004
27 R. Re Manning, *Theology at the End of Culture. Paul Tillich's Theology of Cul-
    ture and Art*, Leuven, 2004

GOD IN FRANCE

Eight Contemporary French Thinkers on God

EDITED BY

PETER JONKERS

&

RUUD WELTEN

PEETERS
LEUVEN – PARIS – DUDLEY, MA
2005

Library of Congress Cataloging-in-Publication Data

God in Frankrijk. English.
  God in France : eight contemporary French thinkers on God / edited by Peter Jonkers &
Ruud Welten.
    p. cm. -- (Studies in philosophical theology)
  Includes bibliographical references.
  ISBN 90-429-1570-6 (alk. paper)
    1. God. 2. Philosophy, French. I. Jonkers, Peter, 1954- II. Welten, Ruud, 1962-
III. Title. IV. Series.

BD573.G6313 2005
211'.092'233--dc22

Enlarged translation of: *God in Frankrijk. Zes hedendaagse Franse filosofen
over God.* Budel 2003, Damon.

© 2005 – Peeters – Bondgenotenlaan 153 – 3000 Leuven – Belgium.

ISBN 90-429-1570-6
D. 2005/0602/17

TABLE OF CONTENTS

GOD IN FRANCE. HEIDEGGER'S LEGACY

PETER JONKERS

1. God in France?

Why a book about God in France? What is the justification for applying a nation-bound criterion to philosophy, especially when it addresses the question of God? After all, this issue has haunted philosophy ever since its origin and surpasses all national, linguistic and cultural boundaries. One of the reasons to opt for this approach in this book is connected with what is usually called the hermeneutic turn in philosophy. As a consequence of this, philosophy can no longer present itself as a *philosophia perennis* (eternal philosophy), claiming to transcend the limitations of time and space because of the universality of thinking and the absoluteness of its object, God. After more than a century of heated debates on the legitimacy of this claim, most contemporary philosophers have come to the awareness that philosophizing is always done by someone and, therefore, always embedded in specific situations and contexts. This inevitable contextuality is also involved when philosophers approach the question of God, whether in France or in any other country. The French thinkers, introduced in this book, obviously share this awareness: their thinking about God is situated in a specific cultural, philosophical, and religious environment. On the other hand, this context also creates a kind of common universe of discourse; it gives colour to the lively discussions in which these thinkers are engaged, both through their work and personal contacts. With the book *God in France,* we want to map out this French universe of discourse and give an account of the discussions going on in it by analyzing the thoughts and ideas of a number of the most important participants specifically concerning the themes of God and religion.

Subsequently, the question arises why this book deals with French thinking specifically, and not German, English or Italian. What is the relevance of this focus? Moreover, this book does not offer an introduction to French thinking as such, but discusses a number of leading contemporary philosophers who, in spite of all the differences between them, are apparently engaged in thinking and writing about God and religion. How should we interpret this engagement, which is quite unexpected from the perspective of the dominant trends in post-war twentieth century? Is it purely coincidental or is it a sign of something else? Of course, the authors of the various chapters of this book will have to make clear the relevance of the thinkers they discuss. But as a first, tentative indication, I want to point to the following. While studying these philosophies, one is struck by their sensitivity to classic religious questions, e.g., what is the way in which God in Himself and His relation to the world can be conceived? how we can name the Unnameable? etc. One should notice, however, that most of the thinkers discussed in this book approach these age-old religious issues from a philosophical perspective. In fact, they use religious ideas in a *heuristic* way: they are convinced that both the content of these ideas and the way in which they are understood in religion can shed new light on important philosophical questions. As such, this heuristic use of ideas that are external to philosophy itself is nothing new: one can think of Descartes' and Leibniz's use of mathematics as a paradigm for all true knowledge, Marx's stress on the importance of economics for a better philosophical understanding of modern society, Heidegger's use of the poems of Hölderlin to express the true sense of Being. But with regard to the thinkers being discussed in this book, the intriguing question is why they use, in an age of secularism and atheism, *religious* ideas? Furthermore, what is the philosophical point they want to make with such ideas? In this introduction, I will try to answer these questions. But besides their philosophical relevance, these interpretations of religious and theological experiences and ideas, symbols and texts also offer unexpected opportunities for a fresh approach to a lot of traditional, sometimes almost forgotten, aspects of Jewish and Christian religion. Without saying that French philosophy is unique on this point, the contributors to this book want to show, nevertheless, that it offers a recognizable, renewing contribution to contemporary philosophy in general, and to philosophical and theological thinking about God and religion in particular.

Of course, the bond between the philosophers gathered in this book largely exceeds their common interest in a current philosophical and religious issue. They all have been educated in a long French tradition of thought, including classical philosophers like Descartes, Malebranche, Pascal, and Bergson, and are marked by it. In the course of the twentieth century, however, a number of new ideas and concepts, most of them coming from other philosophical traditions, have enriched traditional French philosophy and given it its current form. In this introduction,

I want to pay attention, in some detail, to a few of these ideas and concepts, thereby restricting myself to those elements which are particularly relevant to the way in which these philosophers approach the issues of God and religion. In the first place, I will refer to Hegel's philosophy of the absolute spirit, Nietzsche's destruction of metaphysics and Christianity, and Husserl's phenomenology. But besides these, the philosophy of Heidegger has probably had the most profound influence on contemporary French thinking, as I will show in the next sections.[1] In this respect, I will analyze both Heidegger's critique of onto-theology and his attempt to lay bare the realm of the holy as being the only element in which the question of a 'divine God' can come up. The works of these philosophers are not only important to gain insight into the backgrounds of contemporary French philosophy, but also mark current thinking about God and religion in general.

From a wider perspective, one could even argue that, on the one hand, Hegel's idea of thinking the whole of reality, including thinking itself, in terms of a manifestation of the absolute idea which realizes itself through this process and, on the other hand, Nietzsche's radical undermining of the same, make up the concise, philosophical expressions of two fundamental orientations of modern culture. In some sense, they define the domain in which our ideas and concepts of truth and reality, humans and their values receive their content and shape. Therefore, it is not surprising that the philosophers addressed in this book do not want to separate themselves from the profound insights of these great philosophers, who, paradoxically, are all of German origin. On the contrary, they absorb them by interpreting them in their own, French way.

Hegel's philosophy can, for good reasons, be seen as the apogee of metaphysical thinking about God or the Absolute. He states that "the task that touches the interest of philosophy most nearly at the present moment [is] to put God back again at the peak of philosophy, the unique *principium essendi* and *cognoscendi* [principle of Being and knowledge], after all this time in which he has been put *beside* other finite things."[2] To put it in an even more fundamental way, the only content of

---

[1] For a penetrating analysis in support of my thesis on the importance of Heidegger for French philosophy cf. D. Janicaud, *Heidegger en France. I. Récit.* Paris, Albin Michel, 2001, pp. 478-489.

[2] G.W.F Hegel, *Gesammelte Werke. Band 4, Jenaer kritische Schriften.* Hamburg, Felix Meiner, 1968, p. 179 [*Between Kant and Hegel. Texts in the Development of Post-Kantian Idealism.* Albany, SUNY, 1985, p. 299]. See also: G.W.F. Hegel, *Gesammelte Werke. Band 11, Wissenschaft der Logik, erster Band.* Hamburg, Felix Meiner, 1978, p. 38.

philosophy is to think the self-movement of the Absolute or the complete self-revelation of God as a necessary, systematically coherent whole. This becomes pre-eminently clear in the *Science of Logic (Wissenschaft der Logik)* in which Hegel develops the basic concepts of thinking, which are at the same time the fundamental categories of reality. Precisely because the whole point of this science is to think *basic concepts*, it cannot take things too easy by just stating them or 'finding' them in an empirical and coincidental way. On the contrary, these fundamental categories can only derive their foundational character from being developed in a systematic, necessary way from an absolute ground, *viz.*, God or the absolute idea. The completion of this movement coincides with the return to its origin. Philosophy, being the only science that is able to think the unfolding of the absolute idea in all its necessary moments, is therefore the only real science. It appears as a closed whole in which essentially everything can be understood. For all these reasons, Hegel's *Science of Logic* is both ontology, science of Being, and theology, science of God.[3] The importance of Hegel's system and, particularly, the *Logic* in the history of Western philosophy leads to the conclusion that the whole of western metaphysics is dominated by an onto-theological structure. According to Heidegger, this philosophical project reaches its apex in Hegel's philosophy; its full material and cultural realization is technology, which plays a preponderant role in contemporary western society.

Nietzsche's aphoristic writings can be read as the most radical undermining of Hegel's project, his philosophical 'science'. The significance of Nietzsche's work for contemporary French philosophy can hardly be overestimated. In his view, subject and object, God and the world are but fictions and interpretations, the visible outcome of a hidden will to power. Metaphysics is a kind of '*Hinterwelt*', the establishment of an imaginary, 'true' or 'divine' world (cfr. Plato's world of ideas) *behind* ('*hinter*') the real world ('*Welt*') of physical powers in which mankind is actually living. From this perspective, Christianity, which avows its faith in this *Hinterwelt* and links a morality of asceticism and denial of the world with it, is nothing but 'Platonism of the people'. Nietzsche recapitulates his refusal of God and religion in the well-known slogan 'God

[3] This reading of Hegel is to a large extent inspired by Heidegger. Cf. M. Heidegger, Die onto-theo-logische Verfassung der Metaphysik. In: Idem, *Identität und Differenz*. Pfüllingen, Neske, 1957, pp. 31ff. [M. Heidegger, The onto-theo-logical constitution of metaphysics. In: Idem, *Identity and difference*. New York, Harper, 1969, pp. 42ff.].

is dead'. The word 'God' not only stands for Christian religion, but also, more generally, for the whole universe of eternal truths, of univocal references to an objective world, of fixed values towards which man can orientate his life, and of stable social relations. In sum, 'God' stands for everything humans can rely on for their orientation in life. Only when, as is the case in modern culture, this whole reliable universe has reached the end of its life cycle, do humans fully realize the tragedy of its existence. In combination with Freud's rejection of religion as an infantile projection, Nietzsche's ideas have doubtlessly been the most 'fruitful' breeding ground for atheism, which dominates contemporary culture. His 'hammering' at Christian religion has made both philosophical and religious discourse about God a highly precarious, and for many people even implausible, enterprise. It inevitably determines to a large extent the intellectual climate in which all humans, including the philosophers of this book, are living and thinking. In particular, this means that they all, in one way or another, accept atheism as a given element of contemporary culture, implying that they will have to pass through it in order to be able to bring up God in their thinking.

The last philosopher in this line of thinking is Husserl and his phenomenological method. Almost all French philosophers of the twentieth century have been influenced by Husserl. Generally speaking, phenomenology means the theory or study of appearances. In principle, it can examine all kinds of appearances. In this sense, phenomenology of religion studies in an empirical way the phenomenon of religion, which implies that it does not ask for its transcendent origin. Ricoeur uses the term phenomenology in this way.[4] However, Husserl's phenomenology diverges from this empirical approach, since he focuses on the phenomenon of appearing as such. Phenomenology describes consciousness, departing from its orientation to something: consciousness is not a closed entity, but is always consciousness of something. Technically formulated, this implies that phenomenology focuses on intentionality. Particularly through the reception of Husserl's work by Sartre and Merleau-Ponty, phenomenology has earned an important place in post-war French philosophy. Philosophers like Ricoeur, Derrida, Levinas, Henry, and Marion have studied Husserl's writings thoroughly and make use of the phenomenological method in various ways. But in the work of some of them an important shift takes place with regard to their conception of phenomenology. They criticize the central role of intentionality in

---

[4] Cf. The contribution of Theo de Boer on Ricoeur.

Husserl's phenomenology, thus initiating a new, non-intentional phenomenology. Especially where the question of God is concerned, the primacy of intentionality leads to the insurmountable problem that God can
only be thought as the one to which consciousness orients itself, as if He
were a counterpart of man. But then the question arises whether the God
of revelation, the God of the faithful, and of the theologian addresses
Himself to us rather than the other way round?

2. A turn to religion?

The theme that the authors in this book are examining, and which makes
up its systematic core, also asks for some explanation. Traditionally, in
philosophy the issue of God comes up in the context of a specific part of
metaphysics, *viz.*, natural theology. In this discipline, philosophers think
with the help of natural reason only, that is to say, without appealing to
(supernatural) revelation and all kinds of theological premises, about
questions like the relation between the contingency of the world and
God as its absolute ground, the rationality of a governing, providential
principle in the world, the sense of human freedom in relation to God's
absoluteness, etc. Generally speaking, natural theology rests on the presupposition that there is an analogy of being between our philosophical
ideas about (the basic structures of) the world as such and God as its
absolute ground. Since Heidegger, this approach is usually called onto-
theology. In the previous section, we saw that Hegel's philosophy is
generally considered as the fulfillment of this kind of metaphysics. After
Hegel, philosophy has taken a completely different direction and even
explicitly turned away from dialectically comprehending the Absolute
Spirit towards a thinking of reality from the perspective of the material
infrastructure (Marx), the individual (Kierkegaard), the will to power
(Nietzsche), or the positive sciences (positivism). This tendency was
already apparent in the philosophies of the second half of the nineteenth
century, but it only became a general trend in twentieth-century philosophy. To take (again) the example of Heidegger, he is deeply impressed
by the force of Hegel's philosophy and the monumental character of his
conceptual system. But, on the other hand, he explicitly refuses to be
carried away by the dialectical movement of Hegel's philosophy in
which all negativity, obscurity, and externality is eventually 'sublated'
in a complete manifestation of the Absolute. Heidegger tries, in other
words, to overcome metaphysics as onto-theology by taking 'a step

back'. In this way, he wants to lead thinking outside onto-theology, which, ever since Plato, has been the unquestioned essence of western thinking. In this way, he wants to clear the way for what has remained unthought in metaphysics.

Numerous twentieth-century French philosophers carry out a similar movement, to a large extent, under the influence of the pertinent questions raised by Heidegger. They, too, consider Hegel's system as the fulfillment of the project of reason to penetrate into the essence of reality in all its necessary coherence. But, just like Heidegger, they want to deconstruct this ideal of rationality by calling for attention to all kinds of inevitable, but hardly noticed, interruptions of this project. They point to an externality which cannot be integrated in thinking, to a deferment of what thinking considers to be objectively present to the mind's eye, to the dissemination of what intellectual intuition tries to grasp at a glance, to strategies of indirect speech in order (not) to speak about God, etc. However, these philosophers do not consider their critique of metaphysics in general, and of natural theology in particular to be the definitive verdict about man's capacity to speak philosophically about God. They not only see new opportunities to speak about God outside or at least in the margin of traditional metaphysics, but also testify with their work to a philosophical urgency to do so. This is not the result of a kind of apologetic need to save (faith in) God in these 'godforsaken' times. Rather, they consider the way in which the Bible and Christian mystics speak about God as showing a sensitivity to a radical mystery, which, time and again, eludes notice of traditional metaphysics in spite or just because of its thinking force. This sensitivity serves for them as a heuristic means to get a glimpse of aspects of truth and Being, man and values across metaphysical thinking. Therefore, they give expression to this mystery in their philosophies: it helps them to free philosophical thinking of the dominance of instrumental, technical, 'totalizing' rationality and its all too visible consequences in contemporary society. These age-old sources of (Christian) religion testify to a persistent search for God as the radical Other, in combination with an extremely critical reserve with regard to any result that wants to present itself as definitive.

Most of the authors presented in this book not only take a distance from the traditional metaphysical discourse about God, but also see themselves as *philosophers, not as theologians or religious authors*. Therefore, they take a rather distanced attitude with regard to religion and theology as such. As the next chapters will show, this distance varies individually. One of the authors, J. -Y. Lacoste, is a (Roman

Catholic) theologian. There is a chapter on his work in this primarily philosophical book because his theology is heavily dependent on the philosophical insights which are discussed in the other chapters of this book, especially those of Heidegger and Marion. But the large majority of the authors being discussed in this book are philosophers. Some of them, like Ricoeur, Girard, Levinas, and Marion, want to contribute to philosophy of religion, and personally profess Christianity or Judaism. This (implicitly or explicitly) gives colour to their thinking, without implying that they want to be theologians. For example, it is often shown that Judaism colours Levinas's thinking, but he himself repeatedly stressed the strictly philosophical character of his work and refused to be considered as a religious author. Other philosophers, in contrast, like Derrida and Lyotard, have a much more atypical and contrary relation with religion, and are not concerned at all about the religious consequences of their work. In any case, this means that, generally speaking, their use of religious ideas and concepts is not so much for the sake of religion as such, but is primarily motivated by their *philosophical* interest. For all these reasons, it seems to me incorrect to interpret the attention of contemporary (French) philosophy for God and religion as a turn to religion or theology, as some do.[5]

According to Dominique Janicaud, French phenomenology has made a clear shift, taking it to a metaphysico-theological context. Whereas at first, under the influence of Sartre's interpretation of Husserl, the transcendental ego was the central focus of phenomenology, the attention of French phenomenologists shifted after the second World War to themes that break open the classic idea of intentionality. To give an example of this, the later Merleau-Ponty uses the concept of intertwining (*entrelacs*) as a metaphor to show that everything visible is embraced in a latency that is the flesh of things.[6] But above all, he breaks the one-way movement implied by Husserlian intentionality. 'Looking at' is always 'being looked at' as well. Levinas also becomes a critic of Husserl. He stresses the unconditional externality of the Other, thus surpassing the boundaries of intentionality. According to Janicaud, the direction taken by these ways of thinking shows that they are motivated by a non-phenomenological,

---

[5] Cf. D. Janicaud, *Le tournant théologique de la phénoménologie française*. Combas, Editions de l'éclat, 1991 [D. Janicaud, *Phenomenology and the "Theological Turn". The French Debate*. New York, Fordham University Press, 2000]. H. de Vries, *Philosophy and the Turn to Religion*. Baltimore, John Hopkins University Press, 1999.

[6] D. Janicaud, *Le tournant théologique de la phénoménologie française*, p. 13 [D. Janicaud, *Phenomenology and the "Theological Turn"*, p. 24].

'metaphysical' desire. He states that this turn presupposes a meta-physico-theological montage prior to philosophical writing.[7] For Levinas, the radical Other is not a purely philosophical concept, but has also a trace of the God of the Bible within him. In this way, theology enters French phenomenology. But the introduction of this extraneous element implies that the Husserlian patterns of thought no longer determine the course of this kind of philosophy. It has become a phenomenology of what does *not* show itself. After Merleau-Ponty and Levinas, Marion and Henry have continued the so-called 'theological turn of phenomenology'; Marion stresses the original givenness of every phenomenon, and Henry subordinates the classic phenomenological description of the phenomenon to the essence of phenomenality.[8]

Well, Janicaud is obviously right when he states that post-war French phenomenology has taken a much more critical attitude towards the primacy of the transcendental ego, and thus took a completely different direction in comparison to Sartre and the early Merleau-Ponty. But I question his qualification of this development as a theological turn. It goes without saying that important notions in twentieth-century French philosophy — like the flesh, the intrusion of the other in the self, Heidegger's turning (*Kehre*) and Marion's interpretation of it, and the analogy between phenomenality and the absolute put forward by Henry — doubtlessly relate phenomenology to all kinds of questions, which traditionally belong to the field of metaphysics. But, for several reasons, the introduction of these notions cannot and should not be interpreted as a 'metaphysico-theological montage'. First of all, this interpretation puts the philosophical analysis of these notions on par with natural theology, thus uncritically mixing up philosophy with religion and onto-theology. This is especially untenable with regard to the philosophers that Janicaud discusses in support of his interpretation. Of all the points that these philosophers have in common, their persistent attempt to develop a thinking of transcendence that departs from strictly philosophical points of view and their explicit aim to keep it as far away as possible from

---

[7] *Ibid.*, p. 15 [*Ibid.*, p. 27].

[8] *Ibid.*, pp. 19-20 [*Ibid.*, p. 32-34].

[9] At least as far as Henry is concerned, but also more in general, Janicaud finds this theological turn highly problematic. His challenge does not bear on Henry's quite respectable spiritual intention, often of an admirable tenor, "but on his strange stubbornness to install this research (essentially fragile and secret, if not esoteric) at the centre of a disciplinary apparatus whose principles are all formulated in precisely the rational, unifying, Western terms intended to be challenged. Cf. *Ibid.*, p. 21 [*Ibid.*, p. 33].

onto-theology and apologetics, are probably the most important ones. Moreover, Janicaud's reproach of a metaphysico-theological montage fails to recognize that these thinkers really try to renew philosophy. This renewal consists in asking, from a *philosophical* perspective, whether there can be a givenness which goes *beyond* onto-theology, transcending our (power of) thinking, but which at the same time moves us most profoundly and throws us out of balance.

Hent de Vries uses the expression 'the turn to religion' mainly as the title for a new philosophical platform: it does not so much offer an interpretation of recent developments in contemporary philosophy, but rather urges philosophers to make a turn to religion. De Vries comes to this suggestion on the authority of Derrida, or more specifically, from his essay *Faith and Knowledge: the Two Sources of 'Religion' at the Limits of Mere Reason* (*Foi et savoir: les deux sources de la 'religion' aux limites de la simple raison*), to which he attributes an exemplary position in the contemporary philosophical landscape.[10] It would be naïve and illusory to think that the sort of religion to which De Vries wants to return in his book has any reference "to a historical presence, to a delitimable body of writings, or to an intellectual or emotional category that at some time or other may have had the potential of somehow and somewhere remaining itself or intact, regardless of its apparent metamorphoses."[11] Nevertheless, particularly in the work of Derrida and Levinas, he recognizes a lot of motives of thought that can be characterized as religious. The purpose of these (decidedly critical, non-dogmatic and even heterodox) motives is to:

> ...illuminate the unthought, unsaid, or unseen of a philosophical logos that, not only in the guise of modern reason, but from its earliest deployment, tends to forget, repress, or sublate the very *religio* (*relegere, religare,* or relation without relation, as Levinas and, following him, Derrida, would have it) to which these motives testify [...since] the apparent negativity of the unthought (and unsaid or unseen) seeks refuge in the idiom and practices of the positive religions, especially in the most heterodox of their offshoots, those epitomized by negative or apophatic theology, mysticism, messianism, and apocalyptics.[12]

All this shows that De Vries's turn to religion should be interpreted as a way to describe philosophy's renewed attention for all kinds of otherness, which (traditional) philosophical thinking is unable to conceive.

[10] H. de Vries, *Philosophy and the Turn to Religion*, p. 3.
[11] *Ibid.*, p. 8.
[12] *Ibid.*, pp. 5-6.

All speaking and writing includes an *à — Dieu*, a structural orientation towards the totally other or towards the radically singular, that is to say towards 'God' or whatever is coming instead of this figure (term, reference). This path is more plausible and effective than the alleged secularisms, humanisms, and fideisms, which paralyze philosophy, because they deprive it of the idea of otherness. However, the idea that all discourse includes an *à — Dieu* implies the awareness that it is also accompanied by an *adieu,* a farewell to all well-known onto-theological names and concepts of the divine. In other words, a patient attention for God's radical otherness, as becomes manifest in religion, and a farewell to onto-theology go hand in hand. De Vries considers the turn to religion conceived in this way as the essential task for contemporary philosophy.

In his book, De Vries offers a fine analysis of the *philosophical* reasons for contemporary thinking to be interested in all kinds of religious questions. I agree with him that these reasons have to do with difficulties caused by instrumental or technical rationality which have become apparent in our time. But I do not think that the reasons for numerous French (and also foreign) philosophers to be interested in religious issues can be interpreted as a *turn to religion.* By doing so, De Vries unifies all kinds of heterogeneous movements in contemporary (French) philosophy under the heading of a turn to religion. In this way, he seems to deny the crucial differences between the thinkers that come up in his book and also in this book. The attention to religion and/or God revealed in Ricoeur's works is completely different from Levinas and Marion, which profoundly differs from the attention Derrida and Lyotard give to religion and God. Moreover, the ways in which these thinkers do or do not relate to religious traditions is also very diverse, as I have shown above.

This brings me to a second problem. De Vries can only maintain his argument that in contemporary (French) philosophy there is a turn to religion because he explicitly detaches the concept of religion from any personal engagement in a religious conviction, and reduces religious traditions to a semantic and symbolic archive, which can be, to a great extent, formalized and transposed into concepts and philosophemes. If one agrees with De Vries's argument, what, then, is left of the religious character of this kind of religion? In his approach, religion is being restricted to something within the limits of philosophical reason alone. Only those religious aspects, which can be formalized and caught in concepts and philosophemes, find favour in the eyes of philosophical reason. However, the question arises whether this typically enlightened

approach (including a reductionism and formalism with regard to religion) violates religion itself. Is it possible to detach 'religion' from its
connection with a specific religious tradition and community, from its
being embedded in a ritual praxis, from its concrete moral do's and
don'ts? Paradoxically, the objection of De Vries, and some other contemporary philosophers, to classical onto-theology boomerangs. One of
Heidegger's pertinent criticisms of metaphysics as onto-theology was
that it used an idea of God that had become completely detached from
living (Christian) religion, from which metaphysics implicitly or explicitly drew its inspiration. To the God as *causa sui* ('cause of himself' as
being one of the most classic examples of the onto-theological conception of God) "man can neither pray nor sacrifice [...]. Before the *causa
sui*, man can neither fall to his knees in awe nor can he play music and
dance before this god."[13] So read Heidegger's harsh reproach to metaphysics as onto-theology. This is the reason why he is asking for a
'divine' god. But doesn't this reproach apply as much to De Vries's formalized concept of religion? In sum, both De Vries's book and this one
draw attention to a fascinating process taking place in contemporary
(French) philosophy; however, I disagree on whether or not to interpret
this process as a turn to religion.

So, although in my view it is at least premature and probably incorrect
to speak of a turn to religion or to theology, the publications of Janicaud
and De Vries show that, in fact, there is growing attention for questions
with regard to God and religion. But if this is not a turn to religion, how
should this new attention be interpreted since, from the perspective of
the dominant trends in post-war philosophy, it in no way speaks for
itself? We only need to think of humanistic existentialism, which was
not only an expression of radical, philosophical atheism, but which in a
more general sense contributed to the atheistic climate that prevailed in
intellectual circles both in France and abroad. In his pamphlet *Existentialism and Humanism (L'existentialisme est un humanisme)*, Sartre
argues that a choice in favour of man necessarily implies a choice
against God. In particular, the existence of a creating God can in no way
be combined with human freedom. The point of departure of existentialism is subjectivity.[14] This implies that man has no pre-given content or

---

[13] M. Heidegger, 'Die onto-theo-logische Verfassung der Metaphysik', p. 70 [M. Heidegger, The onto-theo-logical constitution of metaphysics, p. 72].
[14] J.-P. Sartre, *L'existentialisme est un humanisme*. Paris, Gallimard, 1996 (reprint),
p. 26.

definition of his essence, but is absolute freedom and indeterminacy. Therefore, human existence differs radically from the way in which things are, which are made on the basis of a concept and with an eye to a certain goal. In the case of man, his free existence precedes any definition of his essence; he only defines himself on the basis of an absolutely free, autonomous project of existence. If not, he is inauthentic and acts in bad faith. Thus, man fully 'invents' himself and is fully responsible for this self-invention.[15] Such a view on man and his freedom obviously excludes the existence of God, for if a creating God did exist, he would have created man according to a pre-given project (the eternal human nature or essence as, e.g., Aristotle says), in the same way as when a human makes things on the basis of a given concept. But thus He would annihilate what makes humans truly human, viz., their free self-determination! Therefore the existence of God is in flagrant contradiction to the authentic existence of man, for whom his existence precedes any definition of his essence. If God exists, man is nothing; if man exists.... In short, existentialist humanism, the choice of man in favour of man, is necessarily a form of atheism.

Merleau-Ponty's position with regard to the possibility of combining the existence of God with human freedom is subtler, but also more ambiguous than Sartre's. He states that if God is understood as the one and only source of sense, having established beforehand the sense of the universe as such, then He chokes the contingent, free process of man giving sense to the world. "Recourse to an absolute foundation destroys the very thing it is supposed to support."[16] Merleau-Ponty compares this absolute source of sense with someone possessing 'a notebook of the master', in which the solutions to all human problems are given beforehand.[17] As a result of this, the earnestness and gravity, which are so characteristic for every human decision, disappear. Human existence thus inevitably becomes a pointless game.

As is common knowledge, in the course of the last quarter of the twentieth century, structuralism somehow replaced existentialism as the dominant trend in French philosophy. Basically, structuralism accuses

---

[15] *Ibid.*, p. 40.

[16] M. Merleau-Ponty, Le métaphysique dans l'homme. In: Idem, *Sens et non-sens*. Paris, Nagel, 1966, p. 166 [M. Merleau-Ponty, The Metaphysical in Man. In: Idem *Sense and Non-Sense*. Evanston (Illinois), Northwestern University Press, 1964, p. 95].

[17] M. Merleau-Ponty, *Eloge de la philosophie*. Paris, Gallimard, 1953, p. 53 [M. Merleau-Ponty, *In Praise of Philosophy*. Evanston (Illinois), Northwestern University Press, 1963, p. 45].

existentialism of being a theology in reverse in so far as existentialism
had simply substituted God for the subject, attributing to the latter the
same central position which used to be the exclusive privilege of God.
However, this critique of the 'anthropotheistic' character of existentialist
humanism certainly did not involve at all that structuralism would take a
more positive attitude towards God and religion. Rather, the anthropologically and morally motivated atheism of existentialism gave way to a
(less militant) scientifically orientated atheism. This is the main argument of the influential book of Jean Lacroix on *The Sense of Modern
Atheism (Le sens de l'atheisme moderne).* In his view, "the systematic
and one-sided use of the structuralistic method is only possible on the
basis of atheistic presuppositions or at least develops an atheistic men-
tality."[18] When man is eliminated from scientific thinking, God goes out
of sight as well. The structuralistic method does not consider man to be
the unique bearer and source of sense, but approaches him only as a
replaceable element in a heterogeneous and discontinuous field of
forces. He does not bring about any meaning himself, but *is being* constituted as a contingent and passing element, as a way in which this field
temporary and contingently has organized itself. On the same grounds,
structuralism criticizes the concept of God as the transcendental referent
of all thinking and acting, as the one who could order and structure this
network. It rejects God as an illusion of consciousness on the basis that
man naively considers all conscious thinking and acting only to be possible if there were a God guaranteeing the pre-established harmony of
the world and the referentiality of our language. Thus, from the proposition that existentialist humanism is *ipso facto* atheistic, one should not
jump to the conclusion that a structuralistic critique of this kind of
humanism would offer new prospects for philosophical and theological
thinking about God. On the contrary, together with the annihilation of
the idea of the subject as the autonomous source of sense, structuralism
has also let God disappear from the philosophical and intellectual scene.

In conclusion, we can say that the philosophical trends that have been
discussed in this section, and which dominated, to a large extent, French
thinking during the second half of the twentieth century, are at odds with
the present philosophical attention for God and religion. This still leaves
unanswered the question of how this interest can be explained.

---

[18] J. Lacroix, *Le sens de l'athéisme moderne.* Paris, Casterman, 1969[6], p. 75.

3. The modern indecision about God

Without the pretension of offering a complete answer to the intriguing question of the reasons for the contemporary philosophical interest in God and religion, I want to propose an interpretation that focuses on an important common feature of French philosophy. In particular, I want to interpret this attention as an attempt to find a solution to some major problems of our culture, specifically concerning our understanding of man and Being, truth and values, as they have been elaborated by Heidegger, in particular[19] We are living in an age in which the influence of technical, economical — in short, instrumental — rationality has become so dominant that it jeopardizes the essence of man as a relational being, the world as the sphere of our existence, truth and value as something entrusted to us, etc. In this situation, the question is how to overcome the dominance of this kind of rationality and the practical effects it produces. A radical rejection of present-day society and culture is no option since that would only strengthen the dominance of instrumental rationality. In order to answer this crucial question, leading contemporary philosophers like Habermas, Taylor, Rorty, and others try out divergent approaches. This variety also holds true for the French philosophers discussed in this book. Nevertheless, their ways of dealing with this question have a common characteristic: in order to deconstruct modernity and develop new, non-instrumental ways of thinking and experiencing, they appeal to elements of religious traditions that always have been at odds with modernity.

I will clarify my point by departing from the attitude of these philosophers towards Heidegger's deconstruction of modern technology and his attempt to overcome the actual dominance of 'calculative thinking', of truth as 'certainty for a representing subject', of the world as an 'object', and of values as subjective constructions. According to Heidegger, only the development of a non-representing, commemorative thinking of Being is capable of doing this. In his view, modern technology does not

---

[19] In accordance with Heidegger, I use these four key words to indicate the basic elements of every age, and thus also of modernity. In his view, every age is founded on a fundamental metaphysical position, which embraces: "(1) The manner and way in which man is man, that is, himself [...]. (2) The essential interpretation of the being of beings. (3) The essential projection of truth. (4) The sense in which, in any given instance, 'man is the measure'." Cf. M. Heidegger, Die Zeit des Weltbildes. In: Idem, *Holzwege*. Frankfurt am Main, Vittorio Klostermann, 1963⁴, p. 95 [M. Heidegger, The Age of the World Picture. In: Idem, *Off the beaten track*. Cambridge, Cambridge University Press, 2002, p. 79].

stand alone, but is only the visible realization of a more fundamental metaphysical position) which he identifies with calculative thinking in terms of subject and object, and with onto-theology. So, Heidegger's attempt to overcome the dominance of technology by paving the way for a commemorative thinking goes hand in hand with his deconstruction of (traditional) metaphysics and his preparation of a non-onto-theological approach to God or, rather, to the gods. With regard to these two issues, Heidegger has influenced contemporary French philosophy profoundly. Even a superficial knowledge of the works of authors like Ricoeur, Girard, Levinas, Derrida, Henry, Marion, Lyotard, and Lacoste suffices to see that they contain a lot of explicit and implicit references to his work. However, their attitude towards Heidegger is very ambivalent. On the one hand, they agree with his critique of onto-theology; on the other hand, they criticize and deconstruct his attempt to prepare a new way of thinking the divine and the divinity situated within the domain of Being.[20] Of course, the stake and the result of these critiques and deconstructions differ individually, as the next chapters will show. Nevertheless, their ambivalent attitude towards Heidegger constitutes an important common motive which needs closer examination. Thus, the question that unites the thinkers discussed in this book is how to relate to both the mysterious attraction and repulsion which Heidegger's work brings about. In this respect, the central systematic question is whether his attempt to overcome calculative thinking by developing a commemorative thinking, including a thinking of God beyond the boundaries of onto-theology, is eventually successful. Or, is this attempt, in spite of itself, stuck in a problematic ontology and theology which, in turn, needs to be deconstructed?

In his essay, *The Age of the World Picture (Die Zeit des Weltbildes)*, Heidegger tries to think the essence of modernity which, in his view, also includes the present time. He mentions several, interrelated characteristics which make up the typically modern aspect of modernity. First of all, there is the rise of the new, mathematically based science, and the transformation of praxis to machine technology. Other characteristics of modernity are art moving into the purview of aesthetics, implying that the artwork becomes an object of experience, and culture becoming the realization of the highest values through the care and cultivation of man's highest goods. To us, a fifth element of modernity is especially important: Heidegger refers to it with the term 'loss of the gods' (*Entgötterung*). He describes it as follows:

---

[20] Cf. D. Janicaud, *Heidegger en France I*, pp. 478-9.

This expression [the loss of the gods] does not mean the mere elimination of the gods, crude atheism. The loss of the gods is a twofold process. On the one hand, the world picture Christianizes itself inasmuch as the ground of the world is posited as infinite and unconditioned, as the absolute. On the other hand, Christendom reinterprets its Christianity as a world view (the Christian world view) and thus makes itself modern and up to date. The loss of the gods is the condition of indecision about God and the gods. Christianity is chiefly responsible for bringing it about. But the loss of the gods is far from excluding religiosity. Rather, it is on its account that the relation to the gods is transformed into religious experience. When this happens, the gods have fled. The resulting void is filled by the historical and psychological investigation of myth.[21]

What does Heidegger mean by loss of the gods, and what consequences does it have for contemporary thinking about God and religion? First of all, it is important to distinguish the loss of the gods from atheism as well as from secularization. The term secularization is primarily used by the social sciences, referring to the (empirically observable) process of social and cultural differentiation which gradually takes place in modernity. As a consequence of this, the close bond between the whole universe and God as its origin and ultimate goal, and the immersion of all spheres of existence in an all-embracing religious order, which was characteristic of the pre-modern period, has vanished. Heidegger, however, uses the term 'loss of the gods' in order to indicate a philosophical interpretation of the dramatic changes that took place during modernity with regard to the relation between God and the world, the holy and the secular. Modern phenomena, such as social differentiation and autonomous science, can only emerge *after* Being is no longer experienced and understood as *ens creatum* (created being), but has become a calculable object, standing alone. Similarly, these phenomena can only come up *after* man has posited his own subjectivity as the unique point of reference for all truth, and has defined the latter as objective certainty. Therefore, the loss of the gods should not be understood from the perspective of secularization, but the other way round; secularization is but a concrete manifestation of the loss of the gods.

Analogously, the loss of the gods should be distinguished from atheism, the elimination of the gods. Atheism, as we understand it nowadays, does not stand alone, but is dependent on so-called theism for its name, meaning and opponents. The term theism only appeared at the

---

[21] M. Heidegger, Die Zeit des Weltbildes, p. 70 [M. Heidegger, The Age of the World Picture, p. 58].

beginning of modernity, referring to a strictly philosophical approach to God. It sets itself up as the discipline that is capable of proving the existence of a personal God on the basis of a purely rational argumentation, without appealing to revelation. It is only from this time on that atheism, in the strict sense of the word, could emerge since, essentially, atheism is the negation of theism. It is a philosophical trend that makes use of the same strictly rational arguments as theism, but with the intent of criticizing it, e.g., by showing that the proofs for God existence do not rest on a solid argumentative bases.[22] Well, with the term 'loss of the gods' Heidegger is referring to an issue that precedes the whole question of theism and atheism: he wonders what change in the relation between God and (philosophical) thinking has made both theism and atheism possible. In fact, they correspond in their transformation of God to an object of representing reasoning. When this occurs, the gods have already fled. Thus, analogous to what was said about secularization, the loss of the gods is (not) a consequence of atheism, but the other way round; atheism (just like theism) only becomes possible after the loss of the gods.

What is the essence of the loss of the gods? As the cited passage from Heidegger's essay indicates, it is a twofold process in which, on the one hand, the world picture christianizes and, on the other hand, Christendom reinterprets its Christianity as a world view. The christianization of the world picture becomes apparent in what Heidegger calls elsewhere the onto-theological structure of metaphysics. Characteristic for modernity is that philosophy took a new turn and orientated itself for its ideal of knowing to the model of exact science. At first, mathematics, and somewhat later physics, became the paradigm of all well-founded, certain knowledge. According to this paradigm, philosophy understands Being as ground, while thinking gathers itself towards Being as its ground in the manner of giving ground and accounting for the ground.[23] Thus, this ground is the ultimate principle on the basis of which the whole of reality can be understood as something radically coherent and transparent. Of course, only God qualifies for being this absolute ground and, consequently, modern philosophy attributed a central position to Him. Heidegger's analysis of this process brings to light the onto-theological structure of the most prominent metaphysical systems of modernity;

[22] Cfr. M. Buckley, *At the Origins of Modern Atheism*. New Haven, Yale University Press, 1987, pp. 13ff.

[23] M. Heidegger, Die onto-theo-logische Verfassung der Metaphysik, p. 48 [M. Heidegger, The onto-theo-logical constitution of metaphysics, p. 57].

concretely, we can think of Descartes' idea of the infinite, Leibniz's principle of sufficient ground, Spinoza's absolute substance, and Hegel's absolute idea.

In Heidegger's view, this turn has far-reaching consequences, not only for religion, but also for philosophy. The crucial issue here is not so much the well-known statement that the God of philosophy has become more and more at odds with the God of the Bible, but something more basic. Because modern philosophy understands God as giving ground, and also accounts for this ground, it, at the same time, takes far-reaching decisions about Being and truth. It conceives them in the light of God as ground. This means that it understands Being as grounded, i.e., as completely manifest presence without any obscurity, and truth as the result of an accounting knowledge on the basis of the availability of this last ground for the knowing subject. These interpretations of Being and truth should not be misunderstood as decisions of individual philosophers, but are made possible themselves by the fact that metaphysics as such essentially has an onto-theological structure. Ever since Plato, this tendency has slumbered in philosophy, and has only come to the fore since modernity. In any case, the modern turn to the idea of the world as a picture put an end to the fundamental openness and historicality, which originally characterized non-onto-theological (or non-metaphysical) thinking about the gods and Being. This is the christianization of the world picture: the basically open, historical and discontinuous destiny of Being as a 'coming to pass' has been reduced to a transparent, representational, objective being, grounded in God as its absolute ground which can be represented by understanding. However, the result of this process is paradoxical: when the picture of the world is christianized, as appears from the dominant position of God in the great metaphysical systems of modernity, the gods have fled and the loss of the gods has become a fact. The christianization of the world has removed the gods from the element of the holy; it has destroyed the unapproachable character of the divinity and, simultaneously, it has annihilated Being as a heterogeneous coming to pass and endless origin.

The other side of the loss of the gods is that Christendom reinterprets its Christianity as a world view. The consequence of this shift is the degradation of the all-encompassing faith in God and divine worship to a detached view of the world competing with other world views. As the title of his essay already indicates, Heidegger examines in *The Age of the World Picture* the essence of the (modern) world picture. In ordinary (German) parlance, this term has a neutral meaning, referring to some

view of or attitude towards the world. But for Heidegger, this term has a
very specific and fundamental meaning. He considers the fact that the
world has become a picture to be the essence of modernity. That is why,
strictly speaking, it is incorrect to contrast the modern world picture with
the one of the Middle Ages and of Antiquity. The interpretation of the
world as a (representational) picture only becomes possible in modernity. What exactly does Heidegger mean by world picture?[24] Let us take
a close look at both elements, world and picture, separately. Considered
philosophically, the word 'world' serves here as a name for beings in
their entirety. This term not only includes nature and history, but also the
world-ground, no matter how its relation to the world is thought. From
the perspective of the christianization of the world view analyzed above,
this means that by conceiving God as giving ground, He gets involved in
the sphere of representational thinking which accounts for the ground.
As a result of this, He turns into something that can be represented,
although his position as the absolute ground of the world is a unique one.
When using the word 'picture', we spontaneously think of a copy of
something, e.g., a photo or a painting. But for Heidegger, 'picture' refers to
something more fundamental. When we say that we try to get a picture of
something, we implicitly use this word in a normative way.[25] The picture
or representation we make of something thus becomes, as it were, the
norm or standard of the thing in itself: the matter itself stands in the way
it stands to us, before us. Consequently, making a picture of something,
or imagining something, does not only have to do with visualization, but
also, and even more basically, with conceptualization. Moreover, this
representation is not an arbitrary product, but is something present for
the mind's eye in all its necessary coherence and totality, i.e., as a system. Finally, the term world picture also has the connotation of the world
(Being as such) being present and available for a representing subject.
"Understood in an essential way, 'world picture' does not mean 'picture
of the world' but, rather, the world grasped as picture. Beings as a whole
are now taken in such a way that a Being is first and only is being insofar as it is set in place by representing-producing humanity."[26]

---

[24] M. Heidegger, Die Zeit des Weltbildes, pp. 81ff. [M. Heidegger, The Age of the
World Picture, pp. 67ff.].

[25] This normative aspect is even more striking in the German expression "wir sind
über etwas im Bilde" (we put ourselves in the picture about something). This expression
constantly plays a part in Heidegger's analysis of the world picture. Cf. Ibid., p. 82 [Ibid.,
p. 67].

[26] Ibid., p. 82 [Ibid., pp. 67-8].

The interpretation of Christianity as a world view is dependent on the world having become a picture for a representing subject. Consequently, the expression 'Christian world view' only gets its sense within the framework of the (modern) world picture. In a certain way, it is the conscious, articulated expression of Christianity. World view means that man is conscious of the fact that he looks at the world from a certain, i.e., Christian perspective. He also attributes a value to his faith, perhaps even the highest value. On the basis of this conscious evaluation, he can enter into a dialogue or confrontation with other world views and other values. But all these world views and the value attributed to them are only possible under the condition that the world as such has already become a picture of which man can make an image or a view. Only against the much larger background of modernity in which man posits himself for the first time as a subject opposed to the world (as object) is he capable of observing or viewing the world in a self-conscious, detached way, of evaluating it in relation to other world views, etc. Thus, the decisive factor is not so much that in the course of modernity, Christianity has entered into a tense relationship with other religious and non-religious world views, but the fact that it has understood itself as a world view. When this occurs, Christianity has already lost its original Christian character.

Why is this so? In its earliest and (in Heidegger's view) most authentic shape, Christian religion is not a world view at all but a way of life, completely dominated by faith. The faithful experience God not only in heaven, or simply as the architect of the world, or as the highest metaphysical principle (supreme being, *causa sui*. etc.), but as the living Father who has entered into history in a concrete way and foretells humanity of its salvation. Moreover, faith is not man's initiative or his construction, but something that is bestowed upon him on the basis of the promise made in the gospel. The faithful believe in God as the one who really acts, who chooses his flock and thus reveals himself as a loving shepherd of his people. This faith is not construed by man; it is received without merit; it is pure grace. However, during modernity this all-encompassing religious mode of existence vanishes because faith becomes a world view. Man takes a detached, observing attitude towards the world and assigns to God a place in it as its first principle. As a consequence of this, it is up to the faithful to consider God and religion to be of (some) importance to life. Religion thus becomes a value which man has to balance against other values (like work, enjoyment, health, etc.). The crucial difference between original, authentic faith and a modern, pious view of the world is that in the former view, faith is a human response to God's initiative, whereas in the latter view, the human subject is the exclusive point of departure on which his religious view of the world is founded. In this way, the subject can also assure himself of the certainty of faith. Concretely, this means that he chooses the world view that fits him best, or construes for himself a new eclectic world view by using elements of the existing ones. Finally, the notion 'place' as such presupposes an organizing subject, which assigns a position to everything and everyone. The result of this evolution is that religion loses its truth and reality, and turns into a religious experience. Man no longer sees God's activity in the world, but only subjectively feels his presence in the interiority of his heart. Here we see again that the well-known opposition between the God of the philosophers and scientists and the God of Abraham, Isaac and Jacob is not of decisive importance. The present-day faithful, who have turned away from all theological and philosophical speculation about God to a (anti-intellectual) religiosity of feeling, are as much victims of the loss of the gods as those who stick to philosophical theism, albeit in different ways. In short, it is obvious that *all* modern forms of religiosity have lost their authenticity ever since they conformed to the premises of the age of the world picture. They all are dominated by the loss of the gods.

On the basis of this analysis, the question arises whether in the age of the world picture, it is still possible at all to think and to speak about God in a truthful way. Heidegger is very pessimistic about the consequences of the loss of the gods: when it has come to this, the gods have fled. As said before, this failing of holy names should certainly not be identified with atheism. Rather, it announces a situation of indecision about the gods: the holy, as the element in which the gods are dwelling, human life that is completely dominated by God's grace, the experience of a world that reveals on every occasion God's activity — all these features of an authentic religious existence have vanished and left a great emptiness. Now man himself has to decide whether or not God exists, on the importance of religion to his life, etc. However, precisely at the moment that he wants to take a decision on these issues, he notices that the things on which he has to decide withdraw and escape his controlling power. This is the situation of indecision about God and the gods. As such, it is not a decision by man, but it is something that happens to him as a destiny, as a consequence of the age of the world picture. At present, man can decide autonomously on many things, almost on everything, but not on the fact *that* he has ended up in this situation.

In this situation of indecision, all thinking about God is both *too late* and *too soon*. We should not understand the statement that our thinking about God is *too late* as a yielding to atheism or agnosticism, and even less as indifference with regard to this issue. The indecision about God is not the consequence of a conscious human decision, but the result of a certain understanding of Being which reigns in our age. In its turn, this understanding is the result of a certain destiny of Being (*Seinsgeschick*). Once the gods have fled, man has thrown away his chances to establish an authentic relationship with God; he is too late. For the same reason, our thinking about God is *too soon*. Precisely because the loss of the gods is not the result of a human decision but happens to man as a destiny, every human attempt to put an end to this indecision high-handedly, e.g., by promoting God and religion again as valuable objects of philosophical inquiry, or by stressing again the value of faith in God, is a confirmation and strengthening of the loss of the gods rather than an overcoming of the same.

The only thing that man can do in this situation is to prepare the leeway in which the divinity can manifest itself again. Only if man lives within the boundaries of this leeway is he able to understand the original meaning of the word God. In a well-known fragment of his *Letter on Humanism (Brief über den Humanismus)*, Heidegger goes more deeply into the nature of this leeway: "The [sort of] thinking that thinks from the question concerning the truth of Being questions more primordially than metaphysics can. Only from the truth of Being can the essence of the holy be thought. Only from the essence of the holy is the essence of divinity to be thought. Only in the light of the essence of divinity can it be thought or said what the word 'God' is to signify."[27] With this remark Heidegger indicates how much preparatory work has to be done in order to understand (again) the meaning of the word 'God'. In general, he describes this work as the 'overcoming of metaphysics'. As said, this is certainly not a Hegelian sublation, but a step back out of (the reign of) metaphysics into its essence; it moves from accepting metaphysics as a given construction (of which Hegel's system is one of the most prominent examples) to its deconstruction. This step back implies that metaphysical thinking is questioned from the perspective of the truth of Being as a coming to pass of unconcealment and concealment.

[27] M. Heidegger, *Brief über den Humanismus*. Frankfurt am Main, Vittorio Klostermann, 1949, pp. 36-7 [M. Heidegger, Letter on Humanism. In: Idem, *Pathmarks*. Cambridge, Cambridge University Press, 1998, p. 267].

In this way, the construction of metaphysics loses its overwhelming, coercive character and appears as a product of its age, as a manifestation of a specific destiny of Being. As far as the question of a more authentic meaning of the word God is concerned, this thinking does not simply accept the fact of the loss of the gods as the inevitable fate of modern culture. On the contrary, it asks more primordially which conception of man and world, truth and values has brought about this destiny and why it can present itself as something unavoidable. Thus, the fate of the loss of the gods loses its coercive character.

However, the overcoming of metaphysics, as a result of which thinking again dwells in the nearness of Being, is but a first, preparatory step in order to think and tell the meaning of the word God in a more authentic way. Precisely because the danger of our thinking about God coming too soon is not yet completely over, more and different preparations are needed. Whenever man truly thinks Being, he experiences the holy. The holy, however, does not coincide with the divinity or God, but rather is the element in which the gods live and can reveal themselves to man. It is the leeway in which the divinity manifests itself. More specifically, the holy is the centre of what Heidegger in another text called the fourfold (das Geviert). By this he understands the four regions of the world in which earth and heaven, the divinities and the mortals gather.[28] All things of the world only get their authentic meaning because they dwell in these four regions and relate them to themselves. To quote a famous example of Heidegger: a jar is only most authentically a jar when one pours it its contents out: water — gift of *heaven* — or wine — gift of the *earth* — to still the thirst of the *mortals* or as a sacrifice to the *gods*. With regard to the divinities, Heidegger says: "[They] are the waving heralds of the divinity. From its covert reigning the God appears in his essence, which withdraws him from every comparison with the present."[29] However difficult it is to interpret this cryptic text, it nevertheless shows that thinking about the holy prepares the leeway in which the God can manifest himself. The divinities do not coincide with the God, but act on behalf of him and invite the mortals to turn themselves towards him. However, the God as such shows himself in no way whatsoever to man, he withdraws from every comparison with the world. So, there is only a relation from man through the divine heralds to the God

[28] For this interpretation cf. J. Beaufret, Heidegger et la théologie. In: R. Kearney and J.S. O'Leary (ed.), *Heidegger et la question de Dieu*. Paris, Grasset, 1980, pp. 28-9.
[29] M. Heidegger, *Vorträge und Aufsätze*. Pfüllingen, Neske, 1954, p. 171.

himself, a relation that is marked by the interplay of concealment and
unconcealment.

In sum, the preparations that are needed to help man in making the
transition from the reign of the loss of the gods to a more authentic relationship to God come down to the following. God can only be thought
after the divinity has been thought, and the divinity in its turn can only
be thought starting from the essence of the holy. Thus, both the question
of the divinities inviting the mortals in the fourfold, and the question of
the withdrawal of God in the loss of the gods can only be asked in an
authentic, original way if one begins from the leeway of the holy. However, man can only get access to this leeway when the openness of Being
has been laid open by a commemorative thinking and when he com-
memoratively dwells in the openness of Being. Here, Heidegger means
that thinking God and thinking Being lie in each other's nearness: man
should put himself under the claim of Being in order to think the holy,
and only starting from this leeway can he think the divinity and, eventually, God.

No matter how one judges Heidegger's thinking about God, it is clear
that he does not only take distance from the representing way of thinking of onto-theology, but from Christian theology as well, which starts
from God's self-revealing Logos in the world. Also, the stress on the
holy as the element in which the divinity dwells is at odds with the
Christian God, who precisely desacralizes the world. Rather, his thinking on this issue is related to the poet Hölderlin, who reads the Gospel
without forgetting Greek myths, which, in his eyes, are as holy as the
Gospels themselves.[30] Heidegger, himself, acknowledges that in the passage from the *Letter on Humanism*, cited above, he speaks only about
the god of the poet and not about the God of Christian revelation.[31]

4. Thinking beyond the loss of the gods?

As is common knowledge, Heidegger's thinking has been of great
influence on the ongoing discussions in continental philosophy, as the
works of all the authors that are discussed in this book prove. This

---

[30] Cf. F. Fédier, Heidegger et Dieu. In: R. Kearney and J.S. O'Leary (ed.), *Heidegger et la question de Dieu*, p. 45.

[31] Dialogue avec Martin Heidegger (Record of a session of the Evangelical Academy of December 1953 in Hofgeismar). In: R. Kearney and J.S. O'Leary (ed.), *Heidegger et la question de Dieu*, p. 336.

indebtedness to Heidegger particularly concerns his deconstruction of onto-theology. When we take into account the radicalness of this deconstruction, how should we interpret the fact that these authors nevertheless want to bring up questions about God and religion in their philosophies? From Heidegger's rather pessimistic perspective, this is highly problematic. Don't the thinkers discussed in this book too easily disregard his warning that in an age in which the gods have fled, all thinking about God is necessarily too soon? Do they listen to his imploring words that in our age it is more appropriate to remain silent about God?[32] And even if the ideas of these thinkers are timely, have they really listened to Heidegger's urgent claim that God should be thought within the domain of the holy since, in his view, this is the only realm in which the divine and the divinity can appear again? To put it in different terms: do these thinkers succeed in finding a realm that is not dominated by the fate of the loss of the gods in which God can be thought and talked about in a new and more authentic way? Or do they fail to take into account this whole issue, thus falling back in the onto-theological way of thinking, which Heidegger precisely tried to overcome? Of course, a complete answer to these intriguing questions, which would also pursue in greater depth the major differences between the thinkers of this book, greatly exceeds the scope of this introduction. Therefore, I will start with a short analysis of their attitude with regard to the problem of onto-theology. I will show that their work can be seen as a continuation of Heidegger's deconstruction of onto-theology. This common frame of reference offers an adequate point of departure to analyze the critique of these thinkers on Heidegger's new approach to think God in the neighbourhood of Being. In particular, I will point to the fundamental objections that his preparations for a new kind of thinking about the holy and the divinity call for in the work of Levinas, Derrida, Marion, and Lacoste. The reason for these objections is certainly not any hidden attempt on their part to revive onto-theology, but rather the conviction that Heidegger's deconstruction of it is not radical enough. In sum, the ambivalent attitude of these thinkers to Heidegger is an important motive in contemporary French thinking about God and religion, and can be interpreted as a way of freeing thinking from the fate of the loss of the gods.

[32] "[M]etaphysics is onto-theo-logy. Someone who has experienced theology in his own roots, both the theology of the Christian faith and that of philosophy, would today rather remain silent about God when he is speaking in the realm of thinking." M. Heidegger, Die onto-theo-logische Verfassung der Metaphysik, p. 51 [M. Heidegger, The onto-theo-logical constitution of metaphysics, pp. 54-5].

In the work of Ricoeur, the influence of Heidegger's critique of onto-theology plays a major role in his struggle with the tradition of reflective philosophy. Its discourse is characterized by universality, univocity, and unity and, as such, it is opposed to the plurality, equivocity, and particularity of the myths. Philosophy sets itself the task of revealing the universal and rational structure which is hidden in the plurality of individual myths and symbols, such as they appear in all religions. This means that in his philosophy of religion, Ricoeur departs from the religious symbols, not from natural theology and its onto-theological implications. The consequence of this approach is not only an enlargement, but also a qualitative change of reflective consciousness. More specifically, it puts the point of departure of reflective philosophy, *viz.*, autonomous thinking, under pressure. With regard to the thinking of God, this crisis becomes manifest in the incapability of reflective philosophy to think the essence of what faith is all about, the Wholly Other who addresses and questions us. Philosophy is situated on the level of immanence and, therefore, it cannot say anything about vertical transcendence. Although reflective philosophy cannot simply be put on a par with Heidegger's concept of onto-theology, there are nevertheless important connections between them. In this regard, we especially have to keep in mind the ideals of rationality, universality and univocity, and the central position of the subject, which reflective philosophy and onto-theology have in common. According to Ricoeur, they are manifestations of the hubris of philosophy. His argument ends in a rehabilitation of non-speculative language, a way of thinking without the totalizing and foundational pretensions of traditional metaphysics. In making this claim, his thought obviously echoes Heidegger's deconstruction of onto-theology.

The work of Girard, too, can be read as a critique of onto-theology, although it should be said that he is closer to Heidegger's philosophy of culture, including his critique of modernity, than to his thinking of Being. As we saw in the previous section, onto-theology is one of the ways in which the loss of the gods has become manifest in our age. From Girard's perspective, onto-theology is a thinking of identity, annihilating the difference between Being and the beings, and reducing God to a being, albeit the supreme being. This comes down to a negation of God's transcendence. In an age in which the world has become a picture, God, too, is conceived after the example of a representational and manageable picture. Thus, in modernity, both the external mediation of mythical religion and the transcendence of the Christian God fail. The only thing left is an internal mediation as the cause of the intrinsically

aggressive character of modern culture which sacrifices nature, the
other, and man himself. This idea of modernity parallels Heidegger's
critique of calculative thinking. In this sense, Girard's critique of the
internal mediation of modern culture and its negation of God's transcendence is a culture-philosophical translation of Heidegger's criticism of
the philosophy of identity or subjectivity, which has come to the fore in
the age of the loss of the gods.

The critique of onto-theology also plays a crucial role in the writings
of Levinas. He links it to the issue of atheism, which serves as a point of
departure for his thinking about God. In this context, the concept 'atheism' refers to a position that precedes both the negation and the affirmation of the divine. More concretely, it is the radical rejection of every
thinking that aims at conceiving God in terms of a participation in man's
doings and goings-on, as well as in terms of any participation in Being.
The last, meaningful sentence of the preface of his book, *Otherwise than
Being or Beyond Essence (Autrement qu'être ou au-delà de l'essence)*,
clearly shows that Levinas takes Heidegger's critique of onto-theology
(although Heidegger does not identify this with atheism) as the point of
departure for his own thinking: "To hear a God not contaminated by
Being is a human possibility no less important and no less precarious
than to bring Being out of the oblivion in which it is said to have fallen
in metaphysics and in onto-theology."[33] From this 'atheistic' perspective, Levinas tries to think a God who does not coincide with the
(supreme) being, but is precisely otherwise than Being. Thus he reacts,
just like Heidegger, against every way of thinking that has the pretension
of being able to thematize God and reduce Him to an object of representing thinking. Levinas concretely has in mind the major representatives of the metaphysical tradition, such as Aristotle, Spinoza, and
Hegel. In one way or another they annihilate God's incomprehensible
infinity by fitting him into a totalizing system. As a consequence, these
philosophers overpower God's transcendence and ignore the infinite difference between man and God. By conceiving God within the network
of Being, they also create the impression that man, as a thinking and acting being, is the unique starting point of all initiative in the world, as
such, he is convinced that he can never be disturbed, thrown off his balance, or displaced by the intrusion of the infinite.

---

[33] E. Levinas, *Autrement qu'être ou au-delà de l'essence,* Dordrecht, Kluwer, 1978,
p. X [E. Levinas, *Otherwise than Being or Beyond Essence*. The Hague/Boston/London,
Nijhoff Publishers, 1981, p. xliii].

Derrida's thinking, too, is tributary to Heidegger's on many points. He even acknowledges that none of the ideas he tries to develop would have been possible without the questions that Heidegger raised.[34] With regard to the issues coming up in this book, he endeavours in his works to deconstruct the onto-theological representation of God as supreme being. He radicalizes the problematic presuppositions of onto-theology by situating them in the larger context of logocentrism which dominates Western thought. The term logocentrism refers to a way of thinking in which truth is of a spiritual nature and, thus, is, in principle, present for the mind's eye. Within logocentrism, God functions as the transcendental referent, warranting a stable meaning for all our speaking and thinking. God ensures the fact that neither confusion nor constantly changing perspectives deregulate our thinking, but that we, in principle, can rely on an objective truth and a stable world. Derrida's intention is not so much to radically refuse this onto-theological and logocentric way of thinking, but to show that it rests on an unfounded prejudice, viz., God as the point of unification, being the source of all sense and meaning. The onto-theological God appears here as the condition of possibility for thinking reality in terms of presence, representability, and objectivity.

Lyotard's 'hidden philosophy of religion' can be taken as an indirect answer to Derrida's question 'how not to speak about God?'. It consists of experimenting with three different new strategies of simultaneously speaking about God and keeping silent about Him, viz., speaking indirectly, speaking with a forked tongue, and ventriloquism. Lyotard's strategy rests upon his basic contention that God cannot be an object of metaphysical thinking, as onto-theology had always presumed. On the contrary, the absolute can only be present in human discourse in a repressed way, thus inevitably transforming and destabilizing it. He illustrates this by focusing on Augustine's narrative of his conversion in the *Confessions*. Lyotard shows that Augustine is not the ultimate subject in the story of his conversion, as onto-theology would contend, but that he (just like every other human being) is the product of the discourse and the writings of God as the radical other; it only gradually becomes his own discourse in a lifelong process of conversion. In sum,

---

[34] J. Derrida, *Positions*. Paris, Minuit, 1972, p. 18 [J. Derrida, *Positions*. London, Athlone Press, 1987, p. 9]. For an intriguing insight into the backgrounds of Derrida's ambivalent attitude to Heidegger cf. D. Janicaud, Jacques Derrida. Entretiens du 1er juillet en du 22 novembre 1999. In: Idem, *Heidegger en France. II. Entretiens*. Paris, Albin Michel, 2001, pp. 89-126, esp. p. 103.

being converted implies that God reshapes my existence completely. It
is not me who speaks, but God himself speaks in my speaking.

Henry's idiosyncratic primal phenomenology can also be interpreted in
the light of Heidegger's critique of onto-theology. According to him,
there is a structural relationship between a radical phenomenology and
Christianity, since both begin from a showing, manifesting, revealing.
The decisive characteristic of revelation is that it cannot be reduced to the
revelation of 'something', as happens in Husserl's phenomenology, but
rather, in a first moment, revelation reveals itself. In Christian religion
this immediacy especially shows itself in God's self-manifestation, in the
"I am who am." This original immediacy of God's self-manifestation has
to be distinguished from the creed of God's revelation as a crucial element of Christian philosophical-theological tradition and a historically
developed church. In Henry's view, the essence of Christianity cannot be
represented and is therefore at odds with any theoretical mediation and
symbolic representation. God is life itself, not life that is constantly
reduced to something other than itself. This implies that God certainly
cannot be conceived in terms of Being, as happens in onto-theology.

As far as Marion is concerned, he bases his thinking about God both
on Heidegger's critique of the confusion of the question of Being and of
God, and on Levinas's objections to the contamination of God by Being.
This already becomes apparent if one looks at the title of his startling
book *God without Being (Dieu sans l'être)*. Marion uses the twin concepts idol and icon to clarify and balance this issue. Idol refers to a
human experience of the holy; it represents the holy as seen only from a
human point of view. The view fixates, and the idol is precisely the point
where the movement of the view stops and fixates itself. As far as philosophy is concerned, this attitude refers to a way of thinking about God
in terms of 'construct' and 'concept', of which onto-theology is a striking
example. As a concept, God is no longer infinite or incomprehensible,
but is being fixated within the boundaries of the human capacity of representing. In accordance with Heidegger's critique of onto-theology,
Marion writes: "The conceptual idol has a site, metaphysics; a function,
the theo-logy in onto-theo-logy; and a definition, *causa sui*. Conceptual
idolatry does not remain a universally vague suspicion, but inscribes
itself in the global strategy of thought taken in its metaphysical figure."[35]

[35] J.L. Marion, *Dieu sans l'être*. Paris, Presses Universitaires de France, 1982, p. 56
[J.L. Marion, *God without Being. Hors-Texte*. Chicago, University Press of Chicago,
1991, p. 36].

Therefore, a way of thinking about God that is not affected by idolatry implies that we should think about God outside the purview of metaphysics.

As for Lacoste, he explains the consequences of Heidegger's critique of onto-theology for theology in a short, dense dictionary-article devoted to Heidegger. Heidegger's phrases "confirm the death of the God of the philosophers [...], and ask for a purely theological reconstruction of theology. [...] Thus, the task for theology is double: on the one hand, it is liberating itself from all relations with metaphysics, and, on the other hand, it is dissociating its destiny from the kind of thinking that, after metaphysics, tries to receive the truth of Being."[36] If theology does not take on this task, it runs the risk of disposing God of his divinity.

The previous paragraphs show that the authors discussed in this book implicitly or explicitly acknowledge the importance of Heidegger's deconstruction of metaphysics as onto-theology. In this way, he laid bare more clearly than anybody else the weak point of traditional metaphysical thinking about God. Moreover, I pointed out that Heidegger's influence on contemporary French thinking is not restricted to the issue of onto-theology in the strict sense, but also relates to the analysis and critique of modern culture, especially the reign of calculative rationality, truth as objective certainty, man as a subject, and values as a human construction. Nevertheless, these authors refuse to comply with Heidegger's call for temporarily keeping silent about God because our thinking of Him would be too soon. They also do not agree with his suggestion that thinking should restrict itself to preparing the leeway in which the holy could appear again. How should this aspect of their attitude to Heidegger be interpreted? Why do they seemingly only follow his path of thinking half-way? What is wrong with his statement that we are only able to think God or the gods appropriately in the nearness of Being, from the realm of the holy? In order to find an answer to these complex questions, I want to examine how Levinas, Derrida, Marion, and Lacoste, in particular, react to this aspect of Heidegger's thinking.

As I already showed in my analysis of the quotation from the preface of *Otherwise than Being*, Levinas's point of departure is a radical rejection of all thinking that conceives God in terms of participation in and community with Being. At first sight, he seems to be in accordance with Heidegger's project to free Being from the forgetfulness in which it has

---

[36] J.-Y. Lacoste, Heidegger. In: J.-Y. Lacoste, *Dictionnaire critique de théologie*. Paris, Presses Universitaires de France, 1998, pp. 522-3.

fallen under the influence of metaphysics and onto-theology. But in the
same sentence of this quotation he places his own project "to hear a God
not contaminated by Being" *next to* Heidegger's as "a human possibility no less important and no less precarious."[37] What does Levinas mean
by this human possibility, and how does it relate to Heidegger's thinking
of Being? At the outset of the second part of his book *God, death and
time (Dieu, la mort et le temps)* entitled *God and onto-theo-logy (Dieu et
l'onto-théo-logie)*, he enters into this issue in detail. Just like Heidegger,
he considers the onto-theological character of metaphysics not as something standing alone, but as an important aspect of the historical manifestation of Being. In accordance with the analysis presented above,
Being manifests itself in modernity as a world picture of which instrumental rationality, truth as certainty, being as representation, and man as
subject are the constitutive elements. In his earlier work, Levinas sum-
marizes, in a certain way, this age under the heading 'totality'. However,
the way in which he wants to overcome onto-theology fundamentally
differs from Heidegger's. He asks whether "the mistake of onto-theology consist[s] in taking Being for God, or rather in taking God for
Being.[38] 'Taking Being for God' occurs when representing thinking
reduces the essential openness of the history of Being, i.e., Being as an
inextricable intertwining of concealment and unconcealment. As a result
of this, thinking understands Being as ('takes Being for') the supreme
being, God, who can be represented and thus controlled by the subject.
On the other hand, however, 'taking God for Being' means that philosophy conceives God exclusively in terms of ('takes Him for') Being. In
this way, philosophy definitively precludes for itself the possibility of
understanding God as otherwise than Being.

    With regard to this issue, Levinas thinks of something very specific:
if philosophy takes God for Being, this inevitably implies that Being
becomes the ultimate source of sense. This shuts the door to a radically
transcendent sense, that is to say, a sense intruding into earthly Being
from outside or above, a sense that does not find its origin in the order
of 'sameness' but in the incommensurable Other. Levinas's thinking as
such aims at showing that an authentic sense-giving thinking, i.e., thinking that looks for a primordial, absolute sense, necessarily implies the
explosion or the subversion of Being, since Being itself and the sense of

---

[37] E. Levinas, *Autrement qu'être,* p. X [E. Levinas, *Otherwise than Being,* p. xliii].
[38] E. Levinas, *Dieu, la mort et le temps.* Paris, Grasset, 1993, p. 141 [E. Levinas, *God,
Death, and Time.* Stanford, Stanford University Press, 2000, p. 124].

Being, as Heidegger already noticed, only manifest themselves as a contingent history of beings and a heterogeneous multiplicity of senses. So, what is actually at stake in Levinas's philosophical project to oppose God to onto-theology is to conceive a new, absolute notion of sense which cannot but lie radically at the other side of Being. This implies that neither onto-theology nor Heidegger's thinking of Being can give access to this primordial layer of sense. We can only trace it through ethics as the unconditional appeal of the radically Other to me. With this, Levinas wants to tell us the following: in spite of his sustained effort (which Levinas appreciates) to overcome metaphysics, Heidegger remains indebted to western metaphysics, which reduces the absolute, transcendent sense of God to the historical understanding of the Being of beings since, according to Heidegger, it is only in the nearness of Being that the holy and the divinity announce themselves.[39]

Levinas still phrases this complex issue in another way: "Is thinking God by way of onto-theo-logy the wrong way of thinking about Being (the Heideggerian thesis), or is it the wrong way of thinking about God? Does not God signify *the beyond Being*? Now that is what, for Heidegger, would be scarcely defensible, although there is a philosophical tradition — Platonic and Plotinian — of thinking of a God beyond Being)."[40] Does Levinas take here the view of a theologian who wants to save the God of the Bible from the hands of philosophical thinking? By no means! His approach is entirely philosophical. He asks for a primordial sense, which is radically transcendent with regard to the ever fluctuating play of diverging sense-contexts, which is characteristic for the Being of beings. According to Heidegger, this fluctuating play is the historical coming to pass of Being, which is the origin of all sense in the world. Going into the sense of Being (an expression that Heidegger often uses) implies that thinking accepts the claim of the coming to pass of Being and expresses its sense. Levinas, however, states that there is a primordial sense which lies beyond the contingency and historicity of the Being of beings; it cannot but lie at the other side of Being, and in that sense goes back to God as the radically Other. This again shows that what is philosophically at stake for Levinas fundamentally differs from Heidegger's philosophical agenda. Levinas does not want to safeguard the sense of the coming to pass of Being against the metaphysical idea

---

[39] E. Levinas, De la signifiance du sens. In: R. Kearney and J.S. O'Leary (ed.), *Heidegger et la question de Dieu*, p. 239.

[40] E. Levinas, *Dieu, La mort et le temps*, pp. 143-4 [E. Levinas, *God, Death, and Time,* pp. 126-7].

of God as a representational, supreme being. Rather, he tries to prevent
Being from absorbing all sense, implying no room would be left anymore for a primordial sense which radically transcends Being. He thus
not only repudiates (together with Heidegger) traditional metaphysics,
but also rejects (in opposition to Heidegger) the commemorative thinking of Being, which thinks more originally than metaphysics does. So, in
Levinas's view, Heidegger's overcoming of metaphysics by a commemorative thinking of Being should itself be overcome in order to be able
to think the intrusion of a primordial, transcendent sense, the Word of
God as the radical Other, in the order of 'sameness' (Being). For Levinas,
'putting an end to onto-theology' therefore necessarily also implies
taking a distance from Heidegger's commemorative thinking of Being.

    Just like Levinas, Derrida also recognizes his indebtedness to Hei-
degger's analysis of the intimate relationship between the metaphysics
of presence and onto-theology. But, again, just like Levinas, he also
mentions a distance (écart) between his own thinking and Heidegger's,
albeit of a completely different nature than the abyss separating Heidegger from Levinas. Derrida shows that Heidegger, in spite of all his
efforts, does not completely succeed in escaping from metaphysical
thinking; formulated in a positive way, this means that he sometimes
remains the prisoner of onto-theology. Well, surely Derrida does not
want to monopolize the merit of having overcome metaphysics and
onto-theology completely. This, perhaps, is impossible, in principle. But
he notices that in the work of Heidegger, there are a lot of hidden ambi-
guities, suggesting a metaphysical rest.

    Derrida offers an example of his deconstruction of the metaphysical
rest in Heidegger's (post-metaphysical) commemorative thinking of
Being in his commentary of the *Letter on Humanism*. More specifically,
he analyzes the passage quoted in the previous section in which Heidegger discusses the possibility of a more original thinking of the divinity
and God, starting from the dimension of the holy.[41] According to Derrida, "in Heidegger's discourse, [one can observe a] dominance of an
entire metaphorics of proximity, of simple and immediate presence, a
metaphorics associating the proximity of Being with the values of neigh-
bouring, shelter, house, service, guard, voice, and listening. As goes

----

[41] Cf. for Derrida's commentary: J. Derrida, Les fins de l'homme. In: Idem, *Marges
de la philosophie*. Paris, Minuit, 1972, pp. 129-164, especially pp. 153ff. [J. Derrida,
Margins of Philosophy. Chicago, University of Chicago Press, 1982, pp. 109-136, especially pp. 128ff.].

without saying, this is not an insignificant rhetoric."[42] Nearness is also the leading metaphor in Heidegger's speaking about the divinity and God: one need only to think of his statement that we can only experience a relation of the divinity to man from the perspective of the truth of Being. According to Derrida, it obviously does not hold to turn Heidegger into a veiled metaphysician, thinking God in terms of representability, presence and supreme being. The nearness that comes up here is not an ontic, but an ontological nearness, that is to say, it pertains to the sort of metaphors Heidegger uses to describe the relation between God and man. For Derrida, the use of one metaphor rather than another is, nevertheless, meaningful. It shows that Heidegger's radical deconstruction of the predominance of presence in metaphysics only aims at urging us to think the presence of the present.

Concretely, Derrida thinks of all kinds of ontological nearness in Heidegger's text — such as man living in the nearness of Being, the theme of homeland (*Heimat*) and homelessness (*Heimatlosigkeit*) man as the shepherd of Being — as standing in the claim of Being, and man's appropriation of the destiny of Being. Particularly as far as this last element is concerned, Derrida points at the relative ease with which Heidegger passes from 'near' (French: *proche*) to 'proper' (French: *propre*). He surely does not want to accuse Heidegger's use of the term 'proper' of referring to one or another transcendental property of man and of thus falling back in a metaphysical way of thinking. But it is clear that Heidegger's notion of the 'proper' points to an involvement of the sense of Being in the sense of man and vice versa: 'Man is the proper of Being, which right near him whispers in his ear; Being is the proper of man, such is the truth that speaks, such is the proposition which gives the *there* of the truth of Being and the truth of man. [...] The proper of man, his *Eigenheit,* his 'authenticity', is to be related to the meaning of Being; he is to hear and to question (*fragen*) it in ek-sistence, to stand straight in the proximity of its light."[43]

With regard to the important issue of the nearness of Being to man, and the way in which he appropriates the sense of Being, Derrida's deconstruction results in an ambivalent position. He certainly does not want to reject Heidegger's line of thought as such, if only because he is convinced that it is impossible to step out of metaphysics and onto-theology 'just like that'. But, by laying his finger on the unreflected evidence of the

[42] Ibid., p. 156 [Ibid., p. 130].
[43] Ibid., p. 160 [Ibid., p. 133].

nearness of Being to man, he shows a metaphysical rest which has
escaped to the attention of Heidegger's commemorative thinking. Even
more precisely, Heidegger's destruction of onto-theology has resusci-
tated this evidence, which had been long forgotten. Under this destruction, executed by his 'commemorative thinking', an even more original
layer of meaning comes to light, namely, the nearness of man and Being.
Well, Derrida wonders whether this evidence in our times doesn't get
derailed. This derailment surely is not a consequence of some human
decision, but can only come from an externality outside the realm that is
common to man and Being. This externality lies outside the circle of
light that the sense of Being casts upon the beings because it is as such
the condition of possibility of the sense of Being. In his later texts, Derrida calls this externality, which he relates to death and violence, God. It
does not coincide with Heidegger's God who becomes manifest in the
realm of the holy and the sense of Being. For Derrida, the term God is
an indication of the extra-sensible, difference, and deferral. This also
makes clear that the orientation of Derrida's commentary on Heidegger
goes in a completely different direction than Levinas's. The main concern for Levinas is to save God, who is otherwise than Being, from the
totalizing take-over by Heidegger's thinking of Being, in short, from
ontology. Derrida, in contrast, questions the evidence of the nearness of
Being, God, and man in order to safeguard the differential character of
Being (the ontological difference), that is to say, the alterity, the openness, the indecision, the deferral, the infinite distance, the dissociation,
etc.[44]

   Marion's interpretation of Heidegger builds on the line of thought of
Levinas and Derrida. In his book *God without Being,* he examines Heidegger's 'new beginning' in which Heidegger sets himself the task of
thinking a divine God or at least preparing the leeway for this. In this
context, Marion sharply criticizes the contested passage in Heidegger's
Letter on Humanism on the possibility of thinking God from the dimension of Being and in relation to the fourfold (*das Geviert*). Marion
thinks that, for Heidegger, the truth about God can only come from the
realm from which truth unconceals itself, namely, from Being, its
enframing and its openness. Thus, Being precedes God. This leads
Marion to the conclusion that there is a second sort of idolatry which is
typical of the thinking of Being as such, and which is even more problematic than the first kind of idolatry, which is characteristic for

---

[44] Cf. D. Janicaud, *Jacques Derrida. Entretiens,* pp. 118-9.

metaphysics as onto-theology (see above).[45] On the basis of this, he gives a penetrating commentary on Heidegger's well-known and often repeated remark that the faithful man, precisely because of his certainty of faith, is perhaps able to *conceive* the philosophical question of Being, but is never capable to fully *commit* himself to it, because of his inevitably faithful interpretation of this question. Marion reverses this reproach and points it towards Heidegger. "Assured of the precomprehension of every possible 'God' as being and of his determination by the anterior instance of Being, Heidegger can well conceive and formulate the question of God (without quotation marks) but can never seriously commit himself to it."[46]

Lacoste, too, gives critical comments precisely on this passage of Heidegger's *Letter on Humanism,* especially as far as the consequences of his thought for Christian theology are concerned. "The transcendence of God yields to the transcendence of Being and its governance; and the kind of theology that takes its place [...]thus is supremely a-theological. [...] The central role that Heidegger attributes to 'serenity' (*Gelassenheit*), in absence of all hope; the subordination of God to a sacredness without a face; a writing on the history of philosophy, in which every Christian reference is left out — these and other features should allow us to affirm that theology has nothing to learn here, except that which it is not at all. Which is, by the way, a very useful lesson."[47] Lacoste's harsh reaction against the very possibility of making Heidegger's thinking of Being productive for theology shows, in an exemplary way, the attitude of a whole number of contemporary French theologians.[48]

In this section I have shown the ambivalent attitude that is characteristic for Levinas, Derrida, Marion, and Lacoste with regard to Heidegger's thinking of Being. The enormous merit of Heidegger's critique of onto-theology for contemporary philosophy and theology should not conceal that his new beginning, his attempt to formulate a more original (and in his view also more truthful) thinking about God, evokes some fundamental objections. The four authors discussed in this section are not the only ones to raise these questions. Some others also have serious

---

[45] J.L. Marion, *Dieu sans l'être,* p. 65 [J.L. Marion, *God without Being,* p. 41].

[46] *Ibid.,* pp. 68-9 [*Ibid.,* p. 43]. On Marion's attitude to Heidegger cf. also: D. Janicaud, Jean-Luc Marion. Entretien du 3 décembre 1999. In: D. Janicaud, *Heidegger en France II,* pp. 210-227.

[47] J.-Y. Lacoste, Heidegger, p. 523.

[48] Cf. D. Janicaud, *Heidegger en France I,* p.480.

problems with Heidegger's thinking concerning this issue. For Girard, Heidegger's notion of holy Being is nothing other than the product of the violence between people. Ricoeur, too, wonders at the fact that Heidegger constantly avoided the confrontation of his thinking about a divine God with Hebrew thinking, whereas the latter, precisely because of its relation to the other and to justice, fundamentally differs from Greek philosophical discourse. In the previous section, I already indicated how much Heidegger's thinking about God is indebted to Hölderlin and his admiration of or nostalgia for the world of the gods of ancient Greece, but pays no attention at all to the God of the Bible. According to Ricoeur, Heidegger's step back out of metaphysics does not adequately take into account the main dimensions of Western philosophical and cultural traditions. In his view, Heidegger fails to recognize "the radical Hebrew dimension of Christianity, which is primarily rooted in Judaism and only afterwards in the Greek tradition."[49]

5. Conclusion

The chapters of this book present and analyze the lively discussions that are taking place in contemporary French philosophy about the issues of God and religion. The purpose of this introduction was, in the first place, to explain some important elements of the common frame of reference within which they are pursued. The question that did not come up in this introduction is the following: does God feel at home in France?[50] To put it more precisely, do the thinkers presented in this book cast a renewing light on the God of religion and are they thus contributing to a fruitful development of theology? The interest, from the perspective wherein this question is raised, is primarily a religious and theological one. As such, it differs from the perspectives of most of the authors being introduced in this book, who are mainly philosophers. This is the reason why I objected in the second section of this introduction to an all-too simplistic interpretation of contemporary

---

[49] P. Ricoeur, Note introductive. In: R. Kearney and J.S. O'Leary (ed.), *Heidegger et la question de Dieu,* p. 17. Cf. also Derrida's remark on this issue in: D. Janicaud, Jacques Derrida. Entretiens, pp. 119.

[50] In this context, it is important to notice that the expression 'living like God in France' means in Dutch, French, and German 'living in clover', 'having a place in the sun'. I have this connotation in mind when I ask whether God feels at home in France.

French philosophy as a turn to theology or religion. Therefore, the aim of this introduction cannot be to fully answer the question whether God feels at home in contemporary French thinking, or, formulated differently, to judge the theological or religious relevance of such thinking. Nevertheless, one cannot ignore the fact that the work of the thinkers discussed in this book does imply a serious challenge to (Christian) religion and theology. This also becomes apparent from the fact that their ideas are being discussed vigorously by many contemporary theologians. The work of Lacoste is only one example of this. Therefore, at the end of this introduction, I want to point to two issues that can be gathered from the various chapters of this book and which, in my view, are of extraordinary importance to present-day religious thinking.

First, there is the question how God's transcendence should be thought in order to prevent Him from falling under the dominance of philosophical thinking of Being, or, to put it differently, in order to prevent Him from becoming an idol, a product of man's imagination. Levinas brings up this issue when he thinks God as a trace, as the one who has absolutely 'passed by'. This idea of God refers to His revelation to Moses in Ex. 33. For theology, this implies that it should always realize that, inevitably, God remains a mystery. Therefore, it should stay loyal to its vocation of being a self-removing discourse about God. Derrida radicalizes this notion of the trace by thinking God as difference and death. By doing so, he spikes the guns of every thinking that approaches God as positivity and definability. In his view, both Heidegger (God in the nearness of Being) and Levinas (God as the trace of the Other) are not yet radical enough. If God occurs, this can only happen in an ungodly way, that is to say, in a human, phenomenal, phenomenological way. Or, in other words, he can only appear as affected by context, relation, background, perspectivism. Lyotard takes a similar stance with regard to this issue as he takes up Derrida's question on how not to speak about God. Marion also discusses this issue extensively via his phenomenological analysis of idol and icon. In opposition to Derrida, however, he explicitly joins in this respect the Christian tradition but without wanting to give up his philosophical perspective. Thinking about Christ as the image of the invisible God (Col. 1:15), he states that the icon deals with a presence, which is of a different nature than the presence of an object. Of course, these ways of thinking God as absolutely transcendent, especially as far as Derrida and Levinas are concerned, give rise to many problems, especially with regard to the problem of incarnation. Ricoeur argues that we cannot know anything at all about a completely absolute Other. If we are unable to experience the totally Other in his radical otherness, we are unable to think or speak about him at all, either philosophically or religiously. Girard, too, tries to make clear with the help of cultural anthropology that both a vertical transcendence, which enlarges the distance between man and God so much that they do not touch each other anymore, and a horizontal transcendence, which causes these two spheres of influence to overlap more or less, create insurmountable problems. Finally, in Henry's radical phenomenology, as a search for the roots of appearing itself, the issue of transcendence takes a new turn again. In opposition to the traditional emphasis on God's transcendence both in philosophy and theology, he stresses the immanence of God's manifestation. In his view, God is Life as such, and reveals Himself from Himself, not as something else, without any exteriority. This approach of (God's) immanence also puts an end to every dialectical relation with transcendence. From the perspective of radical phenomenology, God's essence is his (immanent) self-experience. Well, however diverging all these reflections about God's transcendence are, they give theology a lot to think about, such as the logos about God, the doctrine of incarnation, Christian ethics, etc.

This leads us to a second set of problems with important consequences for theology, namely, the more general methodological question regarding which sources (systematic) theology can draw upon in order to think God and (elements of) Christian religion. In opposition to most traditional forms of natural theology, and in spite of the fact that he is a philosopher himself, Levinas explicitly values the classic texts of his Jewish tradition as authentic sources of philosophical reflection about God. With regard to this, his position is similar to philosophical hermeneutics, which turned away from foundational thinking and tried to think God by means of a philosophical reflection of elements coming from religious traditions and other extra-philosophical sources. Concretely, Levinas concentrates on an attentive reading of the Talmud and the Jewish Bible. However, he strictly separates this reading from his philosophical work. The work of Ricoeur, too, offers a major contribution to this issue. His work *The Rule of Metaphor* (*La metaphore vive*) can be read as an emancipation of perception and imagination from reflective thinking. As a consequence of this, he pays a lot of attention to the specific expressiveness of religious stories and symbols. They 'give to think' and in that sense they precede philosophy. As a literary theorist, Girard, too, opts for such an approach, with the particular purpose of discovering the specificity of Christianity. By means of a comparison of the essential stories of diverging religious traditions, he tries to give a philosophical characterization of Christianity and its essential difference with mythical religions and modern culture. The renewed attention for God is also combined with a renewed interest for and new accents in phenomenology. Besides hermeneutics, phenomenology is an important challenge for theological thinking. Of course, we should keep in mind in the first place the work of Ricoeur, but also the recent works of Marion and Henry deserve to be mentioned in this respect. Marion's central question is how the givenness of God should be thought philosophically. In numerous ways, Christianity shows itself to be a religion of a gift that cannot be objectified. This, of course, primarily holds true for Christ himself, but in a derived sense it is also true for the Gospel as Good Tidings, for love and charity. In his work, Henry offers a phenomenological analysis of this structure of immediacy and connects it to his phenomenological reduction of Christianity. All these examples show that these philosophers point to the crucial importance of extra-philosophical elements, such as religious stories and symbols, in order to think God. Of course, this not only holds true for philosophy, but also for systematic theology.

With this, I have indicated two important sets of problems, *viz*., the specific question of God's transcendence and the more general methodological question of how to think God adequately. Both are of vital importance to religious thought in our times. Of course, the various chapters of this book deal with these problems in a much more detailed and subtle way than this introduction. By briefly indicating them here I did not want to give a definitive answer to whether or not God feels at home in France. I have only given a first impression of the particularly interesting lines that can be drawn between the works of the thinkers that are discussed in this book on the one hand, and Christian religion and theology on the other hand. In an often surprising and sometimes even challenging way, these thinkers take up elements from the Jewish and Christian traditions in order to use them for a clarification of their own philosophical questions. By doing so, they shed a new light on current philosophical problems. Apparently, religion remains an inexhaustible source of inspiration for philosophy, even in an age of indecision about God. But precisely because these thinkers bring up religious ideas in a strange context and from less obvious perspectives, they also shed a new light on religion and theology. It would not be correct to use the

medieval image of philosophy as the handmaid of theology to characterize this (mutual relationship between contemporary French philosophy
and theology) Rather, thinking about these questions offers to both philosophy and theology an opportunity for a crossover, which is mutually
enriching. This book hopes to offer a contribution to this fascinating
process.

PAUL RICOEUR: THINKING THE BIBLE

THEO DE BOER

Throughout the prolific and richly varied works of Paul Ricoeur (born in 1913, hence entering his tenth decade) two distinct moments keep recurring. One is his sustained fascination with religion and theology; the other is his enduring attachment to the (French) tradition of reflective philosophy. Ricoeur has always felt a bond with French Protestantism and has attested to this in many addresses and articles. No less is he an impassioned philosopher. In our culture it seems matter-of-course that there is tension between these two and, as Ricoeur himself indicates, this is true in his case as well. Religion and theology are predicated on faith philosophy presupposes reason. These seem natural enemies. In his intellectual autobiography Ricoeur writes that during his student days he learned to wage, "from one armistice to the next, a civil war between faith and reason, as it was called at the time."[1] He prefers the term 'armistice' rather than alliance because he did not want a kind of fusion or amalgamation between philosophy and biblical faith.

As such, the concept of 'reflective philosophy' does not yet imply an antithesis like this. Re-flection, literally a bending back, refers to the mind bending back upon itself. Sometimes it is a term for inner observation, sometimes it is a synonym for thinking, reflection in the sense of pondering. To this extent the word merely names a method. Human beings are able to think about themselves, about experiences, acts and works. They can also think about religious sentiments, myths and rites. In itself this need not be a problem. But in the Western traditions the notion of reflection is intimately bound up with a philosophy in which the thinker's own consciousness, his thinking I, is central. From Descartes onwards this 'subject' is 'autonomous'. Between this 'philosophy of subjectivity' and religion a tension certainly does exist.

---

[1] Paul Ricoeur, *Réflexion faite. Autobiographie intellectuelle*. Paris, Editions Esprit, 1995, p. 15 [P. Ricoeur, Intellectual Autobiography. In: L.E. Hahn (ed.), *The Philosophy of Paul Ricoeur* (Library of Living Philosophers, 22). Chicago, Open Court, 1995, p. 6]. See also the interview with Ricoeur in: *La critique et la conviction. Entretien avec François Azouvi et Marc de Launay*. Paris, Calmann-Lévy, 1995, pp. 211-56 [*Critique and Conviction*. Cambridge, Polity Press, 1998, pp. 139-171].

Our Western culture features abundant discussion about relationships
between the entities 'faith' and 'reason'. Very often such essays and
treatises are hardly fruitful because the terms function as undefined concepts. Ricoeur's work is exiting because his inquiries extend to these
very concepts themselves. From his earliest work up to the present day
the author conducts a meticulous discussion with himself and, thanks to
his enormous erudition, he dialogues with almost all of the philosophical
and theological literature of the twentieth century. My comments will for
the most part follow the chronological order.

1. Phenomenology of religion

Ricoeur's first major (multi-volume) work, *The Philosophy of the Will*
(Philosophie de la volonté) is, as the title tells us, a purely philosophical
effort. The second part, entitled *Finitude and Culpability (Finitude et*
culpabilité), consists of two volumes, *Fallible Man (L'homme faillible)*
and *The Symbolism of Evil (La Symbolique du mal)*, the second of which
may be considered an indirect contribution to theology.[2] His way of
describing this relationship, however, reveals that he does not view theology as the classical tradition did, where theology is either a philosophical reflection on the idea of god (as 'rational' or 'natural' theology) or
a reflection on revelation (as 'positive' or 'supernatural' theology), and
where natural theology paves the way for supernatural theology.
Ricoeur's perspective cannot be accommodated by either of them. In
The Symbolism of Evil he starts out from a phenomenology of religion as
base for both philosophy and theology.[3]
    Phenomenology of religion, of which Mircea Eliade and Gerardus van
der Leeuw were prominent pioneers, is a new way of thinking religion;
in fact, it is the first empirical approach to religion. The eighteenth century, the time of the early Enlightenment, was a golden age for natural

---

[2] P. Ricoeur, *Philosophie de la volonté: volume I. Le volontaire et l'involontaire*
(Philosophie de l'esprit). Paris, Aubier, 1950 [P. Ricoeur, *Freedom and Nature. The Vol-*
untary and the Involuntary. Evanston (Illinois), Northwestern University Press, 1966];
P. Ricoeur, *Philosophie de la volonté volume II. Finitude et Culpabilité. I. L'homme fail-*
lible (Philosophie de l'esprit). Paris, Aubier, 1960 [P. Ricoeur, *Fallible Man*. Chicago,
Henry Regnery, 1965]; P. Ricoeur, *Finitude et culpabilité, II. La symbolique du mal*
(Philosophie de l'esprit). Paris, Aubier, 1960 [P. Ricoeur, *The Symbolism of Evil* (Religious Perspectives, vol. 17). New York-Evanston-London, Harper, 1967].
[3] P. Ricoeur, *La symbolique du mal*, pp. 25, 288 [P. Ricoeur, *The Symbolism of Evil*,
pp. 19, 309f].

or rational theology. In terms of world-and-life view, Europe had been torn apart by religious wars. Philosophers felt called upon to develop a theology based on reason able to establish a unity overriding creedal discord. They were interested more in the idea of religion than in religion as such. The core of rational theology consisted in the proof of the existence of God, the immortality of the human soul and the morality these implied.

But when, in the course of the nineteenth century, historical consciousness arises, little is left to support the edifice of rational religion. The diversity of religions seems endless. Phenomenology of religion would chart this multitude. Ricoeur calls it 'comparatism'. This is not a disqualification, as if one merely mindlessly collects facts. In *The Symbolism of Evil* Ricoeur himself engages in such comparatism. Phenomenology describes and compares. It further asks for meaning in its findings by looking for parallels among the many symbols and myths. Quite consciously and explicitly, however, it does not ask the 'truth question'. In this phenomenology of religion differs from both Christian and rational theology. The name 'phenomenology' is taken because it borrows the 'phenomenological *epoche*' as practised by the (early) Husserl. Husserl meant to investigate phenomena such as properties like sounds and colours, as given in sense perceptions, without asking about their ontic status. 'Being' was temporarily 'bracketed'. In similar vein, phenomenology of religion investigates religious phenomena without asking about their transcendent origins. The phenomenologist does not investigate God, but 'God' that is to say, the representations of God that people have.

Phenomenology of religion spelled a crisis for rational theology because the supposedly evident basic theses did not reappear in factual reality. Nevertheless, the new religious science too has a politically pacifying import. If in science God must be placed in brackets because truth is unattainable, discrimination of religions no longer has an epistemological base. The separation of Church and State comes to rest on a less speculative but deeper foundation. Not the results of rational thinking, but the operation of the inquiry as such constitutes the basis for tolerance.

The fact that science investigates empirical religions and is not in search of religious axioms implies at least two things: (1) rehabilitation of those religions that can no longer be disqualified as distortions of a rational, original form, and (2) natural axioms or dogmas can no longer claim self-evident authority, which implies recognition of a 'natural' uncertainty. Tolerance is grounded not in evidence but in lack of evidence, i.e. in an a priori and always present awareness that the own conviction, however inspiring, can never be supported with compelling arguments. Religions are multiple by definition. Plurality and time are categories that, as 'irrational', cannot be thought in rational theology (or in the classical concept of *episteme* generally). But this does not mean relativism, as dogmatists and modernists hold; rather, it means that we recognise our post-modern condition. Where reason and dogma fail, the appropriate response is to seek an alternative — a 'well-considered conviction' (to borrow a term from John Rawls) — rather than to bewail relativism.

Descriptive phenomenology precedes both theology and philosophy. For each its function is a preparatory one. Theology and philosophy are two ways to determine one's attitude towards the new empirical materials of religious science. For the moment restricting myself to theology: its position has thereby undergone incisive change. This position does not rest on a preceding rational base, but aligns itself with a contingent tradition and takes a stance in the multiplicity of myths. Phenomenology describes the Adam myth in Genesis and compares it with other myths. Theology builds on this and considers how this myth is related to Christology. An example is St. Paul's thought in the letter to the Romans, where he places the situation of we humans 'in Adam' over against that 'in Christ'. Ecclesiastic theology thus situates the myth in the totality of the proclamation.[4] Does this mean that the basis of theology is irrational? That depends on how one thinks of 'myth' after the demise of rational theology. A major part of Ricoeur's work consists of reflection on this question. A theology that would start out from the myths, that is, the narratives, has a status *sui generis*. Although Ricoeur does not enlarge upon this in *The Symbolism of Evil*, the narrative turn eventually elaborated in *Time and Narrative (Temps et récit)* is already present.[5]

2. Reflective philosophy

Descriptive phenomenology is the starting point for philosophy as well. But something must first be said concerning the status of philosophy.

[4] *Ibid.*, pp. 244, 251f, 253ff [*Ibid.*, pp. 260f, 269f, 271ff].
[5] P. Ricoeur, *Temps et récit, I, II, III.* Paris, Du Seuil, 1983-85 [P. Ricoeur, *Time and Narrative, I, II, III.* Chicago, University of Chicago Press, 1984-88].

According to Ricoeur, philosophy differs from theology in that there is a philosophy that continues the classical tradition of reason (*episteme*), namely as 'eidetics', the analysis of essences.

The first volume in *The Philosophy of the Will*, entitled *The Voluntary and the Involuntary (Le volontaire et l'involontaire)*, is an analysis of the will in the Husserlian manner. As Husserl had inventoried knowledge, so Ricoeur sought to do this for the neglected areas of the will and emotion. He analyses the voluntary, in the three forms of decision, voluntary motion and consent on the one hand, and the involuntary, i.e. aspects of existence that are not subject to the will, such as habits, emotions, character, the unconscious on the other.

Throughout, the analysis brackets the phenomenon of the evil will, because the 'fall' of the will (*la faute*) is something contingent, ineligible for eidetic analysis. The same *epoche* is applied in *Fallible Man*. Here too the 'fault' is bracketed but via an anthropological analysis, Ricoeur seeks to show that human beings are *capable of* the 'fault'. An important element in the argument is the distinction between emotions and desires on the one hand, and passions on the other. Ricoeur looks upon passions as derailed emotions. There is something in human beings on account of which the — as such justified — desire for well-being, influence and honour runs amok. We all know this phenomenon. Humans strive for the infinite. Those who earn a hundred thousand want to earn a million. Two honorary doctorates must become twenty.

Why is it that people take this path? Whence this derailment? Philosophy should thematise not only the structure of the will and of fallibility, but also the enigmatic, factual 'fault' which we call 'evil' hence, the difference between the innocent and the evil will, between salvation and calamity. Can this be done? In practice it seems that philosophy 'forgets' the erring will. In ethics, for example, there is much talk of the need for dialogue, but very little of the willingness to dialogue — 'the dialogue before dialogue', as Levinas calls it. That most linguistic animals simply refuse the dialogue is a fact neglected. It seems as if philosophical means, conceptual analysis, cannot lead to discourse on evil at all. On the other hand, if it does, evil is seen as non-being or as an aspect of finitude. Ricoeur — surely inspired by his faith — always refused to look upon evil as structural. Unlike Karl Jaspers (whom he admires) Ricoeur has never wanted to characterise evil as a constitutive element of the human condition (*Grenzsituation*).

Noteworthy and original is that Ricoeur does not keep factual evil out of philosophy on behalf of purity of method. He adapts method to topic.

If philosophy would treat of evil, it must allow the factual, the 'irrational', to enter. With this, Ricoeur opens the door to hermeneutics. Those who want to know of evil must read and hence interpret. What would we know of jealousy without Shakespeare's *Othello*? What of crime and punishment without Dostoyevski? Here tradition enters philosophy. All these sources are granted admission in a philosophy that would contribute to the 'wisdom' of the nations — a concept that plays a central role in the later 'small ethics' in *Oneself as Another* (*Soi-même comme un autre*).[6] Obviously the Bible is one such source. At this point, then, the phenomenology of religion enters philosophy. All facts gathered and compared are material for interpretation. It is only via the symbolic and mythic tradition that we learn of the evil will. From this point onwards Ricoeur engages in two kinds of philosophy: eidetic analysis and hermeneutics, a philosophy excluding contingent 'presuppositions', and a philosophy embracing them.

Already here I note that this dichotomy poses problems, as evidenced earlier in one area: the analysis of the passions. Ricoeur's Pascalian theory of 'disproportion' in the human being is, compared with other Western-philosophical treatises on the passions, a far-reaching and arresting analysis. Nevertheless — and Ricoeur is not about to hide this — it is inspired by the distinction he makes between a state of innocence and a state of evil. But this shows that the hermeneutic of contingent symbols also impacts on that part of philosophy supposedly resting on eidetic analysis only. The illuminating power of the myth has consequences for 'rational' philosophy. The mutual relationship of the two kinds of philosophy largely determine the development in Ricoeur's thought. In 1960 hermeneutics is still complementary to eidetic analysis. But its position gradually gains greater importance.

Ricoeur's original plan was to present a 'hermeneutics of the fault' in a third part of the *Philosophy of the Will*. He also calls it a philosophy of Transcendence as liberation from evil. But that book remained unwritten, a fact that needs explanation. In the autobiography he calls that announcement an ill-advised promise considering that a number of issues required further study, but I believe that the main reason for

---

[6] P. Ricoeur, *Soi-même comme un autre*. Paris, Du Seuil, 1990 [P. Ricoeur, *Oneself as Another*. Chicago, University of Chicago Press, 1992]. I refer to my analysis of *Oneself as Another* in: Th. De Boer, Identité narrative et identité éthique. In: *Paul Ricoeur. L'herméneutique à l'école de la phénoménologie*. Paris, Institut Catholique de Paris, pp. 43-58.

cancellation (or postponement, see below) is the undecided conflict between faith and 'reason'.

A breakthrough in method is upsetting, not least for a philosopher who would justify every move of his. In 'The symbol gives rise to thought' (*Le symbole donne à penser*), the final chapter of *The Symbolism of Evil*, Ricoeur presents a methodological preview of the planned Part III, so that we have the odd situation that we possess a methodology for a book that remained unwritten. That chapter itself, though, is of great value. On essential points it is in agreement with Gadamer's *Truth and Method* (*Wahrheit und Methode*). There can have been no borrowing, however, since both books were published in the same year, 1960.

A philosopher, Ricoeur says, is expected to go beyond cataloguing and comparing symbols and myths. He is not merely curious, he is involved. Ricoeur admits that already he transgressed the position of the neutral observer in the chapter dealing with the dynamics of myths, to the extent that he starts out from the primacy of the Adam myth relative to other myths (the myth of the original chaos, the evil God over against tragic man, the exiled soul). Unlike the phenomenologist, the philosopher cannot rest content with gathering meanings; he must take a stand. Here Ricoeur speaks of the hermeneutic circle of believing and understanding.

One must believe in order to understand, which means that interpretation is borne by an awareness of the matter at stake in the text. For symbols and myths that would be the sacred (*le sacré*). Such pre-understanding is not a dogmatic prejudice; it is an expectation guiding the interpretation, concretised and criticised as interpretation takes its course. On the other hand, we must understand in order to believe. Here Ricoeur introduces an important concept: 'second naiveté'. We moderns can no longer believe in myths like pre-moderns did, but in understanding we can attain a second naiveté. We can approach this concept — now part of our heritage — via the distinction Ricoeur makes between demythologising and demythicising. At the time Ricoeur participated intensively in the debate on demythologising engendered by Rudolf Bultmann. His position was: Demythologising? Yes. Demythicising? No. We moderns must necessarily demythologise because we can no longer believe in myth as explanation of the world. Mythic time is the original time, which can in no way be integrated in the chronological time of history. As to the myth of the origin of evil: we can no longer believe in the historical fall of the first man causing all human misery.

Ricoeur views the Augustinian doctrine of original sin as an explanatory
theory of the same order. To my mind creationism as alternative for evolution theory is another example, as is the fundamentalist reconstruction
of 'redemptive history' as alternative for modern, historical research.
    Ricoeur holds that precisely demythologising makes it possible to
understand the myth rightly. Recognition of myth *as* myth is an unin-
tended gift of modernity to the believer. We live in an epoch in which a
new understanding of the religious heritage is possible.[7] Demythicising,
however, strips myth's authentic, scientifically irreplaceable message.
Myth is a proto-typical story of what may befall the human creature, and
'donne à penser'. Because of this 'gift to thought', belief as second
naiveté is possible. This is believing through understanding. Accordingly, Ricoeur rejects the idea that a philosophy is not permitted to proceed from presuppositions. Philosophy starts out from an existing language; from the 'fullness of language' or 'full language', a language far
richer than that of science.[8] It is there that we meet the symbols and
myths that nourish thought. Ricoeur is aware that consequently philosophy is embedded in a specific culture, that of the Middle East. As early
as 1960, far in advance of the multi-cultural emancipation of the 1980s,
he recognises as limitation the fact that the Far East and China do not yet
reverberate in our spiritual space.[9]
    Reflective philosophy however, is no less rooted in tradition — in this
case, Ricoeur admits, Greek in origin. Does this mean that philosophy
has its own contingent presupposition? Here we come upon an unre-
solved tension in Ricoeur's thought. Continually he proves to find it difficult to take leave of reflective philosophy's universal pretension. He
refers for example to the philosopher's 'oath' as affirmation of coherence and concept. He would join forces with the tradition of pure reflection that appeals to no myth whatever and in this sense is a direct exercise of rationality. In this connection he says in the final pages of *The
Symbolism of Evil* that the hermeneutic circle must be overcome and that
philosophy of a thinking *in* symbols must switch to thinking *about* symbols and transform the circle to a wager. Thinking in symbols was a
wager already — I bet that I understand humans better with those symbols than without them — but this must now be *verified* in a 'coherent

    [7] P. Ricoeur, *La symbolique du mal*, pp. 13, 154, 325f [P. Ricoeur, *The Symbolism of
Evil*, pp. 5, 162, 349f].
    [8] *Ibid.*, pp. 26, 324, 332 [*Ibid.*, pp. 19, 348f, 357].
    [9] *Ibid.*, pp. 26, 29 [*Ibid.*, pp. 20, 22f].

discourse'. Notwithstanding the contingency of the symbols the task of philosophy is to uncover a 'universal and rational structure'.[10]

For Ricoeur this rational structure refers to general structures of existential experience (comparable to Heidegger's 'existentials'). In *Time and Narrative III* this is worked out in a philosophical anthropology that underlies historical consciousness. No matter how one responds to this analysis[11] — methodically it is a continuation and expansion of the *Philosophy of the Will* — it obviously cannot provide the empirical facts of the tradition with a rational foundation. And so a tension remains in Ricoeur's thought between historical situatedness and general validity (until recently, as we shall see).

That thinking from the myths may come into conflict with reflective philosophy can be gleaned from the closing pages of *The Symbolism of Evil*, where Ricoeur says that the inspiration by myths leads not only to expansion but also to a 'qualitative change' of the reflecting consciousness. After all, we are dealing here with a philosophy of religion, that is, reflection on the bond with the sacred. The task of a philosophy guided by the symbol is to break the magic circle of the self-consciousness. Here the starting point of reflective philosophy, i.e. autonomous thought, faces a crisis. The symbol inspires us to think that thinking itself is not the origin — the very thinking that ought to switch from thinking *in* symbols to thinking *about* symbols. Ricoeur calls this a 'second Copernican revolution'. Naiveté now applies to thinking itself! The act of the *I think* that autonomously posits being must discover that it participates in the very being by which it is questioned. The tension between thought and that which gives rise to thought is lifted in favour of the latter.

In *Freud and Philosophy. An Essay on Interpretation* (*De l'interpretation. Essai sur Freud*), which appeared five years after *The Symbolism of Evil*, we note again the ambiguity of the concept of reflective philosophy. Ricoeur retains the pretension of philosophy as science in the classical sense of *episteme*; characterised by universality, clarity and unity, over against the multiplicity, equivocalness and particularity of the myths.[12]

---

[10] *Ibid.*, pp. 323 ff, 332 [*Ibid.*, pp. 347ff, 357].

[11] See Th. de Boer, Faith, Belief and Narrative. In: H. Vroom and J.D. Gort (ed.), *Holy Scriptures in Judaism, Christianity and Islam. Hermeneutics, Values and Society.* Amsterdam/Atlanta, GA, Rodopi, 1997, pp. 34ff, 37.

[12] P. Ricœur, *De l'interprétation. Essai sur Freud.* Paris, Du Seuil, 1965, pp. 49ff [P. Ricœur, *Freud and Philosophy. An Essay on Interpretation.* New Haven/London, Yale University Press, 1970, pp. 41ff].

But the self-evidence of the 'I think' is *restricted* to the ego as empty
centre. Its concrete contents, whatever these may be, can be subjected to
doubt. Incontestable is only that these are contents of 'my' consciousness. In order to know the 'I' *in concreto* we must study its expression
in the works of culture.

We noted that the mythic legacy is altogether contingent. The question now is whether it is not the case that the apodictic ego is swept
along by that stream of contents. As such one can doubt that the designation 'mine' regarding every content of consciousness must be expli-
cated in the ego-centric way. Would that not be a designation modelled
after one paradigm of ego-involvement, namely, that of the vigilantly
observing scientist? The passions I referred to earlier — and equally
phenomena such as attention, devotion, exaltation, which need not
immediately count as derailments — are part of me as selfhood or (to
use a term from the later Ricoeur) *'ipséité'*, but are not centred around
the I of 'I think'. How can the principle of the self-positing ego hold all
contents together without violating them? Is it not so that this egological
principle, so characteristic for Western thought, is itself contingent?
Implicitly, Ricoeur more or less admits this in the remarkable 'multi-cultural' passage mentioned above. The philosopher has no position in nev-
erland. He speaks from a cultural memory, the Greek memory.[13]

We saw that religious myths in particular plunge the ego into crisis.
They tell of a dimension greater and more original than self-consciousness. Nevertheless, this *cogito*, however abstract and empty, is said to be
'invincible'. With this, a conflict is introduced in the mind of the author,
such that the imagery of 'civil war' is not inappropriate. A 'conflict of
interpretations', one might call it (the title of one of Ricoeur's earlier
books). But in terms of Ricoeur's self-understanding at that time it is a
conflict between an interpretation (of hermeneutics) and a *certainty* (of
reflective philosophy).

3. Theology

Time to return to theology. We saw that both theology and philosophy
(to the extent that they are hermeneutical) are founded in phenomenology. Both depend on empirical materials as source for thought. This is

---

[13] P. Ricoeur, *La symbolique du mal*, p. 29 [P. Ricoeur, *The Symbolism of Evil*,
p. 22f]; P. Ricoeur, *De l'interprétation*, p. 55 [P. Ricoeur, *Freud and Philosophy*, p. 48].

the break with the tradition of rational thought and its self-generated truths. Above, I referred to this as our 'post-modern' condition. Ricoeur does not (yet) use this term. He does say that philosophy can no longer meet the requirement of 'presuppositionlessness'.[7]

A question that needs consideration first is: How does theology actually differ from philosophy? Surely, we may assume that theologians do not just collect and compare meanings, but that they 'think', that is, take a stand. It would seem that theologians *par excellence* are interested in the truth question, hence curious and involved. Must we assume that they operate in the pre-modern manner, feeling quite at home in 'first naiveté'? Although this would be in line with the notions most philosophers entertain regarding theologians, it seems hardly likely that this is Ricoeur's view. It would for example mean that theologians remain blissfully ignorant of historical awareness and its consequent acknowledgement of a plurality of myths.

Next, in the previous section we saw that Ricoeur, in a preview of his 'philosophy of Transcendence', breaks open the 'magic circle of the self-consciousness' and the 'privilege of reflection' — in *philosophy* rather than in theology. But this raises the unavoidable question: How does theology differ from a philosophy that would be taught by symbols? The line of demarcation blurs, though Ricoeur says he wants to maintain it. In this constellation faith and reason cannot be opposed in principle. A philosophy that would understand reflection as a purely methodological concept and would not be contaminated by philosophical prejudices from the Western tradition, such as the idea of the autonomy and self-positing of the ego, is not by definition opposed to theology. Rather, the difference seems to be one of distance regarding specific Christian dogmas (and regarding field of activity and division of labour in vocational theological training). Let us first attend to Ricoeur's own statements on this.

Concerning the status of theology Ricoeur expresses himself in the final chapter of *Freud and Philosophy. An Essay on Interpretation*. There he says that faith introduces a new dimension, an 'interpellation', a 'kerygma', a 'word' (sometimes capitalised). Reflective philosophy, taking its stand in immanence, has no resources here. "To be sure, I speak of the Wholly Other only insofar as it addresses itself to me; and the kerugma, the glad tidings, is precisely that it addresses itself to me and ceases to be the Wholly Other. Of an absolute Wholly Other I know nothing at all. But by its very manner of approaching, of coming, it shows itself to be Wholly Other ...annihilating its radical otherness."[14] I consider this passage well put. One cannot speak of the Wholly Other without referring to it as phenomenon, that is, if it cannot be experienced in the specific modality of radical otherness.[15] There is a threshold, but there is 'a threshold intelligence' as well. This is why Ricoeur can in one breath refer to Van der Leeuw and Eliade as phenomenologists of the sacred *and* Barth and Bultmann as exegetes of the kerygma — all of them have laid bare this dimension, even if they did not work it out.

I explore the problem of the Wholly Other here under the heading 'theology', because of Ricoeur's very clear statement that this dimension of faith cannot be uncovered by the immanent method of reflective philosophy. Yet I should immediately add that the argument does not differ in any way from the lines Ricoeur devoted in *The Symbolism of Evil* to the (never written) philosophy of Transcendence (except that the word 'being' is now replaced by 'the Wholly Other'). Also, he speaks of the circle of believing and understanding in the same way. Once again we note Ricoeur's own inner battle. No other passage in his writings can match the explicitness with which he speaks of the Wholly Other here. Nowhere else do we see him formulate the problem of self-positing more pointedly.

Ricoeur rejects the 'sly move' of introducing the Wholly Other through extrapolation of the ground (*arche*, i.e. the unconscious), and the goal (*telos*, i.e. the culture) of the *cogito*.[16] The archaeology of the subject never reaches beyond that which the *cogito* posited in the past; the teleology halts at the last meaning which gathers up as self-projection of the mind all that went before. No reflection whatever can recover and grasp the religious dimensions *genesis* and *eschaton*. They are 'wholly other', perpendicular to the archaeology and teleology of the subject.

It seems to me that it would help to describe the Wholly Other that Ricoeur intends here as a *vertical* transcendence (or Transcendence). Compared to Kant's horizontal transcendence there is an essential difference. Ricoeur likes to cite Kant who speaks of God as transcendental

---

[14] P. Ricoeur, *De l'interprétation*, pp. 39, 504ff [P. Ricoeur, *Freud and Philosophy*, pp. 29f, 525ff].

[15] In *Soi-même comme un autre* Ricoeur rejects as unthinkable the absolute alterity on which he believes Levinas to insist. Cf. P. Ricoeur, *Soi-même comme un autre*, p. 388 [P. Ricoeur, *Oneself as Another*, pp. 336f].

[16] On the archeology and teleology of the consciousness see Th. de Boer, Ricoeurs Hermeneutik. In: *Allgemeine Zeitschrift für Philosphie*, 16 (1991) 3, pp. 6ff

ideal. For Kant, in the theoretical reason, God is the most comprehensive horizon of thought, always receding and never grasped as object. Objectifying the Wholly Other is — this is Kant's great insight — a diabolic reversal whereby the horizon becomes an object within the horizon. With this, Kant has unmasked metaphysics, which turns God into a highest being. In spite of Ricoeur's appreciation for Kant, though, it should be stressed that for him God is unlike, in particular *more than,* a regulative idea driving thought on towards an unattainable limit. This transcendental ideal is closely bound up with the idea of the autonomous ego. The self-positing ego also stakes out the horizon of experience. For Ricoeur, God is rightly called the 'Wholly Other'. The Wholly Other is a vertical on this horizon, not conceived as limit of theoretical thought. Barth and Bultmann, too, certainly intended something else. Actually, this is the case with the phenomenologists of religion as well. The Wholly Other is perpendicular to experience and hence can present itself within that horizon in anything that may become a 'sign' of the sacred. At any moment the sacred can manifest itself, not as limit of experience but within it — though not as theoretical object: 'the Kingdom of God is at hand'. Precisely this is the contingency of the sacred.

Until now we have mostly referred to Ricoeur's early work. This is not accidental. The religious dimension is remarkably prominent here. This comes to expression especially in the de-centring of the ego, not only of the concrete self, but also of the abstract cogito, i.e. the very point from which reflective philosophy proceeds. In the later works the critique of the ego is there as well, particularly in the dispossession effected by the text, but not in the radical sense as in religion.[17] The subject is dispossessed in the reading, and returns to itself enriched. The questioning appeal of the sacred however may lead to a renouncing of the desire to be (*désir d'être*). What is put into question here is the entire effort of longing to be which Ricoeur, with Spinoza, describes as the core of the subject. Ricoeur speaks of the 'epigenesis' of religious sentiment, overlooked by Freud, which implies a 'conversion' from that longing to be. Such renouncing is no death wish but love.[18]

In his later large works *Time and Narrative* (1983-1985) and *Oneself as Another* (1990) the Wholly Other is no longer mentioned. In the

[17] See my article mentioned in note 16, pp. 21ff.
[18] P. Ricoeur, *De l'interprétation*, pp. 52ff, 513, 526ff [P. Ricocur, *Freud and Philosophy*, pp. 45ff, 534, 548ff].

Introduction to *Oneself as Another* Ricoeur once again emphatically declares that he means to present an autonomous philosophical discourse, reason why, he says, he left out the chapters on biblical hermeneutics with which he ended the *Gifford Lectures*. Biblical faith must be bracketed and the name of God should not mentioned in a philosophical work. As a philosopher, the philosopher is an agnostic. "As a philosopher I cannot say, where the voice of conscience comes from — that ultimate expression of otherness that haunts selfhood! Does it come from a person who is other, but whom I can still *'envisage'*, from my ancestors, from a dead god or from a living God, but one just as absent from our life as the past is from all reconstructed history, or even from some empty place?"[19] Above all, Ricoeur would avoid having theology answer philosophical questions. With this I can agree without reservations. For that would be a presentation in the traditional manner, the scheme of natural and supernatural theology. On the other hand, I see nothing wrong with having philosophy reflect on the gift of 'biblical thought'[20] to thought, and tabling it in the deliberations or 'well-considered convictions' on which democratic societies and inter-religious dialogues ultimately fall back. Meanwhile it is clear why he did not write his book on Transcendence. He dared not cross the threshold for fear of being called a crypto-theologian.

In *Oneself as Another* Ricoeur himself pleads for such an integration of 'world-and-life view' in philosophy implicitly, when he states that ethics, critically tested by rational morality, ultimately falls back on the 'wisdom of the nations', that is, on tradition. This step beyond rational morality back to the ethics of a community (which I analysed elsewhere[21]) is a remarkable development in Ricoeur. *Time and Narrative* still shows him to be much attached to the totalising idea to which I referred above as 'horizontal transcendence'. In practical philosophy this transcendental idea of a totality leading thought takes on the form of a supra-historical standard that must establish unity in the multiplicity of political strivings. It functions as guideline in political action and is aimed at the unity of humankind. It is the practical translation of the

[19] P. Ricoeur, *Réflexion faite. Autobiographie intellectuelle.* p. 82 [P. Ricoeur, Intellectual Autobiography, p. 53]; P. Ricoeur, *Soi-même comme un autre*, pp. 35ff, 409 [P. Ricoeur, *Oneself as Another* pp. 23ff, 355]. See also the Preface by O. Mongin in: P. Ricoeur, *Lectures 3. Aux frontières de la philosophie.* Paris, Du Seuil, 1994, pp. 7-11.
[20] For the expression *pensée biblique* see P. Ricoeur, *La critique et la conviction*, pp. 215, 226 [P. Ricoeur, *Critique and Conviction*, pp. 142, 149].
[21] See the articles mentioned in notes 6 and 16.

regulative idea of pure reason. Ricoeur retains this Kantian idea in *Time and Narrative* because in ethics he cannot rest content with a purely narrative and hence rudderless identity. This idea does not come into crisis until in *Oneself as Another*, where it is reduced to a necessary thought experiment for the rational test of ethics just referred to. The idea of horizontal transcendence, so closely linked up with the autonomous ego, is now abandoned. The totalising perspective is gone. This must have brought Ricoeur to the threshold of post-modernism.

4. Interlude; What is thinking?

Above I spoke repeatedly of 'thought' or 'thinking'. I even suggested that theologians, too, are capable of thinking. But what is thought? Probably no concept is more historically loaded as this one that, like 'reason', pretends to be untouched by any history whatever. To discuss our question we can turn to *The Rule of Metaphor (La métaphore vive)*, a book devoted to the rehabilitation of a competitor of thinking, the metaphor. We met the concept of metaphor in the context of the symbol and the 'fullness of language' as legitimate presupposition in the hermeneutics of religion. At that point Ricoeur had already taken his distance from the classical definition of thinking as *episteme* guided by geometric clarity and distinctness.

The closing chapter of *The Rule of Metaphor* presents a recapitulation of classical theology and philosophy. Ricoeur shows that the doctrine of the *analogia entis*, the analogy of the being of creation and the Being of God, tends to establish theology as genuine science in accordance with the classical standards of *episteme*, distinct from and elevated above poetic biblical discourse. Thinking takes place within the framework of the analogy; the metaphor is the iconic illustration of such thought.[22] This is the classical depreciation of the image as illustration of the concept. The concept clarifies the image; the image illustrates the concept. The implications are far-reaching; substantially the image adds nothing. The substance is always already thought in the concept. The content of the concept is now pictured for sensible creatures.

---

[22] P. Ricoeur, *La métaphore vive*. Paris, Du Seuil, 1975, pp. 344, 351, 355 [P. Ricoeur *The Rule of Metaphor. Multi-disciplinary studies in the creation of meaning in language*. London/Henley, Routledge & Kegan Paul, 1978, pp. 272f, 276, 279].

This theory of metaphor presupposes classical metaphysics and its opposition between the world of sense and the world of thought. This means a disqualification of perception and imagination — a disqualification continuing far into the Enlightenment. Concepts are presumably able to penetrate the invisible order behind visible reality. They grasp the general. The factual and individual cannot be thought; it is irrational, here all you can have are 'opinions'. Doubt regarding this scheme of thought did not arise until the awakening of historical thinking in the nineteenth century, coming to full fruition in what we now call 'postmodernism'. Against this background we understand how essential a step was taken by Ricoeur when he sought to 'supplement' eidetics with interpretation. This step leads him further than he initially realised.

The entire argument of *The Rule of Metaphor* turns on emancipation of perceiving and imagining. The metaphor is not an illustration, no embellishment, but has its own capacity to enlighten. The metaphor does not only have a signification of its own; it also has its own reference. It is a lens that lets us see. Old age is a straw (Aristotle), humankind a thinking reed (Pascal) — no concept can improve on the expressive power here. To be sure, poetic language and analysis differ. Philosophers and theologians ought to write other than poetically. The interpreter must explain and this surely is the job of concepts. To think is to articulate, to expose, to disclose. But conceptual clarity feeds on the preceding creative activity of the imagination providing food for thought. Conceptual analysis clarifies; it is however never exhaustive and therefore the interpretation is never definitive. Those who would leave symbols and metaphors behind in order to reach higher lose the ground on which they stand.

Actually one could ask whether Ricoeur himself is immune to this temptation. When defending the proper nature of philosophical thinking, he describes the interpretation as a 'rationalisation' that ultimately 'eliminates' ('*évacue*') the experience expressed in the metaphor. The new meaning created by the metaphor is not yet conceptual gain; the similar is not yet the identical. As such this is correct, to the extent that conceptual determination distinguishes and fixes meanings. You can compare this to determination of plants. "The botanist's plants are not flowers along the Rhine" writes Heidegger somewhere in *Being and Time (Sein und Zeit)*. Of course, the walker setting out with his *Floral Guide* knows this too. Not for him to cherish the illusion that via determination he will reach a higher-level knowledge of nature and lay bare a rational order behind the phenomena. That would be a rationalisation, 'evacuating' the

experience of the flower fancier. Still, this is what in the early Enlightenment the new natural science was expected to do. Hence the disqualification on the part of thinkers such as Descartes and Spinoza of perception, imagination, the narrative. When at some point Ricoeur places
the domain of the *intellectio* over against that of the *imaginatio,* he
seems to revert to the early Enlightenment dichotomy.[23] Be that as it
may, his essential achievement is that he uncovers the symbolic and
metaphorical ground underneath thought. This is why at an early stage
he already combated demythisising and the rationalisation of the myth
through allegory.

 The Rule of Metaphor is Ricoeur's finest and most revolutionary
work. No wonder that, at times, he seems to shy away from the consequences. For the parties in the civil war these consequences are profound. In virtue of the rehabilitation of pre-philosophical language biblical hermeneutics gains an independence of its own. Whatever clarity a
concept may present, it depends on the meaning created by the
metaphor. The image is not an illustration accompanying the concept,
nor is it a pre-logical stage of a concept that can be replaced by the concept. To pare ideas from an artistic form invariably spells impoverish-
ment. The biblical theology analysing this language is not in need of a
higher, scientific theology filtering out earthly stains and blemishes. In
the next section we will see some implications of this.

 For the opposite party, reflective philosophy, rehabilitation of the
imaginative means a schooling in humility. Analysis sheds light, but
only if it remains subservient thinking. Relevance is lost when thinking
allows the bright light of geometric reason to blind it. It clarifies, but can
no longer be appropriated. Of reflection I said that it is a loaded concept,
because of the dominance of the classical *episteme* concept. Reflection
seeks evident starting points and finds these in the *cogito,* in the 'auto-
position' and in the transcendental ideas bound up with it. But this position cannot do justice to the richness of pre-philosophical experience,
history and language. Rooted in its apodictic certainties, the *cogito* still
pretends that it can know 'true being' behind the phenomena, of both the
world and the self. But the soul under thinking resumes its rights.

---

[23] *Ibid.,* pp. 375ff, 381ff [*Ibid.,* pp. 395ff, 301f].

5. Thinking the Bible

Throughout the period from *Freud and Philosophy* (1965) to *Thinking Biblically (Penser la bible)* (1998) religion is bracketed in the large works. Evidently, the dilemma was either to introduce the Wholly Other and thus enter theological waters, or remain true to philosophy and hence keep silent about Transcendence. In that same period Ricoeur did write a large number of articles on 'theological' or 'biblical' topics.[24] He calls them 'excursions in religious language' or analyses of 'biblical discourse'. In these articles, remaining true to his rule not to confuse things, he wants to pay enduring attention to faith.

The question to which we seek an answer: To what extent has Ricoeur overcome the just-mentioned dilemma? We pick up the thread with the article 'To name God' (1977).[25] Ricoeur starts out with the remark that few authors have the talent to write on 'What I believe'. For his part, all he wants to do is to render account of how he understands that which he has heard. He repeats his conviction that in this field no philosopher can begin without presuppositions, which means that a philosopher cannot 'begin' at all. His presupposition is that the Christian proclamation makes sense, is worth investigating, and that the proof of the text is in applying it in life. His wager is that his risk will be made good a hundred-fold in the increase of understanding, vigilance and joy; and that this is how this contingent beginning will be justified. There is a tradition where God already has a name, and hence I can name Him. The hearing of that Word, 'faith', can be characterised in general religious expressions such as 'ultimate concern', 'absolute dependence' or 'unconditional trust'. In the Christian proclamation however, the religious experience is articulated in language. That is its textuality *(textualité)*.

---

[24] A selection is published in P. Ricoeur, *Le conflit des interprétations. Essais d'herméneutique*. Paris, Du Seuil, 1969 [P. Ricoeur, *The Conflict of Interpretations* (Northwestern University studies in Phenomenology & Existential Philosophy). Evanston (Illinois), Northwestern University Press, 1974]. P. Ricoeur, *Du texte à l'action. Essais d'herméneutique II*. Paris, Du Seuil, 1986, pp. 119-134. [P. Ricoeur, *From Text to Action. Essays in Hermeneutics. II*. London, Athlone Press, 1991]. P. Ricoeur, *Essays on Biblical Interpretation*. Philadelphia, Fortress Press, 1980. P. Ricoeur, Biblical Hermeneutics. In: *Paul Ricoeur on Biblical Hermeneutics. Semeia* 4. *An experimental journal for biblical criticism.* Missoula, MT, University of Montana Press, 1975, pp. 27-149.

[25] P. Ricoeur, Entre philosophie en théologie II: Nommer Dieu (1977). In: P. Ricoeur, *Lectures 3. Aux frontières de la philosophie*, pp. 281-305 [P. Ricoeur, Naming God. In: *Union Seminary Quarterly Review* 34 (1979) pp. 215-228].

The circumstance that in the text God is the referent, should not be taken to mean that He inspires the writer, as if He is the text's original author; rather, God belongs to what the text is dealing with. Revelation should not be understood in terms of the author, because in the very transition from speech to text the author and his particular context are transcended. Ricoeur, then, bids us to read the biblical text like any other text and to understand revelation in terms of what the text is about, its purport. But what are we to make of the prophetic texts that are introduced with the sentence Thus says the Lord? Ricoeur objects when God as first person is disengaged from the historical stories in which he is understood as He. In such cases the reference has to do with constitutive events such as the exodus and the resurrection of Jesus. Prophecy is also about history, about past and future deliverance and disaster. Thus, prophecy, too, has a referent and must be understood in terms of it rather than as the utterance of a speaker. The same is true of poetic language, which reveals something to us that heretofore was hidden.

Ricoeur repeats that Kant put an end to any identification of God with some being. This means the suspension of onto-theological statements along the lines of: God exists, God is immutable, God is omnipotent, God is first cause. But how then are we to speak of Him? What language shall we use? Ricoeur now draws important consequences from the rehabilitation of the metaphor. From the very start he situated thinking about religion in the 'full language' outside the field of science and eidetic analysis. Initially he turned to symbols, a special kind of images in dreams and in religion with two meanings, whereby the literal and perceivable refers, in accordance with a fixed code, to the figurative, for example the canopy of heaven and the majesty of God. Metaphors cover a much larger field, not only poetry, but all of language 'in its fullness'. The ordinary language in which members of a faith community articulate their experiences has its own right and place. This is also the language of the Bible with its many genres: narratives, prophecies, laws, proverbs, prayers, hymns and wisdom writings. 'This is the place where God is named'. This is the source from which biblical hermeneutics draws 'biblical thought'.

Importantly, Ricoeur now calls such pre-philosophical language 'original'. These genres are no 'rhetorical artifice' alien to the content, the philosophical concept of deity. But classical metaphysics claims it is and, driven by the ideal of *episteme,* looks upon pre-philosophical language as ornamental, to be left behind in the analysis of the content or the concept. Admirable in pre-philosophical language is the marvellous

fit of structure and kerygma. Consequently, in the rise to a higher level
via the *analogia entis* something essential is lost!

The language of the Bible is the language of the scheme or model, not
that of the unequivocal concept. The models — king, bridegroom, servant — are not models of God but of the *compagnonnage* of God and
his people. Conceptualisation is not excluded here; hermeneutics with
its circle of believing and understanding does nought else. But the models cannot be subsumed in a system. Later, in *Thinking Biblically*,
Ricoeur says that our guide is not the *quaestio* of the doctrine, but the
lectio, i.e. the order of the text.[26]

Within the framework of 'biblical hermeneutics' Ricoeur now also
speaks far more concretely about the 'Wholly Other'. The Transcendent
is first of all linked to the well-known text of Exodus 3:14, 'I am who I
am'. The name is no definition; it is a sign of salvation. 'I am who I am'
refers to the liberation out of Egypt and can be paraphrased as 'I will
uphold you as I did before'. The name is however also the refusal of any
name.[27] We have no name capable of grasping and identifying God. It is
a rejection of the magical meaning of the name that the Israelites desire
to know. Ricoeur speaks of a 'flight to the infinite' (*fuite à l'infini*) on
the part of the arch-referent 'God', made tangible in the extravagant
point of stories about ordinary life in Jesus' parables. He calls them
'boundary expressions' (*expressions limites*). It is only this specific reference that effects a transformation of meaning, which marks language
as religious language. To use a term of Ian Ramsey: the reference functions as 'qualifier' of the models. We can see them as the religious parallels of philosophical limiting concepts, such as Kant's transcendental
ideas. Except that here the idea does not lead the concepts to an
embracing horizon; rather, the Name or the naming (*nomination*) qualifies or modifies the models. Just as we can say of the Wholly Other
that He breaks through the horizon, anywhere and anytime, just so religious language transcends ordinary language. The boundary expression
marks a point of disappearance, and in that sense the other side of the
boundary, the vertical infinite. This passing over from ordinary experiences to boundary experiences we also find in the application. Love

[26] P. Ricoeur and A. Lacocque, *Penser la bible*. Paris, Du Seuil, 1998, pp. 355, 359
[P. Ricoeur and A. Lacocque, *Thinking Biblically*. Chicago, University of Chicago Press,
1998, pp. 348, 351].

[27] *Ibid.*, p. 165. God is a point of disappearance (*point de fuite*) [*Ibid.*, p. 118].

transcends justice. It too anticipates, anywhere and anytime, the renewal of humanity.

The idea of the Wholly Other — as such without content — is now given substance via Christology. Jesus Christ as the name of God involves that the power of God is understood through the cross and hence through weakness. The omnipotence of the biblical God is denuded of the Greek ideas of immutability and impassivity. The kenosis also holds for the power of the Kingdom of God. This is the 'doctrine of the Trinity for the present day'.

It seems as if all those years that Ricoeur spent on philosophy of language, on metaphor, text, time and narrative now flow into a new space for thinking. He can quit the field of current, reflexive philosophy without relinquishing thought. Does this mean that we have reached the pure reflection I spoke of in the opening paragraphs, not hampered by transmitted philosophical prejudice? Can we call this 'thinking the Bible', to use the title of the work Ricoeur wrote together with André Lacocque in 1998? 'Thinking the Bible' is an attempt to create conceptual clarity in the library which the Bible is, without catching the concepts, pared away from their origin, in a system, and without the pretension that behind the text they reveal the true state of affairs. It is a thinking without totalising and 'foundationalist' pretensions.

Illustrative for the way Ricoeur operates is the chapter entitled 'Loving obedience'. Actually, it is about 'theonomy and/or autonomy'. Four years earlier he wrote an article with this title, and except for some minor adjustments the chapter is the same text. One notable difference is that in *Thinking Biblically* he describes his argument as 'post-modern' and he even speaks of 'we, post-moderns'.[28]

The problem Ricoeur is dealing with here really is the problem of 'moderns after Kant'. To them, the Ten Commandments are the very picture of heteronomy, utterly incompatible with moral autonomy. The problem becomes: theonomy or autonomy, and as such mirrors quite faithfully the dilemma that in Ricoeur separates theology from philosophy. But now his approach is very different. From the outset Ricoeur now states that he is in search of a thinking that overcomes the contradiction; he is after theonomy *and* autonomy.

subject to God's authority

---

[28] *Ibid.*, pp. 163, 169 [*Ibid.*, pp. 116, 121]. Théonomie et/ou autonomie appeared in *Filosofia della rivelazione*. Milan, 1994, pp. 19-36.

He attempts, first, a reconstruction of the meaning of the injunction from the biblical sources. The commandment is situated in all other ways in which the scriptures mention God — the stories, prophecies, hymns, etc. — and in all the ways in which human beings respond 'before God' (*devant Dieu*). First of all, the commandment is embedded in a narrative framework, the story of the exodus. Secondly, there is a parallel with the story of creation, which tells of events outside chronological history in an immemorial past. In this sense the law and the appeal, too, are preliminary, not to be tracked down by a thinking subject. The same holds for the future in the prophetic writings, where the law is inscribed in the hearts. The word remains a word of the Other, though of the Other in us. Ricoeur explicates the statement in 1 John 4, 'God is love', with the help of his theory of metaphor. There is a dissonance between love and the jealous God of the first commandment. In the course of the comparison both emerge changed. The 'absolute dependence' on the human side becomes a 'loving obedience' radiating towards fellow humans. Theonomy is now understood as *l'amour oblige*. Obligating love — the only acceptable form of theonomy.

In relation to modernity this turn is post-modern. It would be mistaken to project this back to pre-modern times. It is up to us, post-moderns, to distinguish between love and obligation. Ricoeur makes this concrete by showing that love is a necessary motive in a situational ethics where rules fall short. A universal obligation calls for extra-ordinary individuals to make a start. As I noted, modern discussion-ethics characteristically takes for granted the factual willingness to engage in dialogue (which is always a personal matter).[29]

This 'Thinking the Bible' — is it theology or is it philosophy? The cover announces the 'contribution of one of our greatest philosophers'. In the text itself, right down to the sub-headings, the term used is 'theology'. Ricoeur also uses the expression 'between philosophy and theology'.[30] Nowadays we call this 'biblical theology' — a kind of thinking just as fragmentary as the exegesis on which it rests, just as contingent and unconcerned with systematics as the proclamation to which it leads. This thinking takes place in a never-ending dialogue with other philosophical-theological 'well-considered convictions'. Here Ricoeur draws the conclusion for the dialogue between religions that in *Oneself as Another* he had already drawn for discussions in ethics. We fall back on

---

[29] *Ibid.,* pp. 178, 183, 187-8 [*Ibid.,* pp. 128, 132, 136].
[30] In the titles in part 3 of *Lectures 3*.

the dialogue between traditions, without the illusion that 'reason' can determine truths behind them.

The answer, then, to my question at the beginning of this section — Does Ricoeur enter theological waters here? — is: Yes he does. Let it be noted, though, that first, this is genuine thinking, be it without totalitarian pretensions; secondly, that the source is original, hence philosophically not suspect; thirdly, that this source has rights equal to those of all other life-views. Accordingly, we are free to call it philosophy, love of wisdom. There was no reason for theological silence in the period from 1965 to 1998.

6. Conclusion

Let us, in closing, inspect once more the fronts in the civil war between reason and faith. On the side of reflective philosophy Ricoeur's thought developed as follows: First, there is the reduction of the autonomous ego to a central point. This restriction is the result of the criticism by the 'masters of suspicion', Marx, Freud and Nietzsche, who 'broke' the *cogito.* The abstract, empty ego is salvaged from this wreckage. This is a development within philosophy, separate from the religious critique of the autonomous self. In the preface to *Oneself as Another* Ricoeur takes a step with far more consequences. There he says that the self-positing cogito has lost all ties with a historical person in dialogue with a 'thou'. Over against this he places a 'hermeneutics of the self (*soi*)'. The empty ego-pole is an artificial entity inside the concrete, acting person, i.e. the self or selfhood (*ipséité*) as it functions within a historical community. This means that we know the self through interpretation. Any kind of apodictic certainty concerning this ego is rejected. The ego 'believes' in himself, in his ability to speak, to act, and to render account. This 'belief' (*créance*) is a belief *in*, in the sense that we believe in freedom of speech, in dialogue or in democracy — not a belief *that*, a belief (*croyance*) or opinion regarding a state of affairs. 'Believing in' is a testimony (*attestation*) with an obligating stake.

The Kantian view that narrative communities are guided by a suprahistorical, transcendental idea, still defended in *Time and Narrative*, is abandoned as well. In an article from 1986 he already criticised 'our predilection for systematic totalisation'.[31] We cannot place historical

---

[31] P. Ricoeur, *Lectures 3*, pp. 212, 226.

life-views in a linear sequence with 'eternal peace' as an asymptotic limit.

As we arrive at this point the question emerges: Is not the idea of the autonomous subject and its transcendental ideas grounded merely in history? Oddly enough, Ricoeur suggests this from the start — we recall his remarks about our Greek-determined cultural memory — though he is not prepared to accept the consequences of this for the *cogito*. Hence the antagonism between reason and its evidences, and faith that acknowledges its own historical roots and is critically opposed to the autonomous subject as ultimate reference. Faith (re)cognises something greater and more original than itself. When the autonomy of the *cogito* is understood as historical legacy and therefore as contingent pre-conception, the situation of reason and faith is in this respect structurally the same. Not only for philosophy of religion but also for philosophical anthropology holds that it depends on pre-philosophical presuppositions, and so is indeed a *hermeneutics* of the self.

Concerning the other front, biblical hermeneutics, my earlier conclusion was that it is a distinct form of life-view thinking. I further point to the fruitfulness of this approach for thinking about God. To begin with, the problem of the evil will is named as problem, and so leads to relevant stances, for example in the discussion on the passions. The old problem of theonomy and autonomy, too, is reconsidered in a new way. In particular I point to the manner in which Ricoeur introduces the problem of Transcendence against the background of the parables. 'Biblical thought', explored with such precision and attentiveness, proves to be — to his own surprise, I should think — a source in the quest for a philosophy of Transcendence.

Lining up both Ricoeurian enterprises, we note that in fact they are not warfronts. Rather, they are parallel undertakings, differing in intent and concern. What is left of the image of a civil war is the dialogue within, vacillating between two ways of thinking that simultaneously are two beliefs. But the two can no longer be opposed as truth over against tradition, reason over against faith, or knowledge over against imagery. Still, enough difference remains. Difference itself, as it were: secular experience over against the Wholly Other, immanence over against Transcendence. For Descartes, founder of modernity in philosophy, certainty about God still guaranteed the surety of the *cogito*. At the present time the existence of the entire Transcendent dimension has become a doubtful entity. To that extent all of us are agnostics. Nevertheless, 'for us, post-moderns' it is possible to break through deadlocked positions.

I can sympathise with Ricoeur's wish to keep the two discourses separate. In this way we witnessed a clear conflict, and especially a sustained analysis of the parties in the conflict. But this separation has disadvantages as well. I should have liked to hear more about the breakdown of the magic circle of immanence, about the decentration of the subject and the suspension of the desire to be. What is the relation between belief in the Wholly Other and the belief in the subject's capacities, including the moral capacities? Can philosophy tell us something about what Eliot called 'the points of intersection of the timeless with time'?

In the closing sentence of the intellectual biography Ricoeur says that he continues to feel obligated, should time allow, to concentrate on the relation between the 'arguments of philosophy' and its 'non-philosophical sources', more precisely, between his agnostic 'philosophy without the absolute' and his 'biblical faith, fed more by exegesis than by theology'. The book on Transcendence, announced by Ricoeur in an unguarded moment, can still, perhaps more than ever, be thought and written.

EVERY MAN HAS A GOD OR AN IDOL.
RENÉ GIRARD'S VIEW OF CHRISTIANITY AND RELIGION

GUIDO VANHEESWIJCK

Does René Girard (°1923) belong to the group of French philosophers being discussed in this book? At first sight, the answer is no. Girard has never been a student of philosophy. His schooling trained him to be an historian. In 1947 he graduated from the École des Chartes in Paris as a palaeographer-archivist. The subject of his thesis was *The Private Life in Avignon During the Second Half of the Fifteenth Century (La vie privée à Avignon dans la seconde moitié du XVᵉ siècle)*. Three years later — in the meantime he had emigrated to the United States — he received his Ph.D. from the faculty of history at the University of Indiana. The topic of his dissertation was *American opinion of France, 1940-1943*. However, he has never really been famous as an historian. He owes his reputation, first and foremost, to his literary analyses, secondly, to his research in anthropology and, finally, to his exegesis of the Bible. Regarding his literary analysis, his first book, *Deceit, Desire and the Novel (Mensonge romantique et verité romanesque)* is worth mentioning. His anthropological research produced the book, *Violence and the Sacred (La violence et le sacré)*. Regarding Biblical-exegesis, there is his opus magnum, *Things Hidden Since the Foundation of the World (Des choses cachées depuis la fondation du monde)*. Time and again, Girard has given expression to his preference for literature over either humanities or philosophy. Human behaviour is, in his view, much less open to elucidation by means of the conceptual structures of discursive philosophy than by means of a Greek tragedy, the Biblical passion-story, or a modern novel. One might retort that Girard's preference for the ethical and anthropological dimensions of literature is typical of current philosophy: leading and less controversial philosophers such as Martha Nussbaum, Richard Rorty, Iris Murdoch, Charles Taylor, and Jacques Derrida all highlight the importance of literary study for philosophical reflection.

However, if we wish to label Girard as a contemporary philosopher, we are in need of stronger arguments. At the very least, there should be a thematic resemblance with other thinkers, which does not, at first sight, seem to be the case. Precisely in an era in which 'the great stories' have been deconstructed, and every effort to form a comprehensive theory is stigmatized beforehand as being 'violent', René Girard comes up with both a comprehensive theory, in which the most diverse phenomena are reduced to the same denominator, and an undisguised apology of Christianity's deep inspiration. Partly due to this obvious contrast with 'post-modern' intellectual fashion, there was not, for a long period of time, any notice made of Girard in the philosophical 'inner circles' of the often talked about Paris salons.[1]

Even regarding the religious theme itself, one may wonder whether René Girard belongs to the list of French philosophers. He was born in 1923 on Christmas day in Avignon, a town with a fascinating but rather ambiguous reputation in medieval ecclesiastic history. Bred in a catholic environment, already as a young man he says farewell to the Catholic Church — atheistic existentialism was in the air at the time. With his first two books, *Deceit, Desire and the Novel* (1961) and *Dostoyevski: from Double to Unity (Dostoievski: du double à l'unité)* (1963), he gained a reputation as a literary critic specialized in the modern European novel. In both these books, he rejects the then fashionable method of analyzing a literary work apart from its historical, social, and psychological contexts. However, these books do not scandalize the intellectual world as much as his later writings do: they stay within a literary context and focus on desire, which was *en vogue* during the 1960s. In his first book, a penetrating analysis of the novels of Cervantes, Stendhal, Flaubert, Proust and Dostoyevsky, respectively, Girard reads these work in terms of an omnipresent 'mimetic' or 'triangular' desire, a first concept that testifies to his idiosyncratic approach.

In the 1960s Girard started examining the domain of the old myths from this perspective of 'mimetic desire'. He saw that desire usually leads to collective violence against a single victim. In this respect, he turns to the great Greek tragedies (in particular, Sophocles' *Oedipus*-cycle and Euripides' *The Bacchantes*) and starts digging into Sigmund Freud's oeuvre. Hence, the mimetic concept is extended in order to

---

[1] The lack of room made for Girard in recent philosophical surveys testifies to his isolated position in current philosophy. See, e.g., A. D. Schrift, *Nietzsche's French Legacy. A Genealogy of Poststructuralism*. Routledge, New York, 1995, in which Girard does not occur at all. This regards even the fifth chapter, 'Why the French are no longer Nietzscheans' in which he refers to the new class of French anti-Nietzscheans, Ferry, Renaut, Descombes, among others. The exception to the rule is Michel Serres. Already from the beginning of his oeuvre, he showed his interest in Girard's work.

include the scapegoat mechanism. Mimetic desire, the scapegoat mechanism, refined by the study of tragedy, and the confrontation with Freud: these four ingredients form, as it were, the backbone of his third book, *Violence and the Sacred*, which appears in 1972. Up to that moment, Girard had hardly written anything on Christianity and the Bible.

In 1978 Girard published his opus magnum, *Things Hidden since the Foundation of the World*. Presented in the form of a dialogue with two psychiatrists, Jean-Michel Oughourlian and Guy Lefort, its format is a triptych: 1) Fundamental Anthropology; 2) The Judeo-Christian Scriptures; 3) Inter-dividual psychology. Not until this book — written at age 55 — does Girard declare himself as a Christian, providing a non-sacrificial lecture of the Bible and of the Divinity of Christ.

Against this backdrop, my presentation of Girard's thought on religion and Christianity consists of three parts. First, I want to show how his renewed acquaintance with the Judeo-Christian tradition marks the contours of the whole of his oeuvre and sheds a completely new light on his earlier books as well. Furthermore, I will show how his idiosyncratic terminology, based upon anthropological, psychological, and literary research, is translatable into a terminology which perfectly fits within the framework of current French philosophy. Finally, I will highlight the typical Christian aspects of Girard's thought by means of his interpretation of one of the most intriguing texts in the Old Testament, the Judgment of Solomon.

1. The significance of Christianity in René Girard's thought

Christianity is sometimes considered to be a western variant of religion which has been unmasked by modern thought. It is against such a reading of Christianity that René Girard, in his most important work, *Things Hidden since the Foundation of the World,* launches a flanked attack. On the one hand, he reads the Bible as an explicit unmasking of pre-modern, mythical religions: myth forms, as it were, the outspoken target of biblical criticism. On the other hand, he interprets the Bible, seen from a contemporary perspective, as a critical stand against a modern society, which is determined by the premises of a market economy. This idiosyncratic interpretation of the Bible only reveals its full significance against the background of the context of Girard's oeuvre as a whole.

1.1 Every culture is mediated

In order to circumscribe the specificity of human culture, René Girard takes as a starting-point the *mimetic* or imitating character of human desire. The fact that the genesis of human culture is largely due to imitation or mimesis has been recognized for a long time, by both philosophers and anthropologists. Aristotle wrote that a human being distinguishes himself from other animals by being more capable of imitation. Typical of Girard's approach is to extrapolate this generally agreed upon role of mimesis concerning the origin of culture to *mimetic desire*. Although mimesis is often a positive force which generates culture ('Eliot writes beautiful poems, I would like to imitate him'), in the case of mimetic desire, things are completely different ('his wife is very pretty, I would like to have her too'). When a mimetic virus affects human desire, it threatens to destroy the established order in society.

Human desire is generally considered to be a spontaneous phenomenon. No two things are more intertwined than a desiring subject and the object of desire. Their relation can always be portrayed by a simple straight line, joining both of them (e.g., I would like to write beautiful poems). The straight line is also present in Girard's thought, but its role is not essential. Above the straight line there is a mediator, radiating toward both the subject and the object (e.g., I would like to write beautiful poems, just like Eliot does). The spatial metaphor which expresses this triple relationship is obviously the triangle. Concrete subjects and concrete objects may change with each adventure, but the triangle remains forever.

Although mimetic desire is itself undoubtedly a universal phenomenon, the form it has taken on in culture is variable, both in its temporal and spatial aspects. In his first book, *Deceit, Desire and the Novel*, Girard shows, by analyzing five great modern novels, how, since the 16th century, mimetic desire in western culture has gradually made a transition from *external mediation*, as one variant of mimetic desire, to *internal mediation*.

Girard speaks of external mediation when the (spiritual) distance is sufficient to eliminate any contact between the two spheres of possibilities of which the mediator and subject occupy the respective centres. Due to the mediator's elevation above the subject, one can speak here of a form of *vertical transcendence*. Girard speaks of internal mediation when this (spiritual) distance is sufficiently reduced to allow these two spheres to penetrate each other more or less profoundly. In this case, one can speak of a form of *horizontal transcendence*. Moreover, both kinds of mediation imply another difference. The subject of external mediation proclaims aloud the true nature of his desire. He worships his model openly and declares himself to be his disciple. The subject of internal mediation, however, denies the origin of his desire. In the quarrel which puts him in opposition to his rival, the subject reverses the logical and chronological order of desires in order to hide his imitation. He asserts that his own desire is prior to that of his rival. So, Girard speaks here — referring to Dostoyevsky — of an *underground desire*.

This distinction between external and internal mediation does not only help Girard in drawing a clear line of demarcation between pre-modern, religious culture and modern, secularized culture, but also gives him the opportunity to situate the significance of Christianity within the evolution of human culture as a whole.

1.2 Religious culture and external mediation

According to Girard, each culture has a religious origin. He defines culture as everything — presuppositions, roles, common ideals, structures, commands and prohibitions, etc. — which enables human beings to exist together without being overcome by chaos, violence, and random murder. Its twofold genesis is amply described in his second book, *Violence and the Sacred*. First of all, culture stems from the disorder, the actual or potential violence that is experienced by hominids when mimetic desire gets out of hand — the contagious force of rivalry making each one resemble each other. These hominids, in the process of becoming human, then make the discovery that convergence upon a victim brings them unanimity and thus relief from violence. Two (or more) people are reconciled at the expense of a third who appears guilty or responsible for whatever disturbs or frightens them. From that moment on, they have a single purpose, which is to prevent the scapegoat from harming them by expelling and destroying him. This victim or scapegoat is carefully elected: preferably, he is marginalized (in a negative way as slave, handicap, criminal, etc. or in a positive way as king, hero, demi-god) so that his elimination may break through the vicious circle of blood revenge.

As soon as the scapegoat has been sacrificed for being the cause of disorder and violence, there occurs — as it were, miraculously — a recovery of order in society. So, sacrifice and scapegoat rituals represent, in a camouflaged form, both disorder, resulting in the original violence of expulsion of the victim, and order, stemming from the newly found relief from conflict and violence. In other words, both disorder and order are the upshot of a *double transference* of the original victimization: those involved in the collective violence transfer the disorder to the victim, but they also transfer their newly found peace to the same victim or scapegoat, ascribing to him the power of yielding peace. In other words, the scapegoat is first held responsible for disorder and disruption in society, and later considered as the foundation of a newly found order.

This age-old scapegoat mechanism is, according to Girard, the foundation of all human culture and religion. By miraculously bringing back unanimity, the scapegoat becomes god-like. The violence at the heart of traditional sacredness is therefore twofold: the negative sacredness of the collective violence that is associated with the dangerous aspects of the god or the hero; and the positive sacredness that is associated with the formation and maintenance of order. Such forms of sacredness have always yielded a relative order and rest. Because people felt their fate to be dependent on this sacral power, which was presumed to bring both welfare and calamity, they established within the community itself all kinds of differences, i.e., all forms of ordering society. No longer fascinated and terrorized by each other, they considered it necessary, due to their relation towards the sacred, to make rules and prohibitions to keep the acquired peace and prevent opportunities for aggression to return.

In other words, external mediation is typical of all mythical-religious cultures. The mediating model is of god-like origin and, as such, extended above human beings; hence, it does not permit jealousy, but it creates room for feelings like admiration, adoration, and submission. All these rules, which are manifest in several rituals of sacrifice, are religious rules that have to be respected due to their sacred origin. According to Girard, this implies that religion, i.e., this heterogeneous whole of orders and prohibitions, myths and rituals, commands and taboos, is at the origin of all institutions, all forms of life and thought, which make up human culture. As a means of defense against the ever-present threat of aggression, religion forms the indispensable binding agency for pre-modern society.

In short, in their efforts to survive, religious societies have always made use of the same 'tactics'. They have been *channelling violence*, inherent in mimetic desire, by means of the scapegoat mechanism which, seen as sacred, has been functioning as a *foundational* and *generative* principle. As such, the sacred God of mythical religion has vindicated even the most appalling forms of cruelty. Fascination with death and violence is often presented as an expression of our nature as *homo religiosus*. Examples of this bond between violence, religion, and transcendence are legion indeed.

1.3 Modern culture and internal mediation

In western culture, Christianity — I will come back to its specific role in culture — has been gradually undermining this 'religious' belief in the sacredness of mythical stories and the efficacy of its sacrificial rituals and, hence, made possible the transition towards modern culture. Those in modern culture who want to ward off the danger of aggression will no longer resort to gods and sacrifices, but will look for human solutions. So, there occurs a gradual transition from external mediation towards internal mediation and towards a society which is no longer based upon religious premises but on economic premises instead. Of course, such a transition has had its consequences on different aspects of human behaviour and more, in particular, on inter-subjective relations.

All that was forbidden by pre-modern morality and was considered as sinful in Dante's medieval world — envy, rivalry, vanity, or, in one word, competition — is registered by the 17th century political philosopher Thomas Hobbes as more or less neutral human characteristics. In *The Fable of the Bees* from the early 18th century, de Mandeville elevates these characteristics to civil virtues, epitomized in the famous slogan "private vices, public virtues." It was, as is generally known, Adam Smith who molded Mandeville's insights into his concept of the "invisible hand." The *homo economicus*, introduced by the father of liberalism, is a rationally calculating being who, only thinking of himself but led by an invisible hand, believes to foster the general interest of society.

The axiom on which liberal political economy is based states that a scarcity of goods causes violence among human beings. All that can vanquish this scarcity, so liberal politicians reason, prevents violence from breaking out and leads to peaceful understanding between people. All that can vanquish this scarcity must therefore be considered as good. In this respect, violence cannot be ascribed to the interaction between human beings, but to nature's scarcity itself. The issue is now: how to vanquish nature's scarcity? The standard story proclaims aloud that modern western society has perfectly succeeded in this challenging task. But is it all so simple?

In *The Realm of Scarcity*, a book from 1988, the Dutch philosopher Hans Achterhuis — strongly inspired by Girard — shows how modern man is gradually experiencing the world as precisely a world of *scarcity*. Modern culture is characterized by a paradoxical situation: human needs are increasing in the same proportion as the opportunities to fulfill them (including welfare) are growing. We do not live in a realm of affluence, but in a realm of self-created scarcity. How can such a phenomenon be explained?

Of course, the feelings that are linked to mimetic desire are as old as human relations themselves. But instead of *channelling* these feelings, as it occurs in pre-modern societies, modern culture has been opting for another strategy: it *gives all opportunities* to mimetic desire. Translated in a recognizable jargon: the principle of rivalry reigns supreme. Although human envy has never been satisfied with less than what another has, so Achterhuis reminds Girard, it is particularly in our modern culture that envy has more elbowroom than ever before.

On the one hand, democratic sensitivity for equality no longer accepts that certain groups or classes possess more than others, by nature. It is precisely at this moment that internal mediation comes to the fore. Internal mediation and rivalry, together with their accompanying feelings of envy, jealousy, and hatred, can only break through if the opportunities for equality between subject and model have been created. Achterhuis amply illustrates how more equality is likely to create more feelings of hatred, envy, aggression, and frustration and how this paradoxical situation makes for the typical psychological disequilibrium and unrest of modern society. The fruits of mimetic desire seem to sour as intersubjective equality increases.

On the other hand, modern money economy made possible a much larger accumulation of wealth than ever before. As long as possession was something *material* and *concrete*, collecting things made sense in so far as one was able to enjoy it. Within this context, it was simply absurd to create more food than could be consumed. Money, on the contrary, is an *abstract* form of wealth and, hence, impossible to limit. Due to the connection of both these aspects, Girard amply described that the mechanism of 'envy' has run wild in modern culture, which leads to a realm of scarcity in which the internally mediated inhabitants inevitably and often un(sub)consciously are imprisoned.

The direct result of this double evolution is a proliferation of artificially created needs: I experience something as a need because I compare myself to someone else and, precisely due to this comparison, I am encouraged to attain what they have (e.g., I want a car which is as expensive as that of my neighbour's, and advertising reinforces the cultivation of this need). Even if the scapegoat mechanism loses its founding status in such a society, it does not prevent all kinds of modifications of the sacrifice mechanism to occur. These sacrificial mechanisms, inherent in this proliferation, are threefold.

First, modern western culture sacrifices *nature*. If one chooses to artificially inflate human needs, one is obliged to fulfill their gratification. In order to do that, modern western culture exploits nature. The mechanical concept of nature, which has become dominant since the 16th century, reinforces this tendency towards exploitation. Currently, increased ecological sensitivity testifies to the untenability of such a concept of nature.

Furthermore, modern western culture sacrifices the *other*. The gap between North and South, between rich and poor is gradually growing. In so far as the world has become a 'global village', no one can pretend to be uninformed about this. But such objective information is of no direct use. In an internally mediated culture, people never compare themselves with others who are far away, but always with others who are nearby and wealthier.

Finally, the modern Westerner is sacrificing *himself*. Because he is internally mediated and, thus, diminishes the distance between himself and the other, he inevitably multiplies the number of mediators. In principle, everyone can, at any time, become a model for the other. Sociologists teach us that people are more influenced by models in their 'peer-groups' (friends, colleagues, fashion, advertising, media, etc.) than by traditional models (church, school, parents). In this way, the image of a fragmented individual within a disrupted society gradually took shape: models come and go, are made and broken. In the meantime, people run, time and again, after new models, always coming too late or, if on time, feel cheated and deceived. Simultaneously, internally mediated subjects obstinately deny the decisive influence of the other: they believe themselves to be acting as fully autonomous individuals, who would feel heavily insulted by the allegation that their desire was influenced by another's desire. Due to this underground character of internal mediation, the modern myth of human autonomy and immediate desire — in Girard's terminology: romantic deceit — has become more or less ineradicable.

Let us recapitulate. With regard to the phenomenon of mimetic desire one can distinguish two variants. Pre-modern cultures, characterized by an outright and, hence, conscious *external mediation*, try to *channel* mimetic desire by means of all kinds of orders and prohibitions connected to religious-hierarchical structures, which are all rooted in the scapegoat mechanism. These cultures live by a vertical form of transcendence. Modern culture, however, characterized by an underground and, hence, unconscious *internal mediation*, aims at the *release of mimetic desire by means of the principle of rivalry and is likely to create envy between people*, which leads to the proliferation of artificial needs. This culture lives by a horizontal form of transcendence.

1.4 The significance of Christianity

What is the role of Christianity in all this? Of course, the God of mythical religion was no projection (à la Feuerbach) of an ideal human type at all. In mythical religions, people are fettered to an ominous godlike force, the cruel and human origin of which is completely unknown to them. They consider this force the only one to be capable of averting human aggression on the condition that its demand of sacrificing a scapegoat is met. For Girard, Christianity has nothing to do with such a religion. The scapegoat is innocent and the gradual realization of this innocence is due to the (indirect) influence of the Judeo-Christian writings, which are scrutinized by Girard in the second part of *Things Hidden since the Foundation of the World*. In his view, Jewish religion is to be interpreted as a struggle with a new ethical awareness and a new image of God. On the basis of a comparison between biblical texts and stories, on the one hand, and myths out of other cultures and religions, on the other hand, he tries to show, in addition to the similarities, the differences between the Judeo-Christian tradition and mythical religions.

Let me give one example of such a comparison. The story of Rome is presented in classic fashion. Its starting-point, not unlike in other myths, is a fratricide. Now, the Roman myth presents the murder of Remus as an action that was perhaps to be regretted, but was justified by the victim's transgression. Remus did not respect the ideal limit traced by Romulus between the inside and the outside of the city and broke the rules. So, Romulus' reaction is justified. In the Jewish Genesis story, by contrast, Cain is presented in a completely different way. He appears as a vulgar murderer who is called to account for his deed by God and is not exonerated from guilt. The condemnation of the murder takes precedence over all other considerations. "Where is your brother Abel?" According to Girard, this change of perspective is of utmost importance.

The title, *Things Hidden since the Foundation of the World* is illustrative in this context. It is borrowed from Matthew 13:13 ("I will utter what has been hidden since the foundation of the world…"), which, in turn, refers to the second verse of Psalm 78. Girard considers the New Testament as the radicalization of the Old Testament: inspired by the figure of Jesus, it is a radical break with a way of life based on sacrifice. In the Old Testament, God has an ambiguous character: the old myths are still influential and the prophets have to fight a continuous struggle against a 'mythic-religious' concept of God (cf. Jeremiah 6:20).

In the New Testament, it is Jesus who unmasks the mimetic, violent character typical of human culture. By means of his words and his attitude, he is confronting us with situations which are experienced as paradoxical because they break through prevailing customs. Only those who are without sin may throw the first stone. When you are struck on your left cheek, turn the other cheek — contrary to the mimetic motion par excellence. And so he offers his right cheek. Furthermore, it is conspicuous that although Jesus functions as a scapegoat, he is — in sharp contrast to the mythical interpretation of the scapegoat — completely innocent: his death by sacrifice is a glaring injustice. By undergoing violence till the end (there was no other possibility), he unveils the violent ground pattern of every mythical religion. After Jesus' unmasking activity, religious mythologisation has become impossible; Jesus has revealed the violent origins of the scapegoat mechanism once and for all. In short, Christianity tries to *unmask* violence, inherent in mimetic desire, by emphasizing the innocence of the godlike scapegoat.

Let me formulate all this from still another angle. Man is, according to Girard, always looking for something that is transcendent. This search for transcendence has taken on two different forms in western culture. It can take the shape of a completely vertical transcendence or external mediation. In this case, we speak of a mythical religion with its belief in a completely transcendent, often violent concept of God, and with its hierarchical concept of man and society. It can also take the shape of a horizontal transcendence or internal mediation. In this case we speak of a secularized culture with its belief in an egalitarian concept of man and society. It is to these two forms of transcendence that Girard refers by the motto which he borrows from Max Scheler and which opens *Deceit, Desire and the Novel*: "every man has a God or an idol."

Against this backdrop, the quintessence of Christianity can be circumscribed by defining its specificity in contrast to both that of religion (with its emphasis on impenetrable transcendence) and that of modern culture (with its emphasis on sheer immanence). Christianity's quintessence becomes manifest both in the domains of ethics and spirituality.

Regarding the ethical domain, Girard focuses upon the sharp contrast between the Christian command of neighbourly love, the pre-modern scapegoat mechanism which generates revenge, and the modern market principle which generates jealousy or resentment. Regarding the spiritual domain, he focuses upon the specificity of the Christian concept of God. The Christian God can never completely fall together with the transcendent God of mythical religion nor wholly express himself in the immanence of this concrete reality. He is, at the same time, transcendent and immanent, Father and Son and Holy Spirit, and his mediation is, in Girard's terminology, never external without simultaneously being internal.

2 The place of Girard in current French philosophy

At first glance, Girard's idiosyncratic terminology seems to be completely at odds with the canonized jargon of current French philosophy. Its central pair of concepts, in particular, with regard to the significance of religion in our culture, is that of *identity* and *difference*. However, anyone who consults Girard's oeuvre will, from the first pages, be confronted with precisely both concepts. This is why a 'translation' in a recognizable philosophical jargon is obvious.

The proliferation of internal mediation and the release of mimetic desire, which Girard sees as predominant in Western culture, testify to what many French philosophers call a 'culture of identity'. They mirror, as it were, the quintessence of a philosophy of identity or subjectivity in which there is no room for any form of transcendence. It is human consciousness in its own right that functions as the only standard for knowledge and action. This well-known analysis of modern culture is even reinforced in Girard's oeuvre for he does not only reveal the predominance of a philosophy of subjectivity that occurs in modern western culture, but the omnipresence of an 'intersubjective' philosophy in which internally mediated subjects, constantly fascinated by each other, are incessantly growing more and more alike.

Of course, religions have always been trying to escape from the danger inherent in a culture of identity, which puts everything on a par. They have been doing this by creating a lot of distinctions in order to establish all kinds of differences. In fact, the establishment of difference — between the Divine and the human, the sacred and the profane — is the hallmark of religion. As well, it is conspicuous that in current philosophy, which reacts against the modern philosophy of subjectivity, a sensitivity for difference is predominant. Heidegger's 'ontological difference' is the starting-point for current (French) philosophy to react against a pure philosophy of identity. Also, Girard follows Heidegger in taking a distance from the thought of identity and in his development of the idea of ontological difference. But where Heidegger stops, Girard goes on: "Heidegger, the inventor of 'ontological difference', never conceived the idea of developing an 'ontology of difference' [...] An *ontology of difference* (italics mine) would mean accepting the philosophical challenge of the disparity of people and the difficulties or opportunities arising as a result."[2] What kind of difference do we establish? This is the central philosophical problem which, according to Girard, we have to cope with today if we want to understand the significance of both religion and Christianity.

In fact, Girard has situated this theme of difference on three levels throughout the whole of his oeuvre. First he deals with difference as applied to mimetic relations between different individual human beings (I want both to be like you and to be different from you). Next, Girard connects this problematic view of intersubjectivity with the relation between immanence and transcendence, a second form of difference. Finally, he focuses upon the differences within the semantic field of transcendence itself: it is precisely Christianity that puts forward a central qualification within the concept of transcendence by emphasizing the trinitary and incarnatory aspects of its image of God.

In this second part, I would like to highlight the thematic kinship between Girard's thought and that of the majority of French contemporary philosophers, whose central theme is that of 'difference'. My point of departure here is Alexandre Kojève's famous interpretation of Hegel's *Phenomenology of the Spirit*. Against the common background of Kojève's and Girard's ideas, the differences between both authors come to the fore. In order to make these divergences more explicit, I will focus upon Girard's interpretation of Nietzsche and Heidegger in general, and their relation to the Christian concept of God, in particular.

2.1 The anthropological reading by Alexandre Kojève

Likewise, Desire directed toward a natural object is human only to the extent that it is 'mediated' by the Desire of another directed toward the

---

[2] R. Safranski, *Martin Heidegger Between Good and Evil*. Cambridge (MA), Harvard University Press, 1998, p. 265.

same object: it is human to desire what others desire, because they desire it. Thus, an object perfectly useless from the biological point of view (such as a medal, or the enemy's flag) can be desired because it is the object of other desires. Such a desire can only be a human Desire, and human reality, as distinguished from animal reality, is created only by action that satisfies such Desires: human history is the history of desired Desires.[3]

Undoubtedly, these words could have been written by Girard. However, they are not. These words are quoted from the famous lectures given by Alexandre Kojève on Hegel's *Phenomenology of Spirit* at the *École pratique des hautes études* between 1933 and 1939, and which were attended by what would become the key thinkers of post-war French philosophy: Raymond Aron, Georges Bataille, Alexandre Koyré, Pierre Klossowski, Jacques Lacan, Maurice Merleau-Ponty, Jean-Paul Sartre, to name a few.[4] Kojève's interpretation of Hegel has, as is generally known, become the point of reference in post-war 20th century philosophy in France. Before 1930, the word 'dialectics' had been burdened with an odium of sin. After 1930, it became a word — thanks to Kojève — that carried prestige.[5] Before 1930, there had been no talk of an Hegelian school whatsoever in France. After 1930, the situation changed so drastically that Merleau-Ponty was able to write these often quoted lines in 1946:

> All the great philosophical ideas of the past century — the philosophies of Marx and Nietzsche, phenomenology, German existentialism, and psychoanalysis — had their beginnings in Hegel; it was he who started the attempt to explore the irrational and integrate it into an expanded reason which remains the task of our century.[6]

Half a century later, these words are all but self-evident. While the generation of French thinkers between 1930 and 1960 stressed its dependence on Hegel, the generation after 1960 heavily opposed him. In 1970, Michel Foucault gave his inaugural speech at the *Collège de France*. On

---

[3] A. Kojève, *Introduction à la lecture de Hegel*. Paris, Gallimard, 1947, p. 13 [A. Kojève, *Introduction to the Reading of Hegel*. Ithaca and London, Cornell University Press, 1969, p. 6].

[4] Although Sartre himself could not attend the lectures (at the time he taught philosophy in Le Havre en Laon), he must have heard of them by way of Aron or Merleau-Ponty.

[5] For more information on the relation between Kojève and French philosophy, cf. V. Descombes, *Le Même et l'Autre. Quarante-cinq ans de philosophie française (1933-1978)*. Paris, Minuit, 1979, pp. 21-70.

[6] M. Merleau-Ponty, L'existentialisme chez Hegel. In: Idem, *Sens et non-sens*. Paris, Nagel, 1948, p. 109 [M. Merleau-Ponty, Hegel's Existentialism. In: Idem, *Sense and Non-Sense*. Evanston (Illinois), Northwestern University Press, 1964, p. 63].

behalf of his generation, he explained how French thinkers, at that
moment, tried to escape from Hegel:

> Our entire epoch, whether through logic or epistemology, whether through
> Marx or Nietzsche, seeks to evade Hegel's imperium.[7]

Obviously, René Girard belongs to the second generation, which, on the
one hand, embroiders the theme of desire borrowed from Kojève's
Hegel-interpretation but, on the other hand, wishes to get rid of Hegel in
its search for answers. Girard must be credited for having coined a new
term for this anthropological structure: *triangular desire (désir triangu-
laire)*. However, the view on inter-human relationships hiding beneath
this term — desire always desires the desire of the other, even when it
seems, at first glance, to refer to a specific object — recurs in the works
of so many of his French contemporaries: Jacques Derrida, Michel Foucault, Jacques Lacan, etc.

2.2 Girard and the thought of difference

Precisely because Girard shares the same anthropological point of departure as Kojève (and Hegel), his criticism hits at the heart of Hegelian
anthropology. While Hegel's (and Kojève's) thought is structured
according to the figure of *identity*, Girard makes use, as an anthropological paradigm, of the figure of *difference*. As such, he is undoubtedly a
typical contemporary thinker. Let me explain this a bit more in detail.

Kojève recognizes that a conflict between human beings is likely to
result in a drama and, eventually, in death (of one or all of them). However, in everyday reality, this dramatic outcome is mostly avoided due to
the fact that there is no equivalence between the partners. One of them
will, confronted with the dilemma between either a possible death or a
life without recognition, choose the latter option. Confronted with the
'master' who is demanding recognition, the 'slave' takes the option of a
dependent life. This split-up between the master and the slave functions,
according to Hegel-Kojève, as the motor of history. Throughout the evolution of their mutual relationship, master and slave do not remain who
they are: they elevate each other dialectically.

Self-consciousness might only arise, in this view, in the course of the
process of recognition itself. In order to find recognition, the subject has
to take distance from the pure immediacy of its endless desire: only then
can it make room for another subject who recognizes me as subject.

---

[7] M. Foucault, *L'ordre du discours*. Paris, Gallimard, 1971, p. 74.

Only the slave, who escapes from the compulsion of desire, is capable of really meeting another subject. Only by abandoning immediacy can he attain self-consciousness, which is mediated by his labour and by his acceptance of the other. Hence, only the slave can attain what the master is, in fact, though in vain, looking for: recognition. The master is demanding recognition from the slave. But forced recognition is not recognition at all; it is only a form of external submission. In principle, the master is not able to get his grip on the slave's subjectivity without simultaneously destroying it and thereby making every form of recognition impossible.

One cannot force genuine recognition; one can only *receive* it. One cannot receive it from a thing, nor from a slave (who is but a thing for the master); one can only receive it from a subject whom one confirms in freedom. In short, there is only real recognition when one subject, which considers itself as a goal-in-itself, *intends* to recognize the other subject as a goal-in-itself as well. The slave is the first to have this experience. By cultivating nature he is making history. By making history he is freeing himself from his nature as a slave and finds recognition in the other-than-himself. For Hegel-Kojève, the dialectic between master and slave is a stage in the journey towards final identity and harmonious unity.

For Girard, however, the figure of dialectic *sublation (Aufhebung)* has lost all its magical force:

> The scandal should be recognized rather than rejected. But this does not mean that we must embrace the scandal in the manner of religious or philosophical thought. There can be no question of returning to mystical formulations or their philosophical counterparts, such as the 'coincidentia oppositorum', the magical power of the negative [...]. There can be no question of returning to Hegel [...].[8]

For Girard, culture always arises from a mimetic crisis. There is a continuous threat of disorder in which the borders between 'I' and 'you' are fading, in which 'I' become 'you' by absorbing 'you' (for that is what 'I' want in my desire) but, simultaneously, stops being 'I'. This chaotic situation in which people — in order to be different from each other — wipe out all differences is both the origin of civilization and the ever-present threat of its end. This process of violent 'indifferentiation'

---

[8] R. Girard, *Des choses cachées depuis la fondation du monde*. Paris, Grasset, 1978, p. 71 [R. Girard, *Things Hidden since the Foundation of the World*. London, Athlone Press, 1987, pp. 62-3.].

(indifférenciation) hangs over man's head as the sword of Damocles. In order to escape from this 'indifference', pre-modern cultures were invariably backsliding into the scapegoat mechanism, while modern Western culture has created a sophisticated 'symbolic order' in which things get their specific sign values.[9] Hence, 'culture' is always — in any form whatsoever — a 'creation' by human beings to avoid backsliding into original violence. But, this effort itself remains extremely ambiguous. For one thing, being human implies the unbearableness of *difference*; for another, remaining a human being implies precisely reinstalling the *difference* between subjects. In this way, the concept of difference plays a key role in Girard's philosophy of culture. It is, as it were, a *perpetuum mobile*: "Differences seem to have vanished, only to reappear in inverted form, thereby perpetuating themselves."[10]

Hence, it is obvious that Girard belongs to the generation of French thinkers who take a distance from Alexandre Kojève's Hegel-interpretation. While Kojève still believes, on the basis of his interpretation of the Hegelian master-slave-dialectic, in the attainment of identity, Girard unmasks, together with figures like Sartre and Lacan, etc., the violent aspects of such a philosophy of identity and places value on difference. In fact, Girard is a typical post-modern author who, by undermining the modern ideal of autonomy and by putting into relief human vulnerability and finitude, rejects a philosophy of subjectivity. Hence, his choice of title for the first part of his first book, *Deceit, Desire and the Novel,* is telling. It refers to the illusory character of a belief in human autonomy shared by the great thinkers of both the Enlightenment and Romanticism.

Like other members of his French generation, Girard is no longer sensitive to the magic of negation: what Hegel-Kojève calls *sublation*, he circumscribes as *exclusion*. How to subsist within difference? This is the central question Girard shares with his famous compatriots, Michel Foucault[11] and Jacques Derrida. Because Girard explicitly refers to Derrida in his two central works, I focus now upon a comparison between both authors.

---

[9] Here, one must situate the congeniality between Jean Baudrillard's and René Girard's views.

[10] R. Girard, *La violence et le sacré*. Paris, Grasset, 1972, p. 298 [R. Girard, *Violence and the Sacred*. London, Athlone Press, 1995, p. 217].

[11] Among others, J.P. Dupuy and P. Dumouchel have pointed out the resemblance between the function of internal mediation in Girard and the efficacy of normalization in Foucault.

2.3 Girard and Derrida

In October 1966, during his tenure as chairman of Romance Languages at John Hopkins University, René Girard, together with Richard Macksey and Eugenio Donato, organized an international colloquium, "The Languages of Criticism and the Sciences of Man," which was to be important for the emergence of critical theory in America. Participants included Roland Barthes, Jacques Derrida, Lucien Goldman, Jean Hyppolite, Jacques Lacan, Georges Poulet, Tsvetan Tvodorov, and Jean-Pierre Vernant. At this symposium, Derrida gave his widely-read and cited paper, *Structure, Sign, and Play in the Discourse of the Humanities (La structure, le signe et le jeu dans le discours des sciences humaines).* For Girard, this paper confirmed that Derrida was a critic to be reckoned with, a feeling that was reinforced further by the publication of Derrida's subsequent essay, *The Pharmacy of Plato (La pharmacie de Platon).*

In *Violence and the Sacred,* Girard highly praises *The Pharmacy of Plato,* in which Derrida analyses Plato's passionate argumentation in the *Phaedrus* against handwriting. Handwriting, according to Plato, facilitates a weakening of memory and prevents philosophy from revealing truth. In Plato's eyes, handwriting is a form of 'alienation'. As a material form out of which breath and life of the process of thought itself have disappeared, it can only provoke misunderstanding. Hence, as Derrida paraphrases, the invention of handwriting, presented as a medicine against forgetfulness, is, in fact, a poisoned medicine, an anaesthetizing medicine. In Greek, both poison and medicine are referred to by the same word: *pharmakon.* Plato rejects such an equivocal medicine; it is a form of 'alienation' which only leads to misunderstanding. He prefers oral instruction of his theory to written representation.

In Derrida's view, however, there is more at stake. A specific interpretation of the quintessence of thought and knowledge is hiding behind Plato's opposition to handwriting. The metaphysical tradition has always interpreted real knowledge in the light of a *presence*: the thinker is present to his own thoughts of which he has a complete overview analogous to the words he is speaking. It is only when they are written down, and so brought within the reach of others, that he is losing control. Girard is enthusiastic about Derrida's interpretation of handwriting's function as *pharmakon*:

> Derrida proves that translations of Plato in modern languages manage to obliterate still further the final traces of the generative operation. For the translations destroy the unity of the term *pharmakon*; they use entirely different words to render *pharmakon*-remedy and *pharmakon*-poison [...] We

have to acknowledge in our time a movement emerging in the opposite
direction, a movement of exhumation, a revelation of violence and its
dynamic of which Derrida's work constitutes an essential moment.[12]

In a later period, Girard will develop the *pharmakon* or writing/poison
aspects of Derrida's analysis of the process of handwriting into the
scapegoat mechanism by putting its efficacy within history and actual
social existence instead of restricting its function to language and inter-
textuality, as Derrida does. Hence, it may not be surprising that six years
later, in *Things Hidden since the Foundation of the World*, Girard's tone
is much more reserved:

> If you examine the pivotal terms in the finest analyses of Derrida, you will
> see that beyond the deconstruction of philosophical concepts, it is always a
> question of the paradoxes of the sacred, and although there is no question
> of deconstructing these they are all the more apparent to the reader. [...]
> This still partial deconstruction confounds our present philosophical and
> cultural crisis with a radical impotence of thought and language. One no
> longer believes in philosophy but one keeps rehearsing the same old philo-
> sophical texts. And yet beyond the current crisis there are possibilities of a
> rational but no longer philosophical knowledge of culture. Instead, decon-
> struction seems content with a pure mirroring of the sacred that amounts to
> nothing, at this stage, but a purely literary effect; it risks degenerating into
> pure verbalism. And what the literary critics and academic disciples of
> deconstruction do not realize is that as soon as one seeks nothing but the
> essence of literature it disappears. If there is really 'something' to Derrida,
> it is because there is something beyond: precisely a deconstruction that
> reaches the mechanisms of the sacred and no longer hesitates to come to
> terms with the surrogate victim.[13]

Andrew McKenna has concisely summarized the difference between
Girard and Derrida: "Whereas Girard advances a theory of violence,
Derrida is concerned with the violence of theory."[14] Derrida limits the
ambiguity of the *pharmakon* to the level of textuality; Girard thinks this
interpretation is interesting but, at most, academic and without commitment. In his view, the play of expulsion is not only situated on the tex-
tual level, but refers to a 'real' expulsion. He sees behind the ambiguity
of the *pharmakon* the working of a scapegoat mechanism as the foundation of human culture.

---

[12] R. Girard, *La violence et le sacré*, p. 41 [R. Girard, *Violence and the Sacred*, p. 23].
[13] R. Girard, *Des choses cachées depuis la fondation du monde*, p. 72 [R. Girard, *Things Hidden since the Foundation of the World*, p. 64].
[14] See the excellent study by A. J. McKenna, *Violence and Difference. Girard, Derrida, and Deconstruction*. Urbana and Chicago, University of Illinois Press, 1992.

Apart from a different view of the relation between language and reality and a different interpretation of the 'pharmakon', both authors give a completely different interpretation of the concept of 'transcendence' as well. Unlike Derrida, Girard unambiguously adheres to Christianity. However, the starting-point here is also identical. Parallel to the undermining of a philosophy of subjectivity, there is also in Girard's work a deconstruction at work of the violent aspects in the tradition of Western metaphysics and in the image of God with which it is closely bound up. The philosophers he refers to in this respect are Nietzsche and Heidegger (and, in line with them, structuralism), with whom he has a love-hate relationship (as he does with Sigmund Freud). He shares their starting-points, but opposes to their conclusions. In order to make this clear, I have to distinguish between a metaphysical and a religious analysis of both authors.

2.4 Difference and transcendence: Girard and philosophy of religion

Girard follows Nietzsche and, especially, Heidegger in their analyses of the 'violent aspects' in classical metaphysics. For Heidegger, metaphysics, as the summit of Western thought, has finally resulted into a reduction of reality so that it has left no room for real transcendence, Being itself. In other words, to grasp the meaning of the *forgetfulness of Being (Seinsvergessenheit)* is to grasp the age-old metaphysical negligence of the *ontological difference (ontologische Differenz)*: that which is different becomes identical, the other becomes the same. Hence, Western metaphysics finds its culmination point in technology; there is no longer any room for Being itself.

However, with respect to both authors' concept of God, Girard repeatedly utters his reservations. Here, I confine myself to two telling examples. In *Things Hidden since the Foundation of the World,* Girard criticizes the interpretation that Heidegger gives in his *Introduction to Metaphysics (Einführung in die Metaphysik)* of Heraclitus' logos as precursor to the logos of St. John. He replaces this interpretation with his own interpretation of the relation between both variants of the logos. In his lecture for the Cérissy-la-Salle-colloquium, Girard gave a penetrating interpretation of the famous par.125 ('Der tolle Mensch') from *Fröhliche Wissenschaft* in which he does not only reject Heidegger's interpretation of this paragraph,[15] but also highlights the sharp

---

[15] M. Heidegger, Nietzsches Wort "Gott ist tot." In: Idem, *Holzwege.* Frankfurt, Klostermann, 1963, blz.193-247 [M. Heidegger, Nietzsche's Word: „God is dead". In: Idem, *Off the beaten track*. Cambridge, Cambridge University Press, 2002, pp. 157-199].

contrast between the Nietzschean concept of god and Christianity's concept.[16]

What is the essence of Girard's criticism? Girard is following Heidegger in so far as he takes a distance from a philosophy of identity and develops the idea of an ontological difference. But, he vehemently rejects Heidegger's interpretation of difference. Girard intends to show that Heidegger's 'sacred Being' is nothing but the product of intersubjective violence: Heidegger's concept of 'difference' is born out of violence itself. The fact that Heidegger, speaking about Being, praises the myth of Dionysus is, for Girard, significant. In his dialogue with Nietzsche and Heidegger, Girard emphasizes, time and again, the contrast between Dionysus and the crucified, putting into relief the specificity of the Christian concept of God. Precisely by stressing this specificity of a God who unmasks violence, and by rejecting the pre(post)modern view of Dionysian sacredness, Girard is strongly isolated in current, French thought.

2.5 Dionysus and deconstructionism

Of course, the influence of Dionysus on the later Nietzsche is well known. The name of this God is probably the last word Nietzsche ever wrote. Influenced by Nietzsche, current French philosophy has given a central role to Dionysus as well. Undoubtedly, this is the case for Georges Bataille. In his last book, *Tears of Eros*, Bataille considers Dionysus as the god of transgression and celebration, ecstasy and madness, eroticism and dissipation. He calls his philosophy a *heterology*, a kind of 'theology' without god in which there is made room for the other. The other is the sacred, appearing in a sacrifice which is sheer dissipation or wastefulness. For Bataille, there is no sacrifice as a consequence of the sacred; rather, it is sacrifice itself (*sacrificium*) that makes it possible for the sacred to appear (*sacrum facere*).

Michel Foucault, the author of the preface to Bataille's *Complete Works (Oeuvres complets)*, points to the congeniality between Bataille's concept of transgression and Heidegger's concept of transcendence, i.e., between his 'heterology' and the thought of ontological difference. Also for Heidegger, there is a contrast between the god of metaphysics and

[16] R. Girard, Le meurtre fondateur dans la pensée de Nietzsche. In: P. Dumouchel (ed.), *Violence et vérité. Colloque de Cérisy autour de René Girard*. Paris, Grasset, 1985, pp. 597-613; cf. also R. Girard, Dionysus versus the Crucified. In: *Modern Language Notes*, 1984, pp. 816-835.

the god to whom we can dance and sacrifice, make music and kneel down. Also for Heidegger, the sacred is primarily disturbing and appalling. A most striking point of congeniality between Heidegger's and Bataille's views is Heidegger's interpretation of the significance of sacrifice in his afterword to *What is Metaphysics? (Was ist Metaphysik?)*. There, Heidegger glorifies the courage to cope with the experience of fear, which makes possible the experience of being. The openness to being, in its distinction to concrete beings, takes shape in sacrifice. In other words, sacrifice is the medium through which the 'other than being' can appear. Dionysus is pre-eminently the god who embodies the other's appearance.

For Girard, Dionysus is not at all the embodiment of merry carelessness but, by contrast, the archetype of furious violence, of chaos threatening man and society. Here, an ethical-religious gap is fixed between Girard, on the one hand, and Nietzsche, Heidegger and French deconstructionism, on the other. Heidegger is, in line with Nietzsche, not only the thinker who reveals violence in its sacred dimension, but worships it as well.[17] Typical of Girard is, as already mentioned, the sharp opposition between the Christian God and sacred holiness. Behind the sacred transcendence of violence is hiding the transcendence of love, which manifests itself pre-eminently in the figure of Jesus Christ. In this sense, Girard's thought is rather congenial to that of the representatives of the new generation of French thinkers who explicitly call themselves anti-Nietzscheans without, however, pleading for a return to Christianity: Luc Ferry, Vincent Descombes, Alain Renaut, etc.

In this respect, it is interesting to note that Luc Ferry in *God-Man or the Sense of Life (L'homme-Dieu ou le sens de la vie)* makes use of the same terminology as René Girard in *Deceit, Desire and the Novel*. Ferry, in order to make a distinction between pre-modern and modern culture, speaks of a transition from *'vertical transcendence'* to *'horizontal transcendence'*, albeit his evaluation of this modern 'horizontal transcendence' is much more positive than Girard's. In passing, one can also refer to the kinship between Girard's interpretation of Christianity as a 'departure from religion' and the interpretation given by Marcel

---

[17] Cf. R. Girard, *La route antique des hommes pervers*. Paris, Grasset, 1985, p. 171: "This is Heidegger's profound and violent meaning when he speaks of the *shepherd of being*. The latter, for some reason, has always made me think of the wolf in disguise of the well known fable. Beneath the pure white coat of the sacrificial lamb, one black paw is showing."

Gauchet in his *Disenchantment of the World (Le Désenchantement du monde)*.[18]

3 Difference in sacrifice: a concrete application.

As already mentioned, the Christian ethical position is at odds with the proliferation of mimetic desire, which is aiming at the identification of everyone and everything: it unmasks the illusionary character of such an artificial form of identity by creating room for what is circumscribed in current French philosophy as 'difference'. But the specificity of the Christian concept of transcendence has its repercussions upon the specificity of Girard's concept of difference. Its specificity manifests itself *par excellence* when his interpretation of the sacrifice is taken into account.

What is the significance of the phenomenon of sacrifice today? It seems to belong to a pre-modern era and holds no meaning for the Westerner of today. At most, it is, perhaps, a weapon in the hands of religious fundamentalists. On the other hand, sacrifice is indissolubly connected to the phenomenon of religion itself; it is at the heart of Christian worship and, as indicated, re-emerges in current philosophy. According to Bataille, the sacred itself appears in sacrifice (*sacrificium*) and is brought about by sacrifice (*sacrum facere*). Also for Heidegger, the sacred is, first and foremost, a disquieting and disturbing force. Sacrifice is truth itself, being at work. The openness for being itself, in its distinction from particular beings, is likely to take shape in sacrifice. In other words, sacrifice is the place where the 'other than being' is located.

Girard has always defined Christianity as an anti-sacrificial religion. In his last book, *The One by Whom the Scandal Happens (Celui par qui le scandale arrive),* he qualifies this terminology (and is even prepared to retain the term 'sacrifice') by throwing into relief the difference

---

[18] From a completely different point of view, one can indeed refer to the congeniality (resemblances and differences) between Girard's interpretation of Christianity and Gauchet's view of Christianity as "the exit out of religion". Cf. for a critical analysis of Gauchet's view: Ch. Taylor, *Foreword.* In: M. Gauchet, *The disenchantment of the World. A Political History of Religion.* Princeton, Princeton University Press, 1997, pp. ix-xv. It goes without saying that the relation between Girard and Levinas and between Girard and Marion is a topic that has been completely neglected in French philosophical thought. For a reference to the relation between these three authors, cf. J. G. Williams (ed.), *The Girard Reader.* New York, The Crossroad Publishing Company, 1996, pp. 282-283.

between Christ's sacrifice and mythical-religious forms of sacrifice.[19] On the basis of his analysis of the Judgment of Solomon, I would like to elucidate the specificity of Girard's concept of sacrifice.

> Then two harlots came to the King, and stood before him. The one woman said, 'Oh, my lord, this woman and I dwell in the same house; and I gave birth to a child while she was in the house. Then on the third day after I was delivered, this woman also gave birth; and we were alone; there was no one else with us in the house, only we two were in the house. And this woman's son died in the night, because she lay on it. And she arose at midnight, and took my son from beside me, while your maidservant slept, and laid it in her bosom, and laid her dead son in my bosom. When I rose in the morning to nurse my child, behold, it was dead; but when I looked at it closely in the morning, behold it was not the child that I had borne.' But the other woman said, 'No, the living child is mine, and the dead child is yours.' The first said, 'No, the dead child is yours, and the living child is mine.' Thus they spoke before the king.
> Then the king said, 'The one says, "This is my son that is alive, and your son is dead"; and the other says, "No; but your son is dead, and my son is the living one."' And the king said, 'Bring me a sword.' So a sword was brought before the king. And the king said, 'Divide the living child in two, and give half to the one, and half to the other.' Then the woman whose son was alive said to the king, because her heart yearned for her son, 'Oh, my lord, give her the living child, and by no means slay it.' But the other said, 'It shall be neither mine nor yours; divide it.' Then the king answered and said, 'Give the living child to the first woman, and by no means slay it; she is its mother.' And all Israel heard of the judgment which the king had rendered; and they stood in awe of the king, because they perceived that the wisdom of God was in him, to render justice (1 Kings 3:16-28).

We have no trouble in recognizing that this text brings in the whole question of the mimetic crisis, the rivalry of doubles, and the issue of *differentiation*. The fact that both women — being harlots — have the same social positions underlines the lack of differentiation. Throughout the whole quarrel that leads to the king's brilliant stratagem, the text makes no distinction at all between the two women. In fact, it does not matter who is speaking since both of them are saying precisely the same thing. This obvious symmetry represents the very essence of each human conflict. That is why the text adds: "thus they spoke before the king."

Consequently, the king decides to end the quarrel by means of a sacrifice: "Divide the living child in two, and give half to the one, and

[19] See the third essay of this book: *Mimetic Theory and Theology (Théorie mimétique et théologie)*. In: R. Girard, *Celui par qui le scandale arrive*. Paris, Desclée de Brouwer, 2001, pp. 63-82.

half to the other." Up to the end, the king respects the symmetry between the *doubles* and hence their 'in-difference'. The symmetry of the terms used corresponds completely to the equality with which the two women are treated. In other words, as he cannot decide the case on any genuine basis, Solomon pretends to have decided to divide the child in two; being incapable of setting apart the antagonistic doubles, he pretends to divide the object of the litigation. So, the child seems to function as the ritual scapegoat, as it occurs in all religions. It is precisely the appointment of the scapegoat that must bring an end to the in-differentiation.

However, the sacrifice which Solomon proposes does not bring an end to the 'in-difference'; on the contrary, it reinforces it. By accepting the king's proposal, the 'wicked' harlot reveals her lack of genuine love for the child. The only thing important to her is possessing what the other harlot possesses. Eventually, she is ready to accept being deprived of the child as long as her opponent is deprived of it in the same way. Obviously, mimetic desire impels her to speak and act: the object of the quarrel, the living child, is no longer important. All that is important is her fascination with her model-rival, which makes her involve this model in her own downfall if achieving any other triumph over the model proves impossible. In short, the wicked harlot sacrifices the child for the sake of the rivalry.

But, the 'good' harlot also makes a sacrifice. Precisely by putting herself in a position of sacrifice for the benefit of the child, she differentiates her behaviour from that of her rival's. Her sacrifice is proof of her motherhood. As such, her sacrifice prefigures Christ's sacrifice. Like Christ himself, she has no inclination at all to sacrifice herself. She wishes to go on living to take care of her child. But she is ready to renounce her child forever, even to renounce her own life, in order to save her child. The good harlot is prepared to substitute herself for the sacrificial victim, not because she feels a morbid attraction to this role but because her answer to the tragic alternative, 'kill or be killed', is 'be killed, so that the child will live'.

In an analogous situation that reveals the ultimate foundation of all human cultures and societies, Christ also accepts death so that humankind will live: it is the only way to denounce the *false identity* of a so-called 'sweet peace' and to install the *real difference*. "So the only way of doing the will of the Father, on earth as it is in heaven, is by behaving like the good harlot, by taking the same risks as she did — which should be done not in a spirit of sacrificial gloom or morbid preoccupation with death but in a spirit of love for true life, so that life may triumph."[20]

In extreme circumstances, adopting a neutral attitude is impossible. One cannot escape from the first kind of sacrifice, which always implies the sacrifice of the other, except by the acceptance of the second form of sacrifice, namely, Christ's sacrifice whereby he dies for his people. Of course, sacrifice is at the heart of Christianity. It is a sacrifice that introduces the kind of *difference* that enables the escape from a violent tendency towards global identification. Hence, the difference which is established by Christ's sacrifice (analogous to the sacrifice of the good harlot) is not a sacrifice that canalizes violence, as in the case of mythical religions. It is a kind of difference that aims at the unmasking — once and for all — of violence which is inherent in the proliferation of all mimetic desire and which manifests itself pre-eminently in current modern market society, the intention of which is to make all of us equal in our striving to possess what others possess.

4 To conclude

In current western culture, Christianity's situation is a precarious one. It is in a rather impossible situation, imprisoned between the modern Charybdis of complete immanence and the anti-modern Scylla of inscrutable transcendence. What does this all mean?

On the one hand, there is a strong sensitivity for the purely immanent aspects of our life in modern culture. The practically oriented attention for 'ordinary life', which has been manifesting itself since the 18th century in the care for the well-being of all people, the importance of personal relations, the demolition of hierarchical structures, etc., this concrete care which is taken for granted by the majority of western people today, seems to be at odds with a care for the spiritual well-being of the soul, which used to be a privilege of the (Christian) happy few. In other words, modern humanism is suspicious of the emphasis that has traditionally been laid upon transcendence by Christianity. In short, although Christianity itself stimulated this kind of practical care for daily life, it simultaneously brought about, in spite of itself, an evolution that made each reference to transcendence rather problematic.

---

[20] R. Girard, *Des choses cachées depuis la fondation du monde*, p. 265 [R. Girard, *Things Hidden since the Foundation of the World*, pp. 242-3].

On the other hand, there is, in our days, undoubtedly, a sense of discontent with prevailing immanence, which manifests itself pre-eminently in current (French) philosophy) Contemporary French philosophers display a strong sensitivity for the 'other', the 'unknown', for something which, in principle, goes beyond the domain of what can be known and be described in verifiable propositions, referring to the domain of what does not belong to the order of knowledge and understanding. In this context, one often hears rumours about the return of transcendence. In general, this openness for transcendence is accompanied by an aloofness to filling up the contents of this transcendence. The 'other' is the empty spot *par excellence*, bearing no form of 'filling up' whatsoever. This principal elusiveness of 'the other' is testified to by the undeniable return of what is called the Dionysian aspect in current philosophy (of religion). This lack of describable characteristics of the Other is, in this view, applicable to the concept of transcendence itself. So, the Christian interpretation of transcendence has, in diverse variants of post-modern thought, become synonymous with a general concept of transcendence which is presumed to be typical of every religion.

It is precisely this identification of the specific Christian concept of transcendence with the general concept of transcendence that has become one of the main targets of Girard's sharp criticism. For Girard, Christian inspiration is, first and foremost, anti-mythological, thereby aiming, in particular, at the religious concept of transcendence. It unmasks the violent aspects of religion, something which has been undoubtedly understood by modern culture. But Christian inspiration is not confined to this unmasking function, i.e., Girard's focus upon its ethical dimension does not imply putting aside the mystery of God's transcendence, something which has not been understood at all by modern culture. The story of Jesus' life precisely shows the real import of what is meant by divine transcendence. Such a reading of the Gospels makes clear the sharp contrast between religion and *well-interpreted* Christianity, the quintessence of which is formed by the image of 'God as Love', not by the 'sacred' which simultaneously exorcises and evokes violence. It is here that the sharp contrast between the concept of difference in French philosophy and in Girard's thought is to be situated.

In line with this central distinction, there is a sharp contrast as well between a one-sided and exclusive form of humanism and a *well-interpreted* form of Christianity, of which neighbourly love is the centre rather than internal mediation, which is the basis of current economical relations in contemporary western society. Parallel to the Christian image of God, which implies both transcendence and immanence and which excludes both sheer external and internal mediation, the Christian attitude of *agapè* does not leave room for the revenge of old religions or for the resentment and hidden envy of always-competing individuals and groups, which are so typical of modern culture.

THIS EXTRAORDINARY WORD.
EMMANUEL LEVINAS ON GOD

JOHAN GOUD

> The ambiguity of transcendence — and consequently the alternation of the soul moving from atheism to belief and from belief to atheism...is not the feeble faith surviving the death of God, but the original mode of the presence of God.[1]

Emmanuel Levinas (1906-1995) is representative of the twentieth century not only because of a life nearly spanning it, but also because of the events that determined his life and his thought. He experienced at first-hand the rise and fall of totalitarian systems that spread over Europe. Witnessing the Russian Revolution in the Ukraine as a boy of eleven years he realized that a new history was emerging. As an adult, having emigrated to France and achieved his doctorate in Strasbourg, he provided philosophical commentary on 'Hitlerism', experienced the Nazi conquest of France and was interned as a prisoner of war. The virulent anti-Semitism of the twentieth century did not pass him by. It affected him as a Jewish boy when he was growing up in Russian Lithuania. Many years later, when the holocaust became a fact, he and his wife and children escaped by chance, and because of help from others, but all the rest of his family in Lithuania died. And finally, this man — who, like many Jews, was formed by various cultures: Russian, Jewish, French and German — witnessed the demise of colonialism, the rise of Arab nations, and the decentralization of world culture. He perceived the problems that arise from this; it is doubtful, however, that he found satisfactory answers to them. When confronted with the question as to how one can explain to a Chinese, for instance, what being Jewish means, he replied that Jewry is not a matter of particularity; it is a universal form of existence. "Everyone is a little bit Jewish (...) Jews are people who know what self-doubt is, who in a way adhere to a religion of unbelievers."[2] This

---

[1] E. Levinas, *Entre nous. Essais sur le penser-à-l'autre*. Paris, Grasset, 1991, p. 72 [E. Levinas, *On-Thinking-of-the-Other entre nous*. London, The Athlone Press, 1998, p. 56].

[2] Chr. Delacampagne (ed.), *Entretiens avec Le Monde. 1. Philosophes*. Paris, La Découverte-Le Monde, 1984, p. 147.

typification clearly assumes the processes of secularization and Enlightenment characteristic of the West. Levinas himself affirms this when he points out, in the same context, that it is precisely in Europe that criticism of Euro-centrism and the idea of *deseuropeanisation (deseuropéanisation)* have developed.

1. Philosopher of Imprudent Consciousness

Levinas commented in an autobiographical sketch from 1963 that his life was dominated by "the presentiment and the memory of the Nazi horror."[3] This pertains to his thinking as well. He seeks to demonstrate the possibility of an *imprudent consciousness* capable of challenging "the inexorable power of being."[4] This imprudent consciousness is not reckless, however. It is aware that it must take the power of being into account at all times and that, as a thinking consciousness, it maneuvers in its center. This is evident in the ambiguity which characterizes the movement. On one hand, consciousness strives for conscious representation and thematic ordering of things and for incorporating the knowledge acquired in this way into the system of the 'said'. On the other hand, it is alert to the movement towards the other which expresses itself in unreserved 'saying'.

In this second aspect we encounter Levinas' 'personalism', as it is called.[5] In the foreword to *Proper Names (Noms propres)*, a book about thinkers and poets who have inspired him, he observes that this marks the end of rationality, which was linked *only* — the emphasis is Levinas' own — to the 'named' or the 'said'. This rationality aimed at knowledge and truths which could be incorporated into a more or less perfect system. He asks himself: Is it possible that, among all the names and commonplaces, it is the *proper* names associated with a face which offer resistance to the disintegration of structures of meaning and give us the ability to speak?[6] The power of the proper name does not have its source

---

[3] E. Levinas, *Difficile liberté. Essais sur le judaïsme*. Paris, Albin Michel, 1976[2], p. 374 [E. Levinas, *Difficult Freedom. Essays on Judaism*. Baltimore, John Hopkins University Press, 1990, p. 291].

[4] E. Levinas, *Quatre lectures talmudiques*. Paris, Minuit, 1968, p. 85 [E. Levinas, *Nine Talmudic Readings*. Bloomington, Indiana University Press, 1990, pp. 70ff.].

[5] See S. Strasser, *Jenseits von Sein und Zeit. Eine Einführung in Emmanuel Levinas' Philosophie.* The Hague, Martinus Nijhoff, 1978, p. 156. In the same context Strasser points to the disruption of this personalism, in Levinas' reflections on the erotic.

[6] E. Levinas, *Noms propres*. Montpellier, Fata Morgana, 1976, pp. 10-11 [E. Levinas, *Proper Names*. Stanford, Stanford University Press, pp. 4-5].

in a mysterious or divine nucleus in the person himself; rather, it proceeds from openness to the other, who is called up by it. Contrary to
Sartre, Levinas does not see the other principally as a threat to personal
freedom, making the state of war a basic human condition. The self is
not of man's own making, neither is it his possession. It is a 'creature',
from the outset called upon to choose the other. Only by responding to
this appeal can it become itself; responsibility for others makes the self
a free and unique person. Man's 'imprudent consciousness' manifests
itself in his ability to provide *acte de presence*, to stand in for others, to
speak. Peace — the opposite of war — is really nothing other than this
ability to speak. "War presupposes peace, the antecedent and non-aller-
gic presence of the other.[7]

Levinas' thought has attracted broad acclaim in Europe and the
United States.[8] This is surprising, because his thought is certainly not
without its difficulties; it is *hors sujet* (out of order), according to this
title of one of his volumes of essays. The important thing is that his
thought is in the very heart of current philosophical discussion, without
being confined by its conditions and limits. It aims to convert Jewish
wisdom into Greek, the language of philosophy, at the same time recognizing that, inevitably, much is lost in the translation. His thought registers the totalitarian features in the way of thinking of Western philosophy; it objects to a cynical view of human nature; it offers an apologia
for subjectivity and dialogue; it is both modern and post-modern. After
the structuralistic death of man, his thought provides new content for the
humanistic ideals of freedom and dignity. Particularly significant in connection with the theme of this volume is that it brings God into discussion again after his anti-metaphysical death — albeit requiring "the
blinking and dia-chrony of enigma."[9]

It does not intend to discuss God in theological terms — at least not
in the narrow sense of God as a theme, and claiming certain knowledge.
Neither does it intend to speak in terms of negative theology, which simply denies the possibility of making any positive assertions about God.
To a certain extent Levinas includes atheism in his thought. His concern

[7] E. Levinas, *Totalité et Infini. Essai sur l'extériorité*. La Haye, Martinus Nijhoff,
1974⁴, p. 174 [E. Levinas, *Totality and Infinity. An Essay on Exteriority*. The Hague-
Boston-London, Martinus Nijhoff Publishers, 1979, p. 199].

[8] See the extensive bibliography prepared by R. Burggraeve, *Emmanuel Levinas. Une
bibliographie primaire et secondaire (1929-1985), avec complement 1985-1989*. Leuven,
Peeters, 1990.

[9] E. Levinas, *De Dieu qui vient à l'idée*. Paris, Vrin, 1982, p. 127 [E. Levinas, *Collected Philosophical Papers*. Dordrecht, Martinus Nijhoff Publishers, 1987, p. 173].

is the relation to an 'altogether other' who withdraws from alternatives of positive or negative theology. In his view of atheism, it is "a position prior to both the negation and the affirmation of the divine, the breaking with participation by which I posits itself as the same and the I." But Levinas is 'out of order' even in his atheism. Indeed, a *witness* concerning God is certainly tenable, albeit as "humility and admission: it is made before all theology." "To bear witness [to] God is precisely not to *state* this extraordinary word.[11] This does not mean, however, that Levinas avoids the use of the word 'God' in his texts. On the contrary, we come across it many times in these texts, even though they do not have the typical character of a witness. One can argue, against one-sided moral and non-religious interpretations, that his philosophical thought hinges on philosophical theology. The foreword of *Otherwise than Being (Autrement qu'être)*, his last major work, formulates the problem he wants to resolve in this complicated book as follows: "to hear a God not contaminated by Being."[12]

2. Manners of Thinking

The question of right method frequently plays a major role in philosophical discourse. A solution to philosophical problems would be greatly facilitated by clarity in method, as held by Bacon, Descartes, Locke and Husserl, to name only a few great thinkers. After what has been said about imprudent consciousness as being 'a movement toward the other', it can hardly come as a surprise that Levinas does not agree. He is not only much more inspired by the content than by the form, but moreover, in his perception, the form in which thought presents itself is constantly disturbed by its content. Responding to a question about his method, he said: "I do not believe that there is a transparency possible in method. Nor that philosophy might be possible as transparency. Those who have worked on methodology all their lives have written many books that replace the more interesting books that they could have written."[13] In

---

[10] E. Levinas, *Totalité et Infini*, p. 30 [E. Levinas, *Totality and Infinity*, p. 58].

[11] E. Levinas, *Autrement qu'être ou au-delà de l'essence*. La Haye, Martinus Nijhoff, 1974, p. 190 [E. Levinas, *Otherwise Than Being or Beyond Essence*. The Hague-Boston-London, Martinus Nijhoff Publishers, 1981, p. 149] — It. By JG.

[12] *Ibid.*, p. X [*Ibid.*, p.xlii].

[13] E. Levinas, *De Dieu qui vient à l'idée*, p. 143 [E. Levinas, *Of God Who Comes to Mind*. Stanford, Stanford University Press, 1998, p. 89].

this section we will therefore not be describing Levinas' method; rather, we will be outlining his manner of thinking on several points. We shall begin by elucidating the way he relativizes method. This will be followed by the delineation of several lines of inspiration in his work. Finally, I shall show how Levinas develops his philosophy of subjectivity.

Levinas relativizes in a big way the value of seeking a method that would make philosophical thought transparent — 'clear and distinct' according to Descartes' mathematical ideal. He sees in it the traditional yearning for "walking in sunlight free of shadow."[14] I shall discuss three of the considerations that led him to reject this.

In the first place, there is his attention to the experiences preceding philosophical thought that are determinative for it. For Levinas, the most important of these pre-philosophical experiences was his encounter with Talmudic Jewry. He was taught in 1947 and 1948 by the mysterious Chouchani, who was also teacher to Elie Wiesel. Wiesel characterized him as 'the wandering Jew'. It was he who quoted him as saying that humankind is not defined by what gives him peace of mind, but by what disturbs it.[15] Levinas was above all impressed by the fact that religion was presented as a source for intellectual discipline.[16] This experience is reflected in his argument for 'adult religion', which does not require people to abdicate intellect and be ruled by revelations. Instead, this religion promotes a piety that can do without explanations and consolations.[17]

The second consideration that relativizes the orientation toward methodology is Levinas' characterization of philosophy as a discipline of questioning. The orientation toward answers and their systematization blinds us to questions that reach beyond the known and the familiar. The greatness of Greek philosophy lay in its discovery of theoretical — in the right sense of the word — query motivated by a respect for the alterity of the known and of the other knowing subjects. This discovery, however, gradually opened the way for theoretical knowledge, whereby

---

[14] *Loc. cit.*

[15] E. Wiesel, *Le chant des morts.* Paris, Seuil, 1966, p. 125.

[16] Levinas does not hesitate to rank Chouchani with Husserl and Heidegger; see Chr. Delacampagne (ed.), *Entretiens avec Le Monde*, p. 142.

[17] See the article from 1957: E. Levinas, Une religion d'adultes. In: Idem, *Difficile liberté*, pp. 25-41 [E. Levinas, A Religion for Adults. In: Idem, *Difficult Freedom*, pp. 11-23].

the particularity of the known disappeared. This was typical of, for example, the '*onto-theology*' that many Western thinkers developed. In such systems, 'God' served as the universal concept that formed the basis for knowledge of all being, or crowned it. Theory in the right sense of the word keeps the 'metaphysical yearning' intact that is directed toward the absolute other. Unlike the theory that would like to have everything appear to perception and vision, this yearning is directed toward 'the dimension of the heights' or 'the invisible'. "To die for the invisible — this is metaphysics."[18]

The third consideration follows on what has just been said. The enigmatic fascinates Levinas. It is this that withdraws itself from the correlation — tending to clarification and clear insight — between the knowing subject and the known object. This evasion, however, does not lead to an absence without problems. It leaves its trace in the disruption that the order of philosophical discourse is experiencing. There have been moments all through the history of philosophy where this enigma has come to the fore. This occurred in Plato when he was speaking of the good; in Plotinus when he dealt with 'the one'; in Descartes when he talked of the infinite. In this respect philosophers had the same experience as believers. One encounters this same perception in religions, although in another form: "To endure the contradiction between the existence included in the essence of God and the scandalous absence of this God is to suffer an initiation trial into religious life which separates philosophers from believers. That is, unless the obstinate absence of God were one of those paradoxes that give access to the highways of the spirit."[19]

In Levinas' philosophical writings we find paradox and enigma particularly in his analysis of the 'trace'. Usually he draws a contrast with the concept 'phenomenon'. Considered as phenomena, things are correlatively bound to our consciousness. They satisfy the appetite for knowledge and light which gets it going. However, it is typical of the trace that it indicates an absolute absence. The manifestation of the altogether other withdraws itself from the light of consciousness and is a 'nocturnal event'. It represents a 'reality' that infinitely transcends the extent of our thought but stimulates and challenges it at the same time. It is often asked how this enigmatic 'reality' can provide an effective challenge.

---

[18] E. Levinas, *Totalité et Infini*, p. 5 [E. Levinas, *Totality and Infinity*, p. 35].

[19] E. Levinas, *En découvrant l'existence avec Husserl et Heidegger*. Paris, Vrin, 1974³, p. 204 [E. Levinas, *Collected Philosophical Papers*, p. 62].

How could it inspire thinking to develop new categories? Is Levinas perhaps being led by a 'heterological' dream[20] that speaks of the other in one way or another without being able to legitimize its own speaking? Levinas responds by dramatizing the relation to the Infinite in the spirit of dialogical philosophy. The absence of straightforwardness and correlation acquires an ethical dimension, that is to say: between the self and the Infinite comes the other who regards me as 'thou' and speaks to me as such. "Does not the invisibility of God belong to … an approach which does not polarize into a subject-object correlation but is deployed as a drama with several personages?"[21]

Levinas' manner of thinking has been developed from various sources. In the first place, there is the inspiration of phenomenology. In this case the pursuance of 'the things themselves' — which his teacher Husserl chose as philosophical guideline — is central in his thinking. It implies the reduction of things perceived to the way in which they — with their horizon of meanings — appear to consciousness. However, in agreement with later developments in phenomenology, Levinas consistently adds a critical comment. For him the most interesting discovery is that some meanings cannot be reduced: the fact that we are corporeal beings, the confrontation with the other. Carrying through on this line in his thought, he arrives at conclusions that lead to a reversal in his view of the original phenomenological perspective. Reduction does not end in a pure ego that is characterized by consciousness of being and beings. The self has to do with the other, is knotted to the other, before the other appears to consciousness. "The other in the same, determinative of subjectivity, is the restlessness of the same, disturbed by the other. This is not the correlation characteristic of intentionality, nor even that of dialogue, which attests to essence by its essential reciprocity."[22] The last part of the sentence points to the second line of inspiration, accompanied in the same breath by the reservations Levinas has.

Levinas became acquainted with the *philosophy of dialogue* partly through Martin Buber. Buber criticized the priority assigned to objectifying knowledge by the Western tradition of thought and established the

[20] J. Derrida. *L'écriture et la différence*. Paris, Du Seuil, 1967, p. 224 [J. Derrida, *Writing and Difference*. Chicago, Chicago University Press, 1978, p. 151].

[21] E. Levinas, *En découvrant l'existence*, p. 204 [E. Levinas, *Collected Philosophical Papers*, p. 62].

[22] E. Levinas, *Autrement qu'être*, p. 32 [E. Levinas, *Otherwise Than Being*, p. 25].

I-thou relationship as being more significant. To see the image of man as he really is, one must first take dialogue seriously. "Without *It* man cannot live. But he who lives with *It* alone is not a man."[23] Although Levinas certainly agrees with this position which takes a critical view of knowledge and culture, he underscores the nonreciprocal in the relation to the other. The other comes to the self from an irreversible position of superiority; I and thou cannot, therefore, be interchangeable. Expressed with more nuances, the concern here is "approaching in such a way that, over and beyond all the reciprocal relations that do not fail to get set up between me and the neighbor, I have always taken one step more toward him (…). In the responsibility which we have for one another, I have to answer for his very responsibility."[24]

The third line of inspiration deserving attention is the *hermeneutical* one. This term, here applied very broadly, refers to the movement of thought that opposes the conscious self having dominant status and the intelligibility of the world being expressed in propositions. Martin Heidegger instigated this movement by proposing the subject to be a 'Dasein' standing in the openness of being and geared toward understanding. Phenomena can appear to us in many and very diverse ways. As we have established several times, Levinas places himself consciously in this line of differentiation within the concept 'intelligibility'. He observes that this thought rediscovers the concrete connections which give our most abstract notions their true meaning. Theological, moral and political thought could derive great benefit from this discovery of concrete and 'fleshly' conditions.[25] He also accepts the passivity and the receptivity that characterize Heidegger's 'Dasein', although he gives them his own, ethical twist. The foundation of 'knowledge and being' is the Me — an I in the accusative — characterized by responsibility. At this most basic level the word ethics perhaps means nothing more than respect for each phenomenon's mode of being and the willingness to do justice to it in its concreteness.[26]

[23] M. Buber, *Ich und Du*. Heidelberg, Lambert Schneider, 1977[9], p. 44 (the final sentence of the first part) [M. Buber, *I and Thou*. New York, Charles Scribner's Sons, 1958, p. 34].

[24] E. Levinas, *Autrement qu'être*, p. 106 [E. Levinas, *Otherwise Than Being*, p. 84].

[25] E. Levinas, *En découvrant l'existence*, p. 134.

[26] In this spirit also A. Th. Peperzak, cited by J. L. Kosky, *Levinas and the Philosophy of Religion*. Bloomington-Indianapolis, Indiana, 2001, p. 57.

Levinas' thought is a philosophy of subjectivity — to a degree following
the line of the philosophy of consciousness dominating French thought
from Descartes onwards. However, he accentuates other points. In his
philosophy of subjectivity, the self is posited as a movement toward the
other. Ethical and theological dimensions come in as a matter of course.
In the nucleus of our subjectivity is found a point that we could never
have intended or thought up, but which is the undoing of the nucleus.
This 'psychosis', the other-in-the-self, does not take away the self's
identity but commits him to it with inevitable summons.[27] In the foreword of *Totality and Infinity (Totalité et Infini)* this book is presented as
a 'defense of subjectivity', although "not at the level of its purely egoist
protestation against totality."[28] In other words, it is not Levinas' concern
to provide an apologia for an ego objecting to totalitarian ways of thinking and acting *for its own sake* (for the sake of its own purity, originality, free choice, salvation). On the contrary, a true, authentic apologia of
subjectivity shows that the self has its origin elsewhere: in the infinite
and then, to be specific, in the other. The apologia concerns a self that
infinitely goes beyond its own limits; it is "founded in the idea of infinity."[29] Remarkable in this idea is that we do encounter it *in* ourselves
and have to concede at the same time that it — in contrast to other
thoughts and ideas — cannot be controlled, and eludes us. In this case
we think infinitely more than we are capable of.

However, a situation can be identified where the idea of the infinite
comes to the fore concretely. It is the *ethical* situation, where I find
myself confronted by an other who eludes all my schematizing; neither
can he be reduced to me in any way whatever. On the contrary, the other
calls me to responsibility and challenges my identity so radically that I
can no longer find a position for myself without the other. Seen in this
way, 'apologia of subjectivity based on the idea of infinity' means:
apologia of the self called to 'goodness', from the outset being obligated
to the other. This procedure of concretizing, essential for Levinas, is
paired with another thought. The infinity who is God cannot be reduced,
restlessly, to the ethical dimension. God's transcendence is different
from the other's transcendence; it precedes moral obligation; it is
'absence' that can be confused with chaos. Levinas calls this chaos *il
y a* (the 'there is'), that is to say: the nightmare of a reality without

---

[27] See E. Levinas, *Autrement qu'être*, p. 180 [E. Levinas, *Otherwise Than Being,* 141].
[28] E. Levinas, *Totalité et Infini*, p. XIV [E. Levinas, *Totality and Infinity*, p. 26].
[29] *Loc. cit.*

subjects, in which there is no sound of a creating word.[30] On one hand, this thought underscores the disinterestedness demanded in the responsibility for the other. Indeed, only the patience of one who suffers in the place of another and expects no reward, will prove to be resistant to chaos.[31] On the other hand, this thought implies that transcendence has other dimensions — coming down to or staying on this side[32] — which can perhaps be articulated by others than saints and prophets, and in other ways. It is important that these varying connotations of transcendence are acknowledged. It means that, although God's eminence or 'glory' realizes its deepest significance in the ethical, it can be supposed elsewhere, too, even if only by its absence. This confirms Levinas in his choice of a manner of thinking that allows for maximum space and that liberates itself "from the pretended sovereignty of objectifying thought, which [...] mocks at the metaphysical adventures of saints, prophets, poets, and simply living men, as if they were only tokens of childishness."[33] The philosopher will have to range himself on the side of the prophets and the poets.

3. Philosopher, Prophet, Poet

The openness to infinity sought by this philosophy of subjectivity is expressed in diverse ways. For instance, it manifests itself in the use of certain forms of thought.[34] The intellectual effort it requires, furthermore, can be seen in the many paradoxes found in Levinas' writings. They point beyond themselves, as it were, and indicate a new orientation. The condition of subjectivity is called "non-condition" and its position, "a surrendering of position".[35] In yet another way, this metaphysical

---

[30] E. Levinas, *De Dieu qui vient à l'idée*, p. 115 [E. Levinas, God and Philosophy. In: E. Levinas, *Collected Philosophical Papers*, p. 166]. See J. D. Caputo, Adieu — sans Dieu. Derrida and Levinas. In: J. Bloechl (ed.), *The Face of the Other and the Trace of God. Essays on the Philosophy of Emmanuel Levinas*. New York, Fordham, 2000, pp. 307-308.

[31] E. Levinas, *Autrement qu'être*, p. 209 [E. Levinas, *Otherwise Than Being*, p. 164]: The *il y a* is an "overflowing of sense by nonsense". "To support without compensation, the excessive or disheartening hubbub and encumberment of the *there is* is needed."

[32] Levinas, too, here uses diverse images: 'transdescendence', a space 'on this side' of the world.

[33] E. Levinas, *En découvrant l'existence*, p. 144.

[34] Such as 'repetition' (concepts being doubled), 'exaltation' or 'emphasis' (magnifying a concept to its superlative).

[35] E. Levinas, *Autrement qu'être*, pp. 143, 163 [E. Levinas, *Otherwise Than Being*, pp. 112, 127].

openness manifests itself in the liberal use of religious and literary sources in his writings. The appeal to *Biblical prophecy* concretizes and strengthens the desire for "the absolute otherness that is *the* other", "the Stranger who disturbs the being at home with oneself".[36] The preference is for *poetical sources* in the confusing area dominated by 'there is', which disengages from everything, and where the other seems to be absent. This section will provide an example both of prophets and of poets.

The main reason why prophecy should be highly valued in connection with philosophy is explained in the foreword of *Totality and Infinity*. Here Levinas refers to the hypocrisy in our civilization. It thinks it can be attached both to the good and to the truth, both to the prophetic ideal and to the philosophic one.[37] His thought is an effort to rise above this hypocrisy. It does not aim to be good and true at the same time; rather, it turns good into a source of inspiration for the desire for truth and restores its prophetic power. In this way Levinas develops a *prophetic philosophy* which combines witness and understanding, inspiration and criticism, Greek and Jew, without leveling the existing huge differences. He sometimes refers to this as *wisdom*. This seems to be a classical philosophical ideal. Levinas, however, does not associate it with classical tranquility of mind. Wisdom is restless, "the wisdom of love at the service of love."[38] The origin of this wisdom that is never wise enough, is the prophetic word. For, in the relation to the other, not only is my freedom cast into doubt and an appeal made to my responsibility, but commandment and admonition resound as well. In the prophetic word, these dimensions of the ethical relation are brought forward. This strain of thought is developed further in *Otherwise than Being*.[39] In this work prophecy acquires a universal significance: All of humanity's spirituality is referred to as 'prophetic'. This means that I respond to the commandment that assigns me to the other even before the Name of God is heard. In my answer I witness to the fact of a prophetic commandment; nowhere else do I encounter it, which "was secretly brought to me." (Job 4:12) In this the Infinite is present and absent at the same time, touches me without exposing himself to me. The origin of human

---

[36] E. Levinas, *Totalité et Infini*, p. 39 [E. Levinas, *Totality and Infinity*, p. 39].
[37] *Ibid.*, p. 9 [*Ibid.*, p. 24].
[38] E. Levinas, *Autrement qu'être*, p. 207 [E. Levinas, *Otherwise Than Being*, p. 162].
[39] *Ibid.*, pp. 190-194 [*Ibid.*, pp. 149ff.] Cf. E. Levinas, *De Dieu qui vient à l'idée*, pp. 123-127 [E. Levinas, God and Philosophy. In: E. Levinas, *Collected Philosophical Papers*, pp. 171-173].

language and spirituality, however, is my saying without reserve —
"Here am I. Send me!" (Is. 6:8)

The quoted verses are examples of Biblical quotations Levinas uses in
the context of his philosophical discourse. They are certainly never
intended as references to be taken as proofs. Neither should they be seen
as evidence of typical Jewish thought. Levinas is very much aware that
philosophical discourse has a character of its own and that Greek, the
language of philosophy, has its own requirements. The Bible quotations
represent the pre-philosophical inspiration that led him to philosophize.
They also serve to relativize the difference — sometimes presented as
absolute — between religious and philosophical literature. In philosophy
one sees dimensions of subjectivity which are also, in their own way,
expressed in religious language. Levinas notes that philosophy is not
essentially godless. It is true that, in philosophy, Bible verses cannot
claim the status of evidence. "[T]he God of verse can, despite all the
text's anthropomorphical metaphors, remain the measure of the Spirit
for the philosopher."[40]

Besides philosophical writings, Levinas has also published many Talmudic lectures and commentaries. They are indirectly, but recognizably,
connected with his philosophical discussions. An example of his Biblical and Talmudic interpretation follows here to illustrate this. The value
of interpretation itself is also brought forward in the illustration.[41]

The following prophecy of Isaiah is the point of discussion: "Since
ancient times no one has heard, no ear has perceived, no eye has seen
any God besides you, who acts on behalf of those who wait for him."
(Is. 64:4) What is the reward, as yet unseen, that is here promised to the
righteous and the wise? One of the opinions about this comes from
Rabbi Jochanan: "It is the wine preserved in the clusters of grapes since
the six days of creation." Levinas adds his own comment. "A fantastic
year for wine! A vintage wine that hasn't been bottled, nor harvested.
Every opportunity for messing with this wine has been prevented. It is
absolutely unchanged, pure wine. The world to come — that is what this
wine is." One can admire the beauty of this image, but what do the
words mean? According to the first explanation, the reward to be
expected, namely the wine of creation, is nothing other than the original
meaning of the Bible. For the one who waits upon God, the true secret

---

[40] E. Levinas, *Éthique et Infini. Dialogues avec Philippe Nemo.* Paris, Fayard, 1982,
p. 18 [E. Levinas, *Ethics and Infinity: conversations with Philippe Nemo.* Pittsburgh,
Duquesne University Press, 1985, pp. 23-24].
[41] E. Levinas, *Difficile liberté*, pp. 92-95 [E. Levinas, *Difficult Freedom*, pp. 66-69].

of the text will be revealed in the world to come — a secret that, against
the kinds of exegesis that look for deeper meanings, will turn out to be
lodged in the original simplicity of the text. "We need to pass through
the interpretation in order to come out beyond interpretation." However,
the Talmud writes up another opinion, expressed by Rabbi Levi. "What
none has seen, that is Eden. But Eden should not be identified with the
garden where Adam lived. For, as Genesis says: A river flowed out of
Eden to water the garden." This second view does not exclude the first
one; it raises a different aspect. The world to come is no return to a lost
paradise. It comes as the resolution of a history leading to it. Eden, the
mystery "that none has seen," and on which paradise depended, will be
revealed only at the end of history. One can conclude, therefore, that history and becoming acquire a positive meaning in this interpretation; they
are characterized by unpredictable fertility. But are such interpretations
not a typical example of pious, arbitrary supposition? Levinas denies
this. Not only is it the case that the meaning of these writings can be
transposed into philosophical language, but it is also in itself applicable
to philosophical problems. The exegete must treat this content of the text
with integrity; for it is rational and even indicative of genius. Pure historical research of texts disallows such respectful treatment of the genius
of the content and views the text as reflecting a peculiar and limited cultural environment. But thought that has genius is "thought where everything has already been thought."

In a subtle, more indirect way, literary sources also contribute to Levinas' philosophy and philosophical theology. He has often pointed out
the significance of the great Russian writers (Pushkin, Tolstoy, Dosto-
ievsky). In his youth he had become well acquainted with their works.
He discovered modern poets such as Blanchot and Celan at a much later
stage in his life. Interpretation is essential for poetry and other expressions of modern art in more than one respect, he observes. Modern
poetry has become 'poetology' — writing about writing. It examines
itself and the material of which it is made up: the system of words, their
rhythm, the secret they evoke. Moreover, the modern poem stands isolated in the world as a given, sufficient unto itself, and exotic. It makes
an appeal to exegesis that allows its manner of being to resound.[42] Exegesis can go even further: It can specify the movement toward the other
which is sought — however hidden — in poetic speech.

---

[42] Levinas delineates this view of modern art and poetry in E. Levinas, *Autrement
qu'être*, pp. 51-53 [E. Levinas, *Otherwise Than Being*, pp. 40-41].

Levinas' assessments of poetry and its possibilities are divergent. He is certainly very interested in it. In poetry, a truth is expressed that separates itself from the actual words. That is to say: In poetic 'said' the 'saying' reaching to the other side remains intact. Here language resounds and sings and seems indifferent to the critical search for the conditions that must be met to make it possible. "He who instigates a transcendental investigation into the conditions for what the poet is saying, puts an end to poetry and is doing philosophy instead."[43] Levinas' doubt and ambivalence are evident in the judgments he expresses in other places. Actually, *Totality and Infinity* supports the age-old philosophic criticism of poets. Poetic language influences us behind our back as it were; it rocks us to sleep by the magic of its rhythm; it makes us a medium of the poem — even though we are active as speakers or readers. It is an entirely different process when discourse originates in an encounter with the other. Ecstasy ends there, ethics begins. "Discourse is rupture and commencement, breaking of rhythm which enraptures and transports the interlocutors — prose."[44] In *Otherwise than Being* other lines are drawn, less taut in this respect. Just like prophecy — as we shall see — poetry here rather becomes the ultimate example of the enigma that language is as such. Language is a tapestry both of what is said and of saying, both of establishing fixed meanings within the perimeters of the system of language and of the ability to transcend the limits of thought — a tapestry that is almost impossible to unravel. "This possibility is laid bare in the poetic said, and the interpretation it calls for ad infinitum. It is shown in the prophetic said, scorning its conditions in a sort of levitation."[45]

An article Levinas dedicated to the writings of the Jewish poet Paul Celan ends in the spirit of the typifications just quoted. Celan, who wrote in German, lived in Paris from 1948 and died in 1970. His poetry, Levinas writes, is "[a] seeking, dedicating itself to the other in the form of the poem. A chant rises in the giving, the one-for-the-other, the signifying of signification."[46] This phrase reflects the main thrust of his interpretation of Celan. Celan's work is a striking example of poetry presupposing a suffering from the anonymous, hopeless reality of 'there is', but looking for the poem that reaches the other, the stranger — a poem that can be a handshake. According to Celan, every poem should

---

[43] According to Levinas in a conversation with me.
[44] E. Levinas, *Totalité et Infini*, p. 177 [E. Levinas, *Totality and Infinity*, p. 203].
[45] E. Levinas, *Autrement qu'être*, p. 216 [E. Levinas, *Otherwise Than Being*, p. 170].
[46] E. Levinas, *Noms propres*, p. 66 [E. Levinas, *Proper Names*, p. 46].

have the remembrance of January 20 imprinted in it.[47] Among other things, he refers to that day in 1942 when Hitler and eleven others decided on the 'Endlösung' — final solution. Poetry that can retain this remembrance will be able to leave all art behind, to forget itself, and to start speaking "in the matter of an *altogether other*." Of this Celan is convinced.

The formulation just named, "the matter of an *altogether other*," reminds one — not by chance — of Rudolf Otto's famous definition of God, which emphasizes His mysterious transcendence, even absence. Celan's astonishment at the absence never leaves him. His poem 'Tenebrae' ends in the prayer: "Bete, Herr./Wir sind nah." (Pray, Lord. We are near.) A commentator remarks that the suffering Christ being addressed here will probably pray nothing other than the words of the cross: "My God, why hast Thou forsaken me?"[48] Celan does not allow himself to be lured away from this godforsaken suffering on the cross or in the extermination camps by any form of religion or mysticism. At the same time, however, he speaks about "the matter of an *altogether other*," he also typifies the poem as a handshake and quotes this statement by the philosopher Malebranche: "Attention is the soul's pure prayer."[49] Levinas cites these expressions and quotes and recognizes in Celan's poetry the attempt to think transcendence. The poet wants to be a movement toward the other, and wants his poem to be that, too, thereby hitting upon the problems that come with the other being a foreigner, whether human or divine. The quest for transcendence gets him involved in the paradox of "a leap over the chasm opened in being, to whom the very identity of the leaper inflicts a refutation. Is it not necessary to die in order to transcend against nature and even against being? Or both to leap and not leap?"[50] Surrounded by reservations, accompanied by negations and contradictions, Celan's thought goes on a quest for the altogether other in its own way. "Does he not suggest poetry itself as an unheard-of modality of the *otherwise than being*?"[51] This question, posed by Levinas at the end of his essay about Celan, brings us back to the central problem in *Otherwise than Being*: "to hear a God

[47] P. Celan, Der Meridian. In P. Celan, *Gesammelte Werke 3*. Frankfurt am Main, 1983, pp. 187-202.
[48] O. Pöggeler, *Spur des Wortes. Zur Lyrik Paul Celans*. Freiburg-München, Alber, 1986, p. 134.
[49] P. Celan, Der Meridian, p. 189.
[50] E. Levinas, *Noms propres*, p. 62 [E. Levinas, *Proper Names*, pp. 42-43].
[51] *Ibid.*, p. 66 [*Ibid*, p. 46].

who is not contaminated by being." How does Levinas himself deal with this 'theological' assignment, and where does he arrive at?

4. God Otherwise Than Being

The fact that Levinas sets himself a theological task does not mean he wants to be viewed as a theologian. Indeed, this is evident from what has been said about his manner of thinking and about the sources of his thought. Levinas is a philosopher who explicates people's metaphysical yearning with great methodical caution. As a phenomenologist he concentrates on describing the human world of experience; the philosophy of dialogue teaches him that the bond between me and the other is of fundamental significance; because of his hermeneutical approach he can take the witnesses of prophets and poets seriously as well. When he uses expressions from the religious and theological sphere (for example, creation, prophecy, God), he is not practicing theology in the usual sense, which means explicating faith connected with a certain tradition. He uses such words because they, better than others, reflect the enigmatic and refractory nature of certain experiences: an experience that we do not have but comes to us, an idea that transcends infinitely our ability to think. In his view, the language of religion adequately describes a dimension of the human world of experience which eludes and transcends our understanding — a dimension that, at the same time, confronts us with fundamental *choices*. Precisely this explains why the philosopher can make use of it, without binding himself to a specific religious tradition and without grasping ahead to the confessional choices that may have to be made.[52]

A second reason makes the specification 'theology' unsuitable. Levinas offers no statements about the theme 'God'. We have, in fact, established that he strongly objects to making God, and everything connected with it, a theme. In his view, making God a theme is characteristic of the practice of theology. He is referring in particular to theologies based on rational argument and systematization developed by philosophers such as Aristotle, Spinoza and Hegel. Levinas rejects these totalizing systems.

[52] Compare M. Heidegger, Phänomenologie und Theologie. In: Idem, *Wegmarken.* Frankfurt am Main, Klostermann, 1978², pp. 61-67 [M. Heidegger, Phenomenology and Theology. In: Idem, *Pathmarks.* Cambridge, Cambridge University Press, 1998, pp. 50-54].

They aim at finding a *concept* of God, speaking *about* God, fitting Him into a narrative or a discourse. That this theology will be 'theo-ontology', a teaching on God's being which categorizes Him as the highest being in the world of beings appearing to man and known by him, is practically unavoidable. It lords over transcendence and fails to acknowledge the infinite difference between me and the Other.

In short, Levinas' thought must be read, valued and perhaps criticized as a philosophy. Otherwise than Buber, he does not regard himself as an 'atypical' thinker; neither theologian, nor philosopher. On the contrary, he sees himself unreservedly as a philosopher in the Western sense, as someone who assumes an audience of *open-minded* spirits, who demand *explicit* ideas at the point where everything is accepted as self-evident. In other words, he addresses 'Greeks'.[53] His speaking about God follows from his analysis of subjectivity; his theology is a form of anthropology (without the atheistic conclusions Feuerbach drew). He makes no ontological statements about human subjectivity. "What is at stake for the self, in its being, is not 'to be'. Beyond egoism and altruism it is the religiosity of the self."[54] Neither does he make an assertion about God's being. However, when he is describing the human condition, he evidently cannot avoid using the word God. Humanity means being responsible for the other person, even before one knows what is wanted. This witness precedes laws and culture; it is like a divine revelation. "God has spoken; who can but prophesy?" (Amos 3:8)[55]

As a continuation of this section, we will pursue Levinas' thoughts on the God who is 'otherwise than being.' First of all we will try to understand the radicalism of his philosophical inquiry. Thereafter we will identify how these inquires are being answered. And finally, we will inquire into the specific nature of philosophical and theological speaking about the enigmatic God.

What does Levinas mean when he says in the foreword of *Otherwise than Being,* that he wants to present the human possibility of 'hearing a God who is not contaminated by being'. Numerous references can be found, spread throughout Levinas' work. But a readymade definition of, for instance, the concept of being, is not provided. To get anywhere near

[53] F. Armengaud, Entretien, pp. 297-298.
[54] E. Levinas, *Autrement qu'être*, p. 150 [E. Levinas, *Otherwise Than Being*, p. 117].
[55] E. Levinas, *Ethique et Infini*, pp. 121-122 [E. Levinas, *Ethics and Infinity,* pp. 113-114]

an understanding, one has to take many paths and circuitous routes. We shall approach the subject here by examining *the question*.

From ancient times, wonder — over the fact that things exist, or that things exist and are not, rather, non-existent — has been considered the source of philosophic thought. Wonder does not attempt to explore things as information, or knowledge; it does not wish to get control of things — rather, it inquires into the ground and connection of phenomena. True philosophy is not about acquiring knowledge, nor is it about answers and conclusions. True philosophy is found in enquiry as such, in seeking, in desiring — to use a term that is important for Levinas. We have seen that he, too, wants to philosophize opposite 'wholly open-minded spirits'.

However, there is a turning-point in the process of open-minded inquiry, a point at which it definitively loses the unengaged attitude to which it is prone. This happens when the other moves me to the core. The inquiry born of wonder changes to a crisis that challenges my existence. The other radicalizes my own inquiry by casting me in doubt and putting me in question. Or, expressed differently, in terms already introduced: The desiring, the question, reveals itself at this turning-point as "the outburst of the 'more' into the 'less', which Descartes called the idea of the Infinite."[56] Jacques Derrida viewed it as a 'total' question arising from a silence that is offered from somewhere outside the violence of history. He added that such a question cannot be put, nor legitimized, in Greek, the language of philosophy. The question arises from another source, a non-Greek one.[57] Although Levinas recognizes the irreplaceable value of 'Greek' as medium for thought and encounter, he retains his radical question. In fact, he intends it to be, among other things, a concrete question. Sometimes he points to the starvation in the Third World as challenging our right to food — and even our right to existence itself. Directed at me, the 'total' question is: Do I have the right to exist, am I not, *as existent*, the murderer of my brother? Questions of this type give meaning to the inquiry about a God 'who is not contaminated by being'. After all, 'being' implies — among other things: Striving to maintain oneself and to acquire an ever greater place under the sun. The other's question identifies the contamination this brings with it.

---

[56] E. Levinas, *De Dieu qui vient à l'idée*, p. 87.

[57] J. Derrida, Violence et Métaphysique. In: Idem, *L'écriture et la différence*, p. 142, 168, 196 [J. Derrida, Violence and Metaphysics. In: Idem, *Writing and Difference*, pp. 79ff.].

The actual question, therefore, coincides with the ethical situation in which I am put into question through the confrontation with the other. Levinas refers to this question or situation also as *conscience*. For him this term does not refer to an inborn moral sense or a source of indisputable insights; on the contrary, conscience is a source of permanent disquiet. The ethical situation is a confusing event, an encounter, an 'intrigue', creating doubt and disquiet. It is a situation that arouses me with a shock, that makes me alert. And this moral alertness, Levinas opines, is a condition for the open-minded inquiry that comprises the origin of philosophy. The disquiet created by the encounter with the other makes possible continued open-mindedness, and therefore also continued philosophical inquiry.

This is the context in which Levinas also speaks of 'God'. The other alarms me and takes possession of me in his *trace*; the ethical situation arises. God is the third party, the Absent One who has "passed by absolutely."[58] Levinas makes this visible in several places by citing the Bible story where Moses does not get to see God face to face, but only after He has passed by, "from behind."[59] This means that God can be no phenomenon that appears to me, that is present in front of me, that I can observe and then describe and make a theme of. This would put an end to the non-reciprocal structure of my relation to the other. At the same time, this would bring an end to the ethical situation which could, after all, only arise by benefit of the *authority* whereby the other makes me uneasy and calls me to account. God's trace, the ethical situation, draws us into an enigma. It is ambiguous: It *signifies* absolute *absence*. God is the enigmatic one who breaks up play as it were, whom I can never catch, the absent one whom I can never know, the He to whom I can never relate directly.

Levinas specifies this enigma more precisely in a few places, in the spirit of the 'drama with several personages' which was mentioned earlier on. It concerns an intrigue with three partners: The I, the Other, and the Infinite. "I approach the infinite insofar as I forget myself for my neighbor who looks at me (…). I approach the infinite by sacrificing myself."[60] Here it is very clear what Levinas is trying to tell us. Following the trace of the God on the other side or 'beyond' being means:

---

[58] Concerning this, see the article 'Énigme et phénomène' in: E. Levinas, *En découvrant l'existence*, pp. 203-216 [E. Levinas, *Collected Philosophical Papers*, pp. 61-74].
[59] Exodus 33: 18-23.
[60] E. Levinas, Énigme et phénomène, p. 215 [E. Levinas, *Collected Philosophical Papers*, p. 72].

sacrificing oneself. In the trace of the Infinite I am pointed to the Other. The relation is radically *non*-rectilinear. The Infinite is found, rather, passes by, beyond my essence, my need to be noticed, my own interests.

One thing and another has already been said about Levinas' motive in specifying the meaning of the ethical situation and thereby speaking of God. The radicalism of the 'total' question has to be interpreted. It is unavoidable that this disquieting inspiration should be translated into Greek, the language of philosophy. The little word God must not, however, lose its recalcitrance, its explosiveness, in the process. It must remain clear that the word goes beyond everything that is usual and beyond every ordering of things. Its original meaning can be found in the trace of God's passing by, in the situation where the prophetic witness says *hinneni*: "Here am I. Send me!" God is present there indirectly, in the witness of the prophet. In this situation the infinite is not found in front of or opposite his witness, but is already past, as an 'implication', a thought in the background, too lofty to push its way to the foreground.[61] That is the original religious situation, preceding all theological discourse. Theology is really only possible as a struggle with pure religiousness; it can confirm this and do it justice only where it fails, or there where the struggle over the manner of speaking is expressed.

Theology — including philosophical theology — is only acceptable if it can maintain a discourse that constantly criticizes, corrects, or even cancels itself. In this respect Levinas sees himself as wholly following the line of Kant, although in a radical way, who established that philosophizing is a form of self-criticism and of self-limitation. But in his own way he also — partly inspired by Celan — continues in the line of Heidegger, who turned philosophy into poetic thinking, no longer bound to the forms of classical discourse.

It is clear that the Absent One is *ultimately* unsayable. It is impossible to keep categorizing him in the field of the 'said'   structured discourse determined by grammar and tradition. In the field of the 'said', clear definitions of themes and conclusive argument count as the highest values. As we established earlier, Levinas relativizes the Cartesian standard of philosophical language as being 'clear and distinct', following the example of mathematics. He objects to the monopoly of uniformity and

---

[61] E. Levinas, *Autrement qu'être*, p. 190 [E. Levinas, *Otherwise Than Being*, p. 149].

logical transparency. This monopoly fails to take into account precisely that which makes of language, a language. Levinas is referring to what precedes language — spoken or written: The ethical relation, a 'saying without said', an openness to the other which is fundamental and unreserved, a willingness to serve him. Even the very clear and distinct philosophical expositions cannot escape this, Levinas posits with grim pleasure. Even philosophical writings are provided with forewords that address the reader in more direct language. Moreover, such writings lead to very diverse, often personally tinted interpretations. In this the philosopher appears to be dependent on the attention, the exegesis and the criticism of *others*.

Philosophy that sincerely seeks the origin of language, the source of all meaning, cannot be satisfied indefinitely with unity of discourse and universality of system. That is why its speaking will be characterized by *alternation,* "an alternating rhythm of the said and the unsaid, and the unsaid being unsaid in its turn…"[62] In so doing it finds itself in a situation of permanent crisis and disquiet. It must be more than only love for wisdom — which is the literal meaning of the word 'philosophy'; that is, it should be the 'wisdom of love at the service of love'. Its critical task is to remind the said of original saying and thereby respect the unsayability of the enigmatic Other.

5. Conclusion

We have become acquainted with Levinas as a philosopher who is out of order, who researches the possibility of a consciousness that allows itself some imprudence. For this reason, following up on phenomenology, the philosophy of dialogue, and hermeneutics, he develops manners of thinking that offer the most space possible, without becoming unfaithful to the standard of rational communication set by the Greek philosophical tradition. He finds, among others, sources of inspiration in Biblical prophecy and modern poetry. Congenial reading allows the first source to provide the philosopher with 'the measure of the Spirit'. The second source appears able to bring to pass, in its own way, a movement toward the 'altogether other' within a neutral, chaotic reality. The philosophical

---

[62] E. Levinas, *De Dieu qui vient à l'idée*, p. 127 [E. Levinas, *Collected Philosophical Papers*, p. 173].
[63] *Ibid.*, p. 7.

theology figured in Levinas' own thinking attempts to show that the word 'God' has significance — whether or not He exists.[63] This theology is marked by the inquiry into 'otherwise than being'. God is the disquieting Absent One, in whose trace I am directed to the other. Theology needs to engage in a reflection that corrects itself unceasingly, going from unsaying to unsaying.

This thought is susceptible to criticism, and knows it. A few questions were touched on in this article. Others can be added. The question arises, whether Levinas is not, in a new, ethical way, giving form to the old universalistic ideal of the world citizen. Does not this indicate, some are asking, that he underestimates the degree in which his own thinking has been conditioned by history and culture? Does he not, incidentally, underrate in a more general sense the fact of humanity's sense of being at home and the tragedy of it?[64] Responding to these questions, one could call to mind Levinas' specification of philosophizing as a ceaseless 'unsaying'. On one hand, it includes the continuing recognition of the independence and sense of being at home with oneself; on the other hand, it includes the challenge of constant self-criticism and of rational communication, thereby taking the independence and maturity of the other seriously.

Another refutation can be that the transcendence of the infinite and other is presented here too one-sidedly as a moral figure. According to some, the necessity for this practically exclusive preference for ethical language is inadequately proven; the face of the other, against the Biblical injunction concerning images, even threatens to become a new idol of infinity.[65] This representation of the matter can be relativized. Levinas is certainly aware of the possibility that God's transcendence will be confused with the anonymity of the 'there is'. Not only prophets, but poets and artists as well, can imply possibilities of other-than-being. The preference for the ethical does not simply exclude other forms by which transcendence is touched on or pointed to. Moreover, one must remember the general importance of concretization in Levinas' view of phenomenology. It allows horizons of meaning to appear which we forget if we limit ourselves to speaking in abstractions. The importance of ethical concretization is, in particular, that it indicates a new orientation.

[64] See Rudi Visker's argumentation in: R. Visker, *Truth and Singularity. Taking Foucault into Phenomenology*. Dordrecht-Boston-London, Kluwer, 1999, especially Chapter 5 (Dis-possessed. How to Remain Silent 'after' Levinas).
[65] Criticism of this nature can be found, for example, in J. L. Kosky, *Levinas and the Philosophy of Religion*, p. XXIII.

Subjectivity is not only unseated by the enigmatic and the incomprehensible, it is also founded by it and is borne by it.[66]

These answers and reactions will not, of course, silence the critics. It
would not be fair to expect that. Being susceptible to criticism belongs
to rational philosophic thinking. To an even greater degree, it belongs to
thought that places itself outside the order of things and wants to reveal
the meaning of 'this extraordinary word',[67] God. Levinas' philosophical
theology contains no system that answers all questions and speaks final
words. On the contrary, it presents us with questions: Prophetic, intense,
disturbing questions. And it does so with taut coherency and unequalled
tenacity.

Translated by Lydia Penner

[66] See above, notes 27 and 28.
[67] See above, note 11.

GOD IS LIFE
ON MICHEL HENRY'S ARCH-CHRISTIANITY

RUUD WELTEN

Phenomenology is the name for a philosophy that is concerned with the appearance of things. Christian revelation implies a phenomenology that is radically different from the phenomenology of the world. Christianity does not concentrate on the visible appearances of the world, but strives after an immediate union with God, who remains invisible from a worldly viewpoint. Nevertheless, Christianity is concerned with appearance, which it calls revelation.

Thinking on Christianity in this way, and the implications of this thought for thinking on God, is prevalent in the later works of the philosopher Michel Henry (1922-2002). Henry was born in Hai Pong (Vietnam) in 1922. He was a professor at Paul-Valéry University at Montpellier. He taught as a guest professor at the École Normale Supérieure and at the Sorbonne in Paris, at the Catholic University of Leuven, the University of Washington at Seattle, and the University of Tokyo.[1] He also wrote five novels. His works have been translated into English, German, Italian, Turkish, Romanian, Spanish, and Japanese. Henry died on July 3, 2002.

Within the context of his philosophy, God cannot be understood without an interpretation of Henry's so-called 'radical' phenomenology. In this introductory study on his later thought, I will pay special attention to this perspective of radical phenomenology. From a theological point of view, Henry's thought is provocative. From the perspective of Henry's

---

[1] His main works are M. Henry, *L'Essence de la manifestation*. Paris, Presses Universitaires de France, 1963/90 [M. Henry, *The Essence of Manifestation*. The Hague, Martinus Nijhoff, 1973]; M. Henry, *Généalogie de la psychanalyse. Le commencement perdu*. Paris, Presses Universitaires de France, 1985 [M. Henry, *The Genealogy of Psychoanalysis*. Stanford, Stanford University Press, 1998]; M. Henry, *La barbarie*. Paris, Grasset, 1987/2001; M. Henry, *C'est moi la vérité. Pour une philosophie du christianisme*. Paris, Du Seuil, 1996 [M. Henry, *I Am the Truth: Toward a Philosophy of Christianity*. Stanford, Stanford University Press, 2003]; and M. Henry, *Incarnation. Une philosophie de la chair*. Paris, Du Seuil, 2000. His last book *Paroles du Christ*. Paris, Du Seuil, 2002, was published posthumously. For a complete bibliography see: www.ruudwelten.nl.

words of christ.

radical phenomenology, formerly obvious theological concepts become inadequate to think about God. God is no longer comprehended in terms of 'transcendence' or 'alterity'. In radical phenomenology, Henry finds a way to describe the original phenomenological structure of revelation. His philosophy is not concerned with all kinds of phenomena of life, but with the very phenomenality of 'Life' itself. According to Henry, it is this Life that Christianity calls God. Therefore, his philosophy is not simply a 'phenomenology of Christianity', but, instead, Henry wants to make plausible that Christianity, at its core and in so far as it starts from revelation, *is* phenomenology. However, Christianity is a phenomenology that cannot be understood in terms of classical phenomenology. Christianity must be understood from its origin, that is: Christ's discourse about himself as we find it in the New Testament.

Although Henry's thoughts on Christianity can be found in some of his earlier works, such as *The Essence of Manifestation (L'essence de la manifestation)* (1963) and even in his work on Marx, in his last three books he focuses exclusively on the Arch-phenomenology of Christianity. In this contribution, my discussion will be limited to Henry's Christian trilogy, namely, *I am the Truth (C'est moi la vérité)* (1996), *Incarnation* (2000), and *Words of Christ (Paroles du Christ)* (2002). In addition to these texts, I will also appeal to *The Essence of Manifestation.*

1. Radical phenomenology

There is a close, intrinsic connection between phenomenology and theology, not for historical reasons, but because both are concerned with revelation. The terms 'showing', 'manifestation', 'revelation', 'givenness' and 'apparition' are substantial forms of both phenomenology and theology.[3] Based on this substantial connection, there is no intrinsic difference between theological revelation and phenomenological manifestation since both are concerned with the meaning and structure of

---

[2] Henry says in a footnote of *I Am the Truth*, p. 279 (Notes): "Let us simply say here that, written with a capital, the term refers to the Life of God; written with a small letter, it refers to our own life. Since life is one and the same, however, these terminological nuances are intended to refer to one condition or the other (divine or human)." Cf. M. Henry, *C'est moi la vérité*, 40.

[3] M. Henry, *C'est moi la vérité*, p. 34 [M. Henry, *I Am the Truth*, p. 23]. M. Henry, *Incarnation*, p. 37.

manifestation. Manifestation is revelation and *vice versa*. Thus, Henry starts not from what is revealed, but from revelation itself, which he often calls 'manifestation'. In this respect, Henry is in line with Descartes: philosophy and theological revelation make manifest the same truth, while their ways remain strictly separate. However, in Henry's work, theology and phenomenology seem to flow together. Yet, upon closer inspection of his 'Christian' phenomenology, we learn that he makes use of theology only as far as it reveals a phenomenological structure. Christianity comprises the insight of radical phenomenology. It contains an Arch-phenomenology. Henry's phenomenology is radical in so far as it concerns a quest for the roots (radix = root) of appearance itself, purified of hermeneutical genesis and theoretical constructivism. His phenomenology is not concerned with phenomena themselves, but with the phenomenality of the phenomena, the appearance of appearance.[4] This is what he calls the "reversal of phenomenology". Husserl and Sartre lingered on in a phenomenology of appearances and descriptions of the constitution of consciousness without ever clarifying the process that underlies the possibility of appearance itself. The so-called 'turn' of contemporary phenomenology is not a turn toward religion, but to the very phenomenological status of appearing,[5] hence: a radical phenomenology.

Paradoxically, to this extent, Henry remains allegiant to the principles of Husserlian phenomenology, which are Cartesian principles indeed: to suspend all formerly accepted opinions by means of the epoché. Henry makes use of the phenomenological reduction in a very special way. More specifically, he does not follow Husserl's intentional analysis.[6] In fact, it is intentionality itself that remains between brackets. Revelation always concerns something that gives itself, something that is not dependent on theoretical construction. For Henry, radical phenomenology is not 'like' Christianity. Moreover, Christianity, according to Henry, is in sharp contrast with the cultural Christianity not meditated by representations. Christianity has nothing in common with symbols or metaphors: "This is because Christianity has to do only with reality, not with the

---

[4] M. Henry, *Incarnation*, §1,2.

[5] Cf. D. Janicaud, *Le tournant théologique de la phénoménologie française*. Combas, Editions de l'éclat, 1991 [D. Janicaud, *Phenomenology and the "Theological Turn"*. *The French Debate*. New York, Fordham University Press, 2000].

[6] Cf. R. Bernet, Introduction. In: Idem, *La vie du sujet. Recherches dur l'interprétation de Husserl dans la phénoménologie*. Paris, Presses Universitaires de France, 1994.

imaginary or with symbols.'"[7] For Henry, the core of Christianity is not marked by mediation and representation but by ultimate reality. We do not find this ultimate reality somewhere outside ourselves but in the Life of our very life itself.

2. A phenomenology of immanence

Christianity calls the eternal Life God. This means that God is neither a transcendent being that exists nor is He, phenomenologically speaking, entirely 'constituted' by consciousness. The structure of Christ's discourse about himself reveals a radical phenomenology: *God is Life*. God is not the life *of* something, but Life itself. God is not an intentional correlate. Henry quotes several biblical verses to support this claim. "The assertion that Life constitutes the essence of God and is identical with him is constantly made in the New Testament. — 'I am the First and the Last; I am the living one' (Revelation 1:17)."[8] The question arises as to whether this is not a highly metaphysical claim based on speculation and religious, not philosophical, authority. How can we meet philosophy in the bible when the bible, as it says, speaks not in the language of the world but of God? Yet, the only starting point for this claim is manifestation itself. Life is nothing less than self-manifestation. Life reveals itself. It is the 'self' that becomes manifest. This is precisely what we learn from the Gospels. This is exactly the meaning of revelation: to manifest itself and nothing other than itself. Christianity makes comprehensible that God is pure revelation and He reveals nothing other than Himself since He is Life. Revelation already implies phenomenology, a turn to manifestation itself. In other words, the structure of phenomenality, manifestation, or revelation is described in the language of the New Testament and not in the parlance of Husserl's phenomenology in which revelation is always revelation *of* something. Husserl's phenomenology is a phenomenology of the world and worldly things. Thus, immanence is not a metaphysical predicate that finds its origins in a theory or construction, but it is the *essence of manifestation* itself. Manifestation is not intentional and not purely intellectual or rational. 'Immanence' is neither the dialectical antipode of transcendence, nor is it the negation of

---

[7] M. Henry, *C'est moi la vérité*, p. 148 [M. Henry, *I Am the Truth*, p. 117].
[8] *Ibid.*, p. 40 [*Ibid.*, p. 28].

transcendence. Transcendence is not the condition for immanence. The only criterion that justifies immanence is a phenomenological one.

Yet, this sounds too abstract and tautological. What does self-manifestation mean? To explain this, Henry quotes Descartes' last book, *The Passions of the Soul (Les passions de l'âme),* on several occasions. In article 26 of this text, Descartes writes:

> "Often when we are sleeping, and even sometimes when awake, we imagine certain things so forcefully that we think we see them before ourselves or feel them within our body, although they are not there at all. But even though we be asleep and dreaming, we cannot feel sad, or moved by any other passion, unless it be quite true that the soul has that passion within itself."[9]

This dreamed sadness, says Henry, is not a representation of a 'real' sadness because it is an experience of itself. This sadness is an original *pathos,* which means it is an experience (e.g., 'suffering'). In *pathos,* there is no subject and object; it is pure self-manifestation. We can only comprehend *pathos* by *pathos* itself: there is no representation of it. I do not 'have' *pathos*: I am *pathos.* This is not the case if I dream of a horse, for example. In my dream, I see a representation of a horse. I am not this representation that is before me. The essence of manifestation is that it coincides with itself. There is no difference, no separation. Indeed, my tears make my grief visible. They represent my grief, but they *are* not my grief. I might be suffering without crying tears. My grief might be expressed in a different way. In other words: suffering, *pathos* is an immanent manifestation. It is experience but it is not experience 'of' something.

The essence of an immanent manifestation, says Henry, is that it does not divide itself or break apart; there is no distance between itself. "In the essence, there is nothing exterior, nothing foreign."[10] Immanence is always preliminary to transcendence. Henry resists all models of phenomenology that start from transcendent relations. Consciousness cannot be reduced to 'consciousness of something' (as Husserl does) or to a 'for-itself' (as Sartre does). (It is interesting that Jean-Paul Sartre recognizes a real immanence in the 'en-soi' (in-itself). But from Henry's point of view, Sartre fails to see that the in-itself is the only essence of

---

⁹ R. Descartes, *Passions de l'âme.* In: Idem, *Œuvres de Descartes XI. éd. C. Adam et P. Tannery.* Paris, Vrin, 1996, p. 349 [R. Descartes, *The Passions of the Soul.* Indianapolis/Cambridge, Hackett Publishing Company, 1989, p. 33].

¹⁰ M. Henry, *L'essence de la manifestation,* p. 352 [M. Henry, *The Essence of Manifestation,* p. 283].

manifestation. For Sartre, only things like chairs and tables are in-itself and, therefore, lacking consciousness). Consciousness cannot be reduced to an intellectual sphere or to a domain of ideas. As in the philosophy of Maurice Merleau-Ponty, consciousness is primarily incarnated. But unlike Merleau-Ponty's philosophy, manifestation is purely immanent. Therefore, what Husserl and Sartre call 'consciousness' is, for Henry, invisible, dark, and opaque. But instead of abolishing this primal sphere of manifestation, like classical phenomenology does, Henry recognizes in this invisibility the origin, the essence of manifestation.

Thus, Henry's phenomenology is not a phenomenology of light. What Sartre rejected as being in-itself is, for Henry, the essence of manifestation. Proceeding from a phenomenology of light, *pathos* is nothing more than a 'black box', something that is not within the reach of phenomenology yet must be presupposed. When consciousness is directed at a tree, it is not the tree that is presupposed but the capacity to direct consciousness at something, namely, the tree. This, says Henry, is the error of classical phenomenology: it is only consciousness, not the tree, that is able to appear. As Malebranche said, things themselves have no capacity to appear at all.

The difference between the theological and the phenomenological meaning of transcendence is abolished by the term immanence: Life is nothing more or less than the continuous generation of itself. This self-generation of Life is a continuous manifestation of itself. According to Henry, this is what Christianity teaches. There is no God in heaven who addresses Himself to mankind. We are already with God since He is nothing but the Life of our life itself. Indeed, God is "*intimior intimo meo,*" in so far as this is not limited to intellectual or spiritual comprehension. Since God is immanent, we are united with Him. For Henry, searching for God means searching for something we have already found but have forgotten. Since I always already live, we do not strive to be God, but to recognize God as the Life of my life.

3. God: the invisible and the night

The terms of immanence, such as autonomy, solitude, the self, inner, or sentiment (though not sentiment *of* something), are terms in which there is no difference, no representation, no alienation or distance. For instance, shame, as a sentiment, makes myself appear to myself. Contrary to Sartre's analysis of shame, in shame I do not merely experience the gaze of the other, but more importantly, the presence of myself to myself. Henry understands shame not as shame for something or someone, but as a sentiment that arises in myself. The error of transcendental phenomenology, says Henry, is that it fails to recognize that the presence of myself to myself is necessary for every intentional relationship with the world. Therefore, affection is not affection that is caused by phenomena; rather, at its core, affection is pure self-affection. Self-affection is a relation without externalisation.

This can be explained further by means of a passage in *The Essence of Manifestation* where Henry speaks of the phenomenon of the night. Night is the zero point of phenomenality.[11] This means that light is not the condition for the night to appear. On the contrary, light makes the darkness of the night invisible. This requires a phenomenology that is different from a phenomenology in which light is the main condition for appearance. Invisibility as a result of darkness withdraws from a phenomenology that makes things appear in the light, yet, manifestation, as such, remains. Night reveals nothing other than itself. It does not reveal the things that are lit. The night is the realm of immanence. Henry reminds us of Novalis' poetry on the night. We might also think of the mysticism of the night in John of the Cross.[12] For both Henry and John of the Cross, the night is not an abyssal darkness: true light shines at night. This true light dazzles the light of the day, or, as Augustine would say, the light of the worldly city. It is not difficult to recognize religious connotations in these thoughts. True light, says Christianity, is different from the light of the world. Henry quotes the New Testament: "In him was Life, and that Life was the light of men. The light shines in the darkness, but the darkness has not understood it."[13] Life is not the light of the world or the light of transcendence. Life is the illumination of God. From the point of view of worldly, transcendental phenomenology, this light remains invisible. Yet, Henry is not a theologian or a mystic. He neither writes a phenomenology that is 'typical' for mysticism, nor does he describe a mystical 'path'. Only the phenomenological consequences of these thoughts make these biblical words crucial. Western thought, which is not governed by Christianity but hostile to it, says Henry, has made light a paradigm. This becomes clear in the

[11] *Ibid.*, §50.
[12] Cf. R. Welten, The Night in John of the Cross and Michel Henry. A Phenomenological Interpretation. In: *Studies in Spirituality*, 2003.
[13] M. Henry, *C'est moi la vérité*, p. 101 [M. Henry, *I Am the Truth*, p. 87].

phenomenologies of Husserl and Heidegger. Following the Greek model of *phainomenon*, they have structured phenomenology as a philosophy that brings phenomena to light. Even Heidegger's *Aletheia*, which means 'unconcealment', implies disclosure according to terms of light.

4. Meister Eckhart

Let us take a closer look at Henry's reading of mysticism. Already in *The Essence of Manifestation*, Henry presents a possibility for a phenomenological understanding of Christianity. Henry's 1963 magnum opus contains two important paragraphs on Meister Eckhart's *Sermons*. Eckhart preaches the union of the soul with God.[14] This union or unity (*Einheit*) reveals something about the relationship between God and man rather than something about God. The soul is understood as an action of God. In fact, this action *is* God and is constantly active.[15] Man becomes one with God if man empties his soul of his own presence. This, says Henry, is precisely what Eckhart means by mysticism. We can reach this unity by humility and poverty.[16] Humility and poverty 'disqualify' the values of worldly affairs. Within this attitude, the world, as the mere phenomenological field of exteriority, is suspended. Let us take a closer look at this implied phenomenology.

From a phenomenological perspective, the external world is presented to us by *images*. Images are on the side of the world. An image is always an image of something, thus, it results from intentionality. Resistance against the image is a very important theme in the sermons of Meister Eckhart. Those who want to unveil the truth must separate themselves from images. Henry interprets this attitude as a phenomenological distinction between immediacy and mediation. His attention focuses on the distinction that Eckhart implies between two different phenomenologies which are, in fact, two different ways of *looking*. Eckhart says:

> "The soul has two eyes, one inward and one outward. The soul's inner eye is that which sees into being, and derives its being without any mediation from God. The soul's outer eye is that which is turned towards all creatures, observing them as images and through the 'powers' [of the soul]. Any man who is turned in on himself, so as to know God by His own taste

---

[14] M. Henry, *L'essence de la manifestation*, p. 385 [M. Henry, *The Essence of Manifestation*, p. 309].
[15] *Ibid.*, p. 386. [*Ibid.*, p. 310].
[16] *Ibid.*, p. 393. [*Ibid.*, p. 315].

and His own ground, that man is made free of all created things, and is enclosed in himself in a very castle of truth."[17]

It is the outer eye that sees by means of images. The inward eye, in contrast, is turned towards the 'inner', which is not just a new domain of images or imagination. In phenomenological terms, the inner domain is immanent, whereas what is outer is transcendent. For Eckhart, God can only be found in an immanent, inner domain: 'He is found within.' That is within which dwells in the ground of the soul, in the intellect, and it does not go outside and does not look at any one thing.[18]

There can be no image without likeness, but there *can* be likeness without images.[19] God, who is found in the inner, is without image. He cannot be mediated by images or imagination. The inner or the soul is equal to God. This equality is not meditated through images. When two things are equal, one is the 'image' of the other. One represents the other. However, the image of God is *einfaltig* or simple, in 'one form.'[20] This means God's image is without meditation, without representation. The two ways of looking are distinct because of intentionality or the absence of intentionality: the outer eye is turned towards the outer world whereas the inner eye is not turned towards something outside at all. The phenomenology implied by the inner eye cannot be described by an intentional phenomenology such as Husserl's. The inner eye is not turned towards something, which is the condition of phenomenality according to Husserl. Hence, we need a so-called 'non-intentional' phenomenology to describe the phenomenal structure of the inner eye, which is, at the same time, a phenomenology without images or any kind of representations. It is not transcendental or directed towards something. It is immanent; it is 'inner-without-outer'. Moreover, this immanence is the phenomenological structure of the *unio mystica* itself. For Eckhart, unity is achieved through the disengagement of images. "If I am to know God, that must occur without images and immediately. [...] If I am to know God without 'means' and without image or likeness, then God must become practically 'I', and 'I' practically God...."[21]

[17] Meister Eckhart, *Deutsche Predigten und Traktate*. Zürich, Diogenes, 1979, p. 203 (Predigt 11) [Meister Eckhart *Sermons & Treatises. Volume II*. London, Element Books, 1979, pp. 141-2 (Sermon 66)].

[18] Meister Eckhart, *Deutsche Predigten*, p. 207 (Predigt 11) [Meister Eckhart, *Sermons*, p. 146 (Sermon 66)].

[19] Meister Eckhart, *Deutsche Predigten*, p. 225 (Predigt 16) [Meister Eckhart, *Sermons*, p. 124].

[20] *Loc. cit.*

[21] Meister Eckhart, *Deutsche Predigten*, p. 402 [Meister Eckhart, *Sermons*, p. 289].

As a result, Henry speaks of the ontological identity of the soul with God. This is the essential content of Eckhart's thought.[22] The conditions for this unification are stated by Eckhart explicitly: love, poverty, and humility. According to Henry's interpretation of Eckhart, the internal structure of the absolute is understood as the *excluding* of the world. The world is presented by images and therefore the soul must free itself from images because: God works without means and without images, and the freer you are from images, the more receptive you are for his inward working, and the more introverted and self-forgetful, the nearer you are to this.[23]

Henry concludes that the unity Eckhart advocates, the unity that can be reached through the exclusion of the world and its images not only implies a unity with God but, moreover, the experience of this unity is the essence of revelation itself. Henry uses the term 'revelation' here in a mere phenomenological way. 'Unity' is manifestation without exteriority. As becomes clear in Henry's later works, this revelation is not just a manifestation counterpart to the phenomenality of the world; rather, this revelation is the condition of the world's phenomenality. This original manifestation precedes all possible secondary manifestations.[24]

5. Truth

In Eckhart, we find an insight that is fundamental for *I am the truth*: "The most proper words that we can speak pertaining to God, are 'Word' and 'Truth'."[25] God is Truth. What does this mean? Why not: 'God is true' or 'it is true that God exists'? The reason is because Christian 'Truth' has nothing to do with logical reasoning. Henry states that science and Husserl's transcendental phenomenology are, in fact, 'worldly' forms of wisdom and, due to their structures, incapable of teaching us something about Life. Nevertheless, when reading Henry, it is important to keep in mind the first two sentences of *I am the Truth*: I do not intend to ask whether Christianity is 'true' or 'false', or to establish, for example, the former hypothesis. Rather, what will be in question

---

[22] M. Henry, *L'essence de la manifestation*, p. 387 [M. Henry, *The Essence of Manifestation*, pp. 310f].
[23] Meister Eckhart, *Deutsche Predigten,* p. 421 [Meister Eckhart, *Sermons*, p. 8].
[24] M. Henry, *L'essence de la manifestation,* pp. 414-5 [M. Henry, *The Essence of Manifestation*, pp. 331-2].
[25] Meister Eckhart, *Deutsche Predigten*, p. 199.

here is *what Christianity considers as truth* — what kind of truth it offers to people, what it endeavours to communicate them, not as a theoretical and indifferent truth but as the essential truth that by some mysterious affinity is suitable for them, to the point that it alone is capable of assuring them salvation.[26]

Henry is not concerned with the external truth or falsity of the claims made by Christianity. Instead, he wants to stress a radically different concept of truth when examining Christianity. It is possible to say that the claims of Christianity are true or not true, but to do so situates us in a merely worldly (external) comprehension of truth. Henry describes the *Truth* of Christianity from within, phenomenologically understood from its inner structure.

What, then, is this special conception of Truth (as distinguished from worldly, logical truth)? According to Christianity, Truth has nothing in common with the empirical truth of the sciences. This radical difference between two conceptions of truth is already found in the *First Letter to the Corinthians*, where the wisdom of the world (*sophia tou kosmou*) is separated sharply from the wisdom of God (*sophia tou theou*). What is wisdom in the eyes of the world is foolishness in the eyes of God and *vice versa*. Jesus says that he has come to the world to bear witness to Truth (John 18:37). What the Truth of Christianity reveals cannot be understood in terms and in light of the phenomenality of the world. Henry wants to unveil the phenomenology that underlies this dichotomy.

Contrary to the Christian view, worldly phenomenality is the comprehension of phenomenality as developed in Western philosophy and science. Galileo's mathematisation of nature is responsible for the alienation of knowledge. Modern science reduces its objects to concepts and models so that the object is alienated from itself.[27] After Galileo, objects lose their qualities of real experience and become mathematical unities. Within the scope of Galilean science, Life is not something that is autonomous. Life is submitted to external, mathematical laws. In his book *Barbarism (La barbarie)*, Henry elaborates on this theme, which originates in Husserl's *Crisis of European Sciences and Transcendental Phenomenology (Krisis der europäischen Wissenschaften)*.[28] Despite his

---

[26] M. Henry, *C'est moi la vérité*, p. 7 [M. Henry, *I Am the Truth*, p. 1].

[27] M. Henry, *Incarnation*, p. 143.

[28] M. Henry, *La barbarie*; E. Husserl, *Die Krisis der europäischen Wissenschaften und die transzendentale Phänomenologie*. Hamburg, Felix Meiner, 1996 [E. Husserl, *The Crisis of European Sciences and Transcendental Phenomenology*. Evanston, Northwestern University Press, 1970].

severe and radical criticism of Husserl's primacy of intentionality, Henry remains motivated by Husserl's thought.[29] Yet, in *Barbarism*, Henry shows how the alienation of immanent self-manifestation not only finds its origins in science, but in transcendental phenomenology as well. Henry makes use of Husserl's criticism of the sciences against Husserl himself. But, like Husserl, in the disintegration of the sciences, in science's alienation of objects from themselves by the reduction of objects to mere concepts and countable unities, Henry recognizes the real cause of the abyssal disintegration of human knowledge, which results in the disintegration of culture. We live in a world of mediations and representations void of *pathos*. Galilean science has nothing in common with Life: it is deprived of odour, sensation, sound, and sight. Henry recalls Pascal's famous words: "The eternal silence of the infinite spaces frightens me."[30] When we enter the doors of a monastery, we retire from the sounds of the world. This silence, says Henry, refers to an audible world. But in the world of mathematics, in a Galilean world, there are no sounds at all from which silence is a retreat. Mathematics is eternally silent with no audible counterpart: its objects were never and will never be there. The bodies of Galilean science are bodies without feelings and passions. They have nothing in common with Life, nothing in common with our lives as human beings.

This view of knowledge as something outside itself is symptomatic of modern science. Every science is a science of its object; thus, it is directed to something outside itself. The biologist, for example, claims to study life, but because his science is a science of objectification, he constantly forgets Life itself. This has been the general argument against science in the phenomenological tradition since Husserl, Heidegger, and Merleau-Ponty. Even in the work of Emmanuel Levinas, the face of the other is a countenance that cannot be reduced to scientific terms. Obviously, we do not need Michel Henry to formulate these arguments generally found in phenomenology. But his criticism strikes at science and at classical phenomenology as well. Since transcendental phenomenology is always already externally oriented, it loses its contact with immanent self-manifestation. Therefore, an alternative to science and objectification is not found in classical phenomenology. Instead, a true alternative is found in Christianity, not as a 'belief', but as a radical phenomenology. When science studies a human being, it reduces him to

---

[29] Cf. James G. Hart, A phenomenological theory and critique of culture: A reading of Michel Henry's *La Barbarie*. In: *Continental Philosophy Review* 32 (1999) pp. 255-270.
[30] M. Henry, *Incarnation*, p. 147; B. Pascal, *Pensées*, §206 (after Brunschwig).

bones, cells, atoms, physical, psychological, or sociological behaviour. But all these visible phenomena have nothing to say about Life. The core of this criticism strikes at every possible transcendental method in so far as Life can only be 'understood' as itself. Life cannot be understood from a distance, either by means of scientific objectification or intentional analysis. Life is immanent self-manifestation, self experience. Life is *pathos*.

Contrary to Galilean and transcendental phenomenology, radical phenomenology discloses the inner structure of manifestation as self-manifestation. Henry recognises this phenomenological structure in the 'arch-intelligibility' of the Gospel of John. What is at stake is not a theologisation of phenomenology, but the disclosure of the inner phenomenological structures that remain incomprehensible within the scopes of exegesis and theology. Henry claims that this 'arch-intelligibility' does not reveal a new theology, but a new phenomenology, not taught in the history of phenomenology.

In the absolute meaning of the word, 'truth' is purely phenomenological. The starting point for marking a difference between the Truth of Christianity and the truth of the world is not given by religious belief or theology, but by the determination of different phenomenological structures, such as those that became clear in the theme of the 'night'.[31] What does this difference consist of, *phenomenologically speaking*? In short, the structure of the truth of the world is the structure of Husserl's phenomenology: exterior to the self and determined by intentionality and transcendental relations. As became clear above, things appear as objects. From Parmenides to Husserl, Western philosophy acknowledges just one form of manifestation, namely, object-manifestation. This 'ontological monism' makes invisible the essence of manifestation itself.[32] Primacy was always assigned to the appearance and, as a result, philosophy turned out to be a science of objects. Within this conception of philosophy, manifestation implies object-manifestation; self-manifestation remains beyond reach. In other words, an appearance is always an appearance *of* something. Subjectivity's identity is only possible on the basis of the fact that something appears for-itself. Consequently, 'truth' pertains to something that appears within this transcendental structure. The inevitable result is that truth becomes alienated from itself because 'truth' *is* not itself; it is nothing more than a predicate or judgement.

[31] M. Henry, *C'est moi la vérité*, p. 34 [M. Henry, *I Am the Truth*, p. 23].
[32] M. Henry, *L'essence de la manifestation*, pp. 59-164 [M. Henry, *The Essence of Manifestation*, pp. 49-133].

Something is true. This 'something' is exterior to truth itself. This phenomenal exteriority is the world itself. Things appear in the world; the world is the realm of appearance. Yet, seeing already presupposes a distance. Following Eckhart, Henry disregards this transcendent structure of subjectivity and phenomenality, and roots phenomenality or apparition in itself. What does this mean? The appearance of an appearance is immanent. Instead of being an appearance of something else, an appearance reveals itself.

Contrary to Husserl's phenomenology, Henry's radical phenomenology aims at the appearance of an appearance, and not at the phenomenon as such. Henry understands Husserl's famous 'back to the things themselves!' not so much as a turn towards phenomena, but as a turn to appearances as such. Henry corrects Husserl: "Back to the appearance itself!"[33] According to Henry, Husserl forgot the fundamental question that underlies his whole project: the question of how appearances can appear. In spite of his claim that he aimed to get rid of assumptions, Husserl's phenomenology is based on an assumption: Husserlian phenomenology starts from the appearance of the world and consciousness without questioning the possibility of the appearance as such.

The language of the New Testament, and especially in the Gospel of John, points to a radical phenomenology in which God reveals Himself. Henry wants to show that the difference between the Christian idea of Truth and the worldly, scientific idea of truth is, fundamentally, a phenomenological difference. The revelation of God is pure self-revelation. This is the Truth according to Christianity. This Truth differs radically from the truth of the world. The Gospel of John makes this difference clear: Jesus prays "not for the world" (John 17:9); his kingship is "not of this world" (John 18:36).[34] Phenomenologically speaking, this points to an immediate givenness as such, and not to a givenness that is built on theological constructions. Here we have the paradox of Henry's thought: we are only able to understand this radical phenomenology if we leave every theological assumption behind. The New Testament does not speak theology, but phenomenology.

---

[33] M. Henry, *Incarnation*, p. 45.
[34] M. Henry, *C'est moi la vérité*, p. 38 [M. Henry, *I Am the Truth*, p. 26].

6. Life

Life, then, is nothing more than self-manifestation and the only way to comprehend this self-manifestation is to comprehend it in and by Life itself. Life is not a thing among other things. Life is "the very fact of self-revealing, self-revelation as such."[35] Therefore, it makes no sense to say that this is a metaphysical assumption since the only criterion is phenomenological, which means: revelation gives itself. Henry does not say that we have to believe the New Testament or have to become Christians in order to see the Truth. He says that the phenomenological structure of Christianity reveals self-manifestation. Therefore, we can recognize God in Life and in Life alone. "Saying this we already know what God is, but we do not know it through the effect of some knowledge or learning — we do not know it through thought, against the background of the truth of the world. Rather we know it, and can know it, only in and through Life itself."[36] In fact, Henry's earlier works on Maine de Biran, Kandinsky, and Marx give an answer to the question, 'in what does this self-revelation consist?'[37] Since Life is one and the same, it is not limited to Christianity. There is no suggestion that we can only understand Henry's later 'Christian' writings if we undergo a personal conversion. God is neither the cause of Life, nor is He an image of it. God is Life. He is "the living God" (I Timothy 3: 15).[38] Life is neither a metaphor nor a concept or an object (like it is for the biologist); Life is pure, immanent pathos.

It seems strange that Henry says Life does not reveal itself in the world.[39] The content of Life is Life itself, which means that images or appearances in the world cannot represent it. What we see in the world, what is visible, obeys the laws of worldly phenomenality, that is, according to the laws that Husserl has described, such as the primacy of intentionality. But Life is independent of intentionality. More specifically, Life precedes intentionality. Life is self-experience, self-manifestation,

---

[35] *Ibid.*, p. 39 [*Ibid.*, p. 27].

[36] *Ibid.*, pp. 27-28 [*Ibid.*, pp. 27-28].

[37] M. Henry, *Philosophie et phénoménologie du corps. Essai sur l'ontologie biranienne.* Paris, Presses Universitaires de France, 1965/2001; M. Henry, *Voir l'invisible. Sur Kandinsky.* Paris, Éd. Bourin-Julliard, 1988; M. Henry, *Marx. I. Une philosophie de la réalité*; II. *Une philosophie de l'économie.* Paris, Gallimard, 1976 (rééd. dans la collection 'Tel', 1991).

[38] M. Henry, *C'est moi la vérité*, p. 40 [M. Henry, *I Am the Truth*, p. 28].

[39] *Ibid.*, p. 43 [*Ibid.*, p. 30].

and it is radically non-intentional. Therefore, Henry says that invisibility precedes visibility.

The process of Life is a self-generation (*auto-génération*).[40] This self-generation cannot be understood without self-affection: the constant endurance of Life itself. "Life self-engenders itself as me. If, along with Meister Eckhart — and with Christianity — we call Life God, we might say: 'God engenders himself as me'."[41] As mentioned above, this 'endurance of itself' is called *pathos* and this endurance is invisible, nocturnal, and falls into oblivion. In other words, the self-generation is totally phenomenological. It is *radically* phenomenological in so far as it pertains to the manifestation of appearance itself. Therefore, '*pathos*' is independent of sensorial experience. If pathos was sensorial, it would be externally constituted; it would not be a self-manifestation, but the manifestation of something outside itself. For the very same reason, *pathos* is always already 'synaesthetic': the mutual sensual differences (hearing, seeing, feeling, etc.) are not constitutive of self-manifestation. Henry elaborates on this in his work on the theoretical ideas of the painter Wassily Kandinsky. In abstract art, says Henry, 'abstraction' means the withdrawal of representations of the world. The contents of Life become visible in abstract art: colour, sound, and melody are movements of Life itself, not secondary qualities of the phenomena of the world. In abstract art, the invisible becomes visible.[42]

Again, it seems strange that Henry says Life does not reveal itself in the world. But can we find the real impetus of this statement in our uncritical confirmation of the paradigm of visibility? Are we not overpowered by the visible world in such a way that the invisible seems to be unimportant? Life, says Henry, involves oblivion (as the later Heidegger said about Being). We already live before we think about Life. We see things. In this seeing we forget the very act of seeing since we always already 'see something'. Seeing, itself, remains invisible. We are in the world, focussed on our occupations, and this focussing is only possible because we forget Life itself. Like the night, oblivion is not a negation but an original manifestation. Oblivion, night, and invisibility belong to each other: they are the original manifestations of Life itself.

[40] M. Henry, Chapitre 4: L'auto-génération de la Vie comme generation du Premier Vivant. In: Idem, *C'est moi la vérité*, pp. 71-89 [M. Henry, Chapter 4: The Self-Generation as Generation of the First Living. In: Idem, *I Am the Truth*, pp. 53-68].

[41] M. Henry, *C'est moi la vérité*, p. 132 [M. Henry, *I Am the Truth*, p. 104]. Meister Eckhart, *The Essential Sermons, Commentaries, Treatises, and Defenses*. New York, Paulist Press, 1981, p. 187 (Sermon 6).

[42] Cf. M. Henry, *Voir l'invisible. Sur Kandinsky*.

7. Birth

Radical phenomenology and Christianity are congenial in structure. According to radical phenomenology, human beings cannot find their true being in their egos alone. The ego always remains tributary to Life. The ego lives but it cannot create Life by itself. "In reality, it is this Life that is finite and incapable to give Life to itself, and to maintain it by its own means."[43] Since, according to Christianity, Life is God, man is always tributary to Him. This is the full significance of Christianity's comprehension of Son-ship. "The more the ego is concerned with itself, the more its true essence escapes it. The more it thinks of itself, the more it forgets its condition of Son."[44] The Father is Life. Man is the Son of Life. Man is the Son of God. The First Living (*le Premier Vivant*) is God the Father, nameless and invisible because He cannot be reduced to a phenomenon in our world. The Father constantly generates the Son within Himself. Therefore, Henry calls the Son the Arch-Son (*l'Archi-Fils*) because the Son is 'from the same age' as the Father. He is the first-born, but not in the sense of being the eldest child of a worldly family. His birth is not a birth in the world.

Here we come to a highly innovative part of Henry's philosophy, namely, his conception of birth. In the language of worldly affairs, the word 'birth' means to come into being, to come into the world. Christianity, says Henry, radically ruptures the worldly notion of birth. Within the world, 'birth' remains impossible. "In the world and in the externality of its 'outside', no 'Living' is possible — and consequently no livings either."[45] Within the world, things appear, they come and go, they appear and they die. But the Truth of Life cannot be understood within worldly models of appearance. This is why Christianity correctly speaks of revelation. To be born, says Christianity, is not to come into the world but "to come into life."[46] If we follow Henry's interpretation, the account of the birth of Jesus in the Gospel of John is not reducible to a worldly birth (i.e., the Christmas story), in contrast to the accounts in the Gospels of Matthew and Luke. The birth of Jesus, as Henry understands it, pertains to the coming-into-flesh of the Word, the incarnation. As we find in John (1:3), the Word is Life from which everything comes into being. It becomes clear why Henry's Arch-phenomenology of *I am the*

[43] M. Henry, *Paroles du Christ*, p. 7.
[44] M. Henry, *C'est moi la vérité*, p. 182 [M. Henry, *I Am the Truth*, p. 144].
[45] *Ibid.*, p. 92 [*Ibid.*, p. 71].
[46] *Ibid.*, pp. 78-79 [*Ibid.*, p. 59].

Truth principally relies on the Gospel of John, and less on the Synoptic gospels. Christ's discourse about himself rejects all worldly categories. He is not of the world, his father is not an earthly father. "Do not call anyone on earth 'father'; for you have one Father, he in Heaven."[47]

'Coming-into-Life' cannot be understood in chronological time (on a temporal line of 'birth', 'life' and 'death'), but as a second birth (*la seconde naissance*). Paradoxically, this means that birth in the world is preceded by the second birth, which is a coming into consciousness of the fact that we do not generate our own life. Contrary to the life of the ego, Life engenders itself. Therefore, Henry makes a distinction between the weak and strong meaning of self-affection.[48] In fact, 'weak self-affection' is elaborated by Descartes in his *Meditations* when he concludes: "I think therefore I am." Contrary to Husserl, Henry takes this to be the starting point of phenomenology. *I think therefore I am* is the purest self-affection possible.[49] From a Husserlian point of view, Descartes has failed to achieve a transcendental phenomenological subject in so far as Descartes' *cogito* represents a psychological statement. Henry maintains that Descartes' *ego cogito ergo sum* implies a full phenomenological subject, not because of its transcendental disposition but, on the contrary, because of its pure *self-affection*. Consciousness, according to Henry, is not consciousness of something outside the self, but the pure consciousness of being affected. In the weak self-affection of the Cartesian *cogito,* we do indeed find a pure form of affection, but not a pure form of self-generation. Descartes' *cogito* is affected by itself, but it does not generate or create itself. The *cogito* is generated and created (when Descartes moves to the idea of infinity in the third *Meditation*). "I experience myself without being the source of this experience."[50] Hence, a weak form of self-affection always remains tributary to absolute self-affection, which is Life and what Christianity calls God.

Man experiences that he lives, but he *forgets* his Life. In the light of the world, Life remains invisible. It is only when man forgets himself that he then faces Life, which is God. Thus, Henry does not fully reject

---

[47] Matthew 23:9, quoted in M. Henry, *C'est moi la vérité*, p. 95 [M. Henry, *I Am the Truth*, p. 73].

[48] M. Henry, *C'est moi la vérité*, pp. 135-141 [M. Henry, *I Am the Truth*, pp. 106-111].

[49] M. Henry, The Soul according to Descartes. In: Stephen Voss (ed.), *Essays on the philosophy and science of René Descartes*. New-York/Oxford, Oxford University Press, 1993, pp. 40-51.

[50] M. Henry, *C'est moi la vérité*, p. 136 [M. Henry, *I Am the Truth*, p. 107].

weak self-affection. Rather, his point is that Christianity discloses and is the ultimate source of our self-affection, a self-affection that precedes all weak affections. Weak self-affection forgets this strong self-affection. Only by self-oblivion can man discover his Son-ship. This thought reminds us of the *Selbstvergessenheit* in Eckhart, cited above. Belonging to our state of self-affection is our forgetfulness of the condition of the possibility of our self-affection.[51] This 'hypostasis' (my term) from weak to strong self-affection is called a second birth (*seconde nais-sance*). This implies a difference between worldly *birth* and *creation*, which can only be realized by God.

In the second birth, *pathos* becomes belief (*foi*). As Henry understands it, belief is neither a collection of chosen ideas, nor is it an attitude towards the world of life, nor is it a rational content of consciousness. In other words, belief consists not in believing in something. Belief has nothing to do with a world-view or an opinion that is formed under psychological or social conditions. Rather, belief is the *pathos* that affects itself and 'knows' it is created.

8. Incarnation

As we have seen, incarnation is one of the most important themes in Henry's thought. Henry elaborates on the theme of incarnation in his study of Maine de Biran: *Philosophy and Phenomenology of the Body (Philosophie et phénoménologie du corps)*[52] and, almost fifty years later, it is the main theme of *Incarnation. A Philosophy of the Flesh (Incarnation. Une philosophie de la chair)*. For Henry, the theme of incarnation is inextricably bound up with Christianity and the phenomenology of the body.

In *Incarnation*, Henry recognizes the original, immanent *pathos* in the flesh: a bodily subjectivity that consists of self-affection. Flesh does not become manifest as a result of intentionality or (Heideggerian) *ek-stasis*. Flesh is invisible because it is *pathos*. The human being is no longer understood as essentially a 'thinking thing'. There is an embodied sphere of manifestation that precedes idea-governed 'consciousness'. At

[51] M. Henry, J'oubli par l'homme de sa condition de Fils: «moi, je»; «Moi, ego». In: Idem, *C'est moi la vérité*, pp. 168-191 [M. Henry, Chapter 8: Forgetting the Condition of Son. 'Me, I'/'Me, Ego'. In: Idem, *I Am the Truth*, pp. 133-151].

[52] M. Henry, *Philosophie et phénoménologie du corps*.

first sight, Henry remains close to the philosophy of Merleau-Ponty who, like Henry, also spent his earlier years studying Maine de Biran.[53] Like Merleau-Ponty, Henry's phenomenology of the body and flesh does not concern an 'ontological region', as if it were separate from a phenomenology of the mind or being. Both philosophers, influenced by Biran, maintain that intellectual consciousness is not the ultimate essence of our life as human beings. We are bodies, and experience is always already bodily experience so that neither the body nor experience can be reduced to intellectual schemes or mere materialism.

Yet, Henry's thought on the body cannot be simply equated with Merleau-Ponty's phenomenology. For Merleau-Ponty, the flesh (*la chair*) is neither fully immanent nor fully transcendent: I am already in the world that I touch and see. Here is where the paths of Merleau-Ponty and Henry part. According to Henry, the flesh is absolutely immanent and precedes my relations with the outer world. The flesh is bodily subjectivity within itself, in itself. Moreover, Henry starts from a Husserlian dualism between the body (*corps*) and the flesh (*chair*). The body is the object as comprehended by the Greeks and which is observed by modern sciences. ~~The body is the object of biology or medical science~~. But, as we have seen above, this objectification cannot reach the realm of Life since it reduces everything to countable entities. As a subjective experience, 'feeling sick' is reduced by the medical scientist to an illness that bears a Latin name. My experience is classified and is nothing more than an object. Science cannot *a priori* observe the self-experience of my body because life is only attainable by life itself. To understand what life is, I have to live. Self-experience, self-affection, or self-manifestation cannot be understood by looking through the lens of a microscope. The body that the scientist observes is 'dead' because it is deprived of self-experience and, thus, from its self-manifestation. The body, in this case, serves only as an example of object-manifestation. An absolutely immanent sphere of subjectivity is marked by the self-manifestation that is called flesh. Contrary to the idea of the flesh developed in Merleau-Ponty's later works, the flesh is not in the word, at the crossing of the visible and the invisible; instead, the flesh is fully invisible.[54] The living

---

[53] M. Merleau-Ponty, *L'union de l'âme et du corps chez Malebranche, Biran et Bergson*. Notes prises au cours de Maurice Merleau-Ponty a l'école Normale Supérieure (1947-1948). Paris, Vrin, 1978. This remarkable resemblance can partially be explained by the influence of Henri Gouhier, one of the most important scholars of Maine de Biran at the time. Both Merleau-Ponty and Henry knew Gouhier personally.

[54] Cf. Maurice Merleau-Ponty, *Le visible et l'invisible*. Paris, Gallimard, 1964 [M. Merleau-Ponty, *The Visible and the Invisible*. Evanston, Northwestern University Press, 1968].

flesh *lives*, which means: it endures itself, it is a manifestation of itself. In contrast, the body, as an object, feels nothing, is dead. The body is an object, and not the centre point, of experience and knowledge. (On the operating table of a surgeon who is only concerned with his scientific task before him, the anaesthetized patient, numb to any bodily feeling, is nothing more than an object: body and soul are separated as the soul plays no part in the body's objectification.) As a result, that which becomes visible as a result of intentionality is always an object, even if it is my own body. Looking in the mirror, I can see the tears in my eyes, but I cannot see my grief. The tears *are* not my sorrow and grief. To assert that they are is to fall into behaviourism. My grief is totally imma-nent, invisible. Nevertheless, it *manifests* itself.

All living beings on earth are body and flesh. All living beings are incarnated. For Henry, it is not the material body as such that matters, but the *being alive* of this body, or: the experience, the endurance of being alive. What becomes incarnated in the flesh is Life. And Life, says Christianity, is God. Man is born out of a body; hence, as described above, true birth is to come to Life.

In fact, the flesh is nothing more or less than what we have already described as *pathos*. Christianity understands the incarnation as this coming to Life. According to Henry, incarnation is not an event that was realized only in the birth of Jesus. Man is incarnated. Jesus is the Arch-Son. "The central affirmation of Christianity regarding man is that he is the Son of God," says Henry.[55]

Despite the fact that the flesh is not reduced to a phenomenon, the flesh is understood phenomenologically in a radical way: manifestation takes its root in the appearance of an appearance. This appearance is not translated into images, representations, or intellectual knowledge, but is *pathos*, the endurance of oneself. Hence, this endurance of oneself not only points to the origin of phenomenality (manifestation), but also to revelation. Life is revealed in and with the flesh. Life is never an intel-lectual abstraction, but always already concrete. It is embodied and already there. The question Henry elaborates is not how Life (the Word) becomes flesh, but how flesh becomes living. The flesh is not a Merleau-Pontian 'flesh of the world', since it is not of this (visible) world; rather, the flesh is non-intentional self-manifestation.[56] Henry would agree with St. Augustine that the city of the world is the city of God.

[55] M. Henry, *C'est moi la vérité*, p. 120 [M. Henry, *I Am the Truth*, p. 94].
[56] Henry against Merleau-Ponty, M. Henry, *Incarnation*, §21.

The revelation of the flesh cannot be understood in external, alien terms. Flesh always reveals itself to itself and this revelation cannot be understood in terms outside itself. Henry calls a body without *pathos* 'the loam of the earth' (*limon de la terre*). This loam consists of nothing but bodies, not flesh.[57] Since the body does not experience itself, it is exclusively material. Dead material. Out of loam, one cannot create life, but only dead forms. What, then, is Life? Life means to experience/feel oneself (*s'éprouver soi-même*).[58] Only flesh feels itself.

Henry refers to the prologue of John which says that "the Word (*logos*) has become Flesh" (John 1:14). How must we understand Henry's interpretation? Flesh originates not in the loam of the world but in the Word. Logos, here, is not the logos of Greek thought where it refers to the word of reason. In the Word, flesh finds confirmation of all its inseparable characteristics. That the flesh is inseparable means that I can never disengage myself from it. Flesh is not composed of cells, molecules, or atoms. Instead, it is composed of feeling hungry, suffering, pain and pleasure, passion and sloth, power and enjoyment. In short, flesh is made up of non-intentional experience, *pathos*. Thus, the Word is immanent not to the body in general, but to the immediate manifestation of the body. This self-experience, this self-manifestation *is* the Word, the Logos. The loam of the earth is devoid of the Word.[59] This manifestation is non-intentional, unknowable in a scientific way (as being an object), and invisible. This manifestation is what Henry recognizes as the Arch-intelligibility of the Gospel of John. Incarnation refers to the flesh that has become living and, thereby, the flesh that has become Word.

9. New paths

Within the philosophy of Michel Henry, God is no longer the Absolute Other. "He is more intimate to me than I am to myself" says Augustine. It becomes clear that, within Henry's thought, the quest for God does not concern a specific theological problem, but strikes at the roots of phenomenology. Christianity comprises this radical phenomenology from its beginnings. However, we might question whether the title 'Christianity' is even adequate. As Henry says frequently, he is speaking of

[57] *Ibid.*, p. 27.
[58] *Ibid.*, p. 29.
[59] *Ibid.*, p. 29.

Christ's discourse about himself.[60] So why should this Arch-discourse
be called 'Christianity'? Henry's thought seems to imply a radical phenomenological reduction of the cultural and ecclesiastical canon of what
Christianity is, a 'bracketing' of tradition, ecclesiastical dogmatism, and
history. Christ's discourse about himself does not engender a 'Christianity' just as Marx's words do not constitute 'Marxism'. Perhaps it would
be better to say that Henry's phenomenology is a philosophy of 'Arch-
Christianity' (Urchristentum). This term usually pertains to the state of
Christianity before it became ecclesiastically instituted. It refers to the
experience of those people of the first century who heard the living
teaching of Christ first hand, the Evangelists. Henry's Christianity is not
a religion of the Eucharist and liturgy, of councils and church buildings.
Although he never turns against this religion of Christianity, the phenomenological reduction he realizes requires turning 'back to the things
themselves', which means turning 'back to the living Word itself'! It
means not only turning back to the sources, but, more importantly, back
to the Words of Christ. It is noteworthy that in his very last book which
bears this title, the heading 'Christianity' no longer plays the role it did
in I Am the Truth. Henry does not say what 'Christianity says…', as he
does in I Am the Truth; he merely appeals to what Christ says in the
Scriptures. He appeals neither to theology nor phenomenology, but only
to the living words of Christ himself, without developing these words
into a system of thought. A new beginning. But not the beginning of a
new doctrine, a new politics. It is a beginning that remains always in a
state of beginning. Back to the beginnings without any subsequent
changes to the power of these words. In Words of Christ, Henry talks
and listens as if Christianity has never happened, as if he has just discovered these new words. He writes about these words to understand
them on the basis of Christ's own pretensions, and not on the basis of
any science whatsoever.

Yet, Henry's philosophy contains much more than a 'phenomenology
of Christianity' because his readings force phenomenology to change
itself. Phenomenology is not the method to analyse Christianity; rather,
Christianity contains the Arch-structure of radical phenomenology. The
phenomenological reduction, according to Husserl, aims to bracket the
knowledge of the world in order to return to pure consciousness.[61] This

[60] E.g. M. Henry, C'est moi la vérité, p. 92 [M. Henry, I Am the Truth, p. 71];
M. Henry, Paroles du Christ, p. 11.
[61] E. Husserl, Ideen zu einer reinen Phänomenologie und phänomenologischen
Philosophie.Erstes Buch: Allgemeine Einführung in die reine Phänomenologie. Den

seems to be exactly what Henry achieves regarding Christianity: only pure givenness, purified of theoretical and metaphysical speculation is warranted, phenomenologically speaking. Henry's Christianity is not Christianity as it has been historically developed; all historical facts are bracketed. This very same operation led to a methodological atheism in Husserl's *Ideas*. In Henry's phenomenology, however, it discloses a radical, immanent comprehension of God.

Against the idea of absolute transcendence, the idea that the origin of religion is an "immemorial past that never has been present,"[62] as Levinas says, Henry makes possible the idea of an absolute presence, the idea of *parousia*. Since God is Life, He is always already present. And, similar to the view of the mystics, it becomes possible to understand why God is not 'outside' us but 'deeper than my inner self'. There are no *traces* of God outside of us. Life is not a trace of God because Life is fully present. Henry's philosophy of Christianity is a phenomenology of *real presence*.

The question remains: Does Henry successfully disclose the phenomenological structure of Christianity or, rather, of religion in general? With the idea of the immanence of *pathos*, Henry might be closer to the idea of 'non-duality' in Indian *Advaita Vedanta* philosophy than to the cultural Christianity of the church. As we find in Yoga, man does not 'believe' in ideas, but turns towards his *pathos*. In Islamic Sufism, for instance, we find the famous words of Mansur Al-Hallaj: "I am God — I am the truth." Perhaps, we have opened a new door for the study of comparative religion. Once on the track of radical phenomenology, it seems feasible that we find the very same radical phenomenological structures in other religions. Can we find the self-manifestation of Life in Upanishad literature, for example? If so, there seems to be no need to identify radical phenomenology with Christianity specifically. Instead, there seems to be some value in attempting to elaborate on the radical phenomenological similarities between the world religions in general.

Henry remains absolutely solitary in his intellectual position: far from transcendental phenomenology, far from theology, and also far from the post-modern thought of his fellow countrymen. Yet, his philosophy bears the promise for a radical new comprehension of religion.

Haag, Martinus Nijhoff, 1976 [E. Husserl, *Ideas Pertaining to a Pure Phenomenology and to a Phenomenological Philosophy*, First Book. *General Introduction to a Pure Phenomenology*. Dordrecht/Boston/London, Kluwer, 1982, pp. 57-62].

[62] E. Levinas, Énigme et phénomène. In: Idem, *En découvrant l'existence avec Husserl et Heidegger*. Paris, Vrin, 1949/ 94, p. 216.

GOD AS WAR.
DERRIDA ON DIVINE VIOLENCE

RICO SNELLER

1. Introduction

Could there ever have existed a philosopher who, without having the intention of spreading vulgar atheism or putting forth blasphemous critique of God, had the audacity to associate God with Difference, Desert, Violence and War, or even with Pubic Hair or Excrements? The French philosopher Jacques Derrida (1930-2004) had this audacity. Being at odds with a Judaism that had been carved into his flesh by circumcision, struggling with the burden of the great Book, called Torah, and battling against strangling phylacteries (*tefilin*), seduced by the great Husserl and Heidegger and wholly taken with French tradition — from Descartes to Mallarmé —, he unburdened himself recently by confiding to his French audience that he had decided *not to decide* on whether to have himself, like his father, be buried wrapped up in the *tallieth* (prayer shawl) he had once been given by his grandfather. "I have decided that the decision would not be mine, I have decided not to dictate anything regarding my death. Thus, I render myself to the truth of my decision: a verdict is always the other's."[1]

Jacques Derrida, modern or post-modern French philosopher: has he ever been otherwise engaged than with the question of *God*? And what would it mean were this true? Would it mean that he was a crypto-theologian, and that he contributed in his own proper way to the perpetual theological or philosophical debate on God, on the question who or what God might be? Or would it mean that he was engaged — just like Jacob, wrestling with the Nameless one on the banks of the Jabbok[2] — in a combat with someone for whom even the *name* 'God' would risk to name him *prematurely*? And if these things were all true, what would this mean for philosophy? Is philosophy able to guard itself against

---

[1] H. Cixous et J. Derrida, *Voiles*. Paris, Galilée, 1998, p.47 [H. Cixous and J. Derrida, *Veils*. Stanford, Stanford University Press, 2001].

[2] Genesis 32: 22-32.

'God', against that which is named by the very name 'God', or against
that which is designated by this name? And will it indeed be possible, as
a philosopher, "not to get mixed up in theology" as Descartes would
have it? Will it in fact be possible as a theologian to stubbornly remain
entangled in *ontotheology* — that presents God as a supreme being and
brings him within the reach of our thinking. Shouldn't philosophy help
to free oneself from ontotheological illusions as, for instance, Levinas
would have it?

In this article, I will insist on the ways, in which Derrida introduces
God in French philosophy, or otherwise, evacuates him out of it. I will
address the question as to the way in which Derrida provides a space for
an *alterity* that interrupts thinking, and cannot be adequately grasped by
thinking — that is: grasped by means of a concept, an idea or a mental
picture —, but without which thinking cannot expand either.

First, I will elaborate the way in which Derrida — mainly in the wake
of Heidegger — opposes ontotheology, that is: opposes an image of God
that pictures him as a highest being, a being that would be accessible to
thinking *before* it would have *done* something to thinking or to the
thinker himself.

Second, I will dwell upon the peculiar fact that Derrida *re*adopts the
word or the name 'God', yet conferring heterologous shades of meaning
to it. I will principally confine myself to his associations of God and
'violence' or 'war', and I will show that the word 'difference' (*différence, différance*) is the common denominator these *un*common names
can be reduced to. I will also try to make a reasonable case for the fact
that the identification of God and violence exactly raises the question of
theodicy.

2. Language and Difference

Why would it, in fact, be impossible to not only address but also answer
unambiguously the question as to Derrida's philosophical convictions
with respect to God? Would this not be because the question's very
articulation, as a matter of fact, is always presupposing something? The
question presupposes a certain concept of God. As a rule, this presupposition entails the concept of an infinite and almighty Being, that leads an
independent and separate existence. Derrida denies repeatedly the existence of such a Being. In this, he essentially continues the Heideggerian
critique of ontotheology and the Nietzschean verdict about God's death.

In this section, I will try to draw up Derrida's objections to ontotheological representations of God, that is: of God conceived as a Supreme Being. A critical stance towards these ontotheological representations already characterizes Derrida's earliest texts, and it continues to do so up to and including his latest writings. The metaphors he uses to expound his resistance against God-as-a-Supreme-Being are mainly taken from writing practices or from theories on the relationship between the spoken and the written word. Note for example the following important terms in Derrida: scripture or writing *(écriture)*, meaning, sense *(sens)*, sign *(signe)*, signifier *(significant)*, and signified or significance *(signifié)*.

2.1 'God', Logos and Logocentrism

Western thought, Derrida argues, continuously appears to be wholly oriented by one and the same philosophical paradigm, viz. the *spirituality of truth, and its accessibility to human spirit*. We usually call this Western, philosophical-theological paradigm the *commensurability of thinking and being*: both being and thinking can (and are to) be measured by the same measure, they can (and are to) be compared to each other on account of their similar structure. It was Parmenides who first drew up this paradigm: "Thinking and being are the same." In this respect Derrida speaks of the 'epoch of the logos'.

Within this (*logo-centric*) paradigm, Derrida affirms — and he seems to be original in this[3] — the *spoken* word has always taken precedence over the *written* word. This seems to be evidence itself, for does not he who tries to express his own thoughts, while speaking, appear to be most near to these very thoughts? He who speaks can at any time re-state his words more precisely or in more detail and, when mistaken by his audience, resume (re-assume) and confer new verbal expressions to their mental predecessors. Once the words have been written down, however, the bonds between them and their original, underlying thoughts become very loose, not to say wholly interrupted. The written word — Derrida repeatedly shows, referring to innumerable examples taken from the history of philosophy and theology — is only a faint shadow of the preceding, living word. It can give rise to misunderstandings, its author being

---

[3] One would then have to neglect specific medieval cabbalistic currents, for example the one around Isaac the Blind (12th Century) taking *written* Torah to be pre-existent and to be even prior to creation (which had been made up of Hebrew letters); one might even refer to the earlier *Sefer Jetsira* ('The Book of the Creation'). See a.o. G. Scholem, *Major Trends in Jewish Mysticism*. New York, Schocken Books, 1995 (1941).

unable to adequately and immediately intervene. The spoken word being already a mediation — that is, of pure, immediate thought —, how much more this applies to the written word! The *spoken* 'signs' or 'signifiers' are fleeting and, once expressed, instantly evaporate. *Written* signs or signifiers are durable, steady and, in fact, hampering: they block or obfuscate the appropriate access to (spiritual) truth. This access consists of an act of (spiritual) apprehending, and not only of an act of simply reading letters.

The following passage, which I borrow from one of Derrida's earliest writings, makes clear how Derrida associates the concept of 'God' to the aforementioned paradigm and to the 'epoch of the logos' or 'the history of metaphysics'. 'God' turns out to be the very accomplishment of this history:

> The epoch of the logos thus debases writing considered as mediation of mediation and as a fall into the exteriority of meaning [*sens*]. To this epoch belongs the difference between signified and signifier [...]. The difference between signified and signifier belongs in a profound and implicit way to the totality of the great epoch covered by the history of metaphysics, and in a more explicit and more systematically articulated way to the narrower epoch of Christian creationism and infinitism when these appropriate the resources of Greek conceptuality. [...]
> The signified [...] refers to an absolute logos to which it is immediately united. This absolute logos was an infinite creative subjectivity in medieval theology: the intelligible face of the sign remains turned toward the word and the face of God [*la face de Dieu*]."[4]

So, God guarantees the intelligibility or the comprehensibility of sense or meaning. Without 'God', the grasping of such meaning is impossible. Suppose I am thinking about, say, the past, about someone else's sayings, about a particular moral problem. What I will be doing then, is comprehending 'meanings'. These meanings — for example, that what *really* happened in the past, the *factual content* of my interlocutor's remarks, the *concepts* of 'right' and 'wrong' as well as the *concrete human behavior* I am referring to by means of these concepts — are what they are *in* or *for God*. Their sense or meaning is included in God. If there were no God, nothing would be stable: either in the past or at present, let alone in the future. Without God, it would be impossible both for me and for my interlocutor to ever determine a proper meaning, to ever determine what I myself or my interlocutor really means by

⁴ J. Derrida, *De la grammatologie*. Paris, Minuit, 1967, pp. 24, 25 [J. Derrida, *Of Grammatology*. Baltimore, John Hopkins University Press, 1974, pp. 12, 13].

saying something. Moreover, it would be altogether impossible to reach any definitive agreement upon what should be ultimately considered as evil and what as good. Do not all these things (concepts, events, matters of fact, meanings etc.) coincide with what they are or have been *in God's eyes*? Is not God He who knows what is or has been 'really' going on? Is it not He who prevents confusion or irreducible perspectivity to have the last word, and who guarantees truthfulness to truth and realness to reality? Is not the conviction that all sense or meaning is located *in God* the final point of reference for all my thinking? Is it not exactly *this* I am referring to when speaking? And also: is it not exactly this I am referring to — but *indirectly*, this time — when writing? My spoken — and *a fortiori*, if necessary, written — verbal signs always refer to this ultimate sense, Derrida holds. "The sign and divinity", he continues, "have the same place and time of birth. The age of the sign is essentially theological. Perhaps it will never *end*. Its historical *closure* is, however, outlined."[5]

Two remarks are required here. First: to be true, Derrida speaks here about 'medieval theology', but that does not prevent the trust in the logocentric paradigm referred to, from having much wider implications. Derrida not only mentions Plato and Aristotle, but also Descartes, Rousseau, Jaspers, and even Heidegger, and modern semiology and linguistics. Nietzsche, however, seems to be excepted. For Nietzsche, Derrida suggests, has made a decisive contribution to liberate writing from its domination by logos, truth, meaning, and finally, of course, by the Meaning par excellence: 'God'. Nietzsche, according to Derrida, has been led much more by the effects of (the letter of) his texts than by their (cognitive, thetic) content. What mattered to him was much more the *production* of meaning, the proliferation of new, alternative meanings, than the scrupulous conservation of one single predominant meaning. Derrida seems to have in mind approximately the same thing, especially (?) when he *re*considers the *name* 'God' after having abandoned any ontotheological *concept* of God.

Secondly, I would like to indicate here that Derrida does not in the least expect theology or logocentrism — 'theo-logocentrism' — to be definitively refuted or concluded. He is prepared to admit that we cannot do without its conceptuality. The point Derrida wants to make is that this ontotheological conceptuality necessarily presupposes something it cannot prove. This presupposition, he argues, consists of the assumption of

---

[5] *Ibid.*, p. 25 [*Ibid.*, p. 14].

a final instance that assures all comprehensibility, of the premise of a unifying quality that gives rise to sense or meaning as such. That is logocentrism. Without such an Assurance, and without its accessibility assured by the Assurance itself, Derrida affirms, we are bound to writing. That is, we are bound to something that is said to obfuscate things, something that is supposed to be dead in itself without the clarifying assistance of the original author; something, to put it briefly, that without such an Assurance is suddenly *not less* precise, exact or adequate anymore than the spoken word is. Indeed, without such an Assurance it would be very tempting to conceive of the spoken word as just a *kind* of writing or scripture. For, are not audible signs (spoken words or letters), just as visible signs (written words or letters), only discernable in that they differ from others? And is not the spoken word equally susceptible to misunderstanding, as the speaker is not wholly able to master his audience's frame of reference or its hermeneutic horizon? And finally, is it not striking that many a philosopher, from Plato on, when trying to explain the process of thinking and the role memory plays in this process, so often appeal to metaphors of writing (for example, when they talk about the 'wax tablet' or the 'slate' of memory our daily experiences are 'stored' onto)? What do these scriptural metaphors tell us in fact about the alleged purity and originality of a thinking that is supposed to have or generate pure thoughts? Does not the appeal to a metaphoricity of writing with regard to thinking reveal that I will only be able to reflect if my thinking is originally impure, that is: if it does not wholly coincide with itself, nor ever exactly know *what* it really thinks? (One should recall here Freudian psychoanalysis, which suggested that human conscience is not capable of grasping itself entirely, and which is determined by unconscious desires.)

2.2 Deferral, Difference, Trace

In order to point out the 'fundamental' character of writing, Derrida proposes to use the word 'trace' instead of 'sign'. Why does he do so? Whereas the concept of the 'sign' implies the designation of a significance, the notion of 'trace', by contrast, — at least as used by Freud, Nietzsche or Levinas — does more justice to the jumble of references, to the inapproachability of true, fixed meanings, and finally: to the permanent deferral (*différance*), brought about by deferring differences, of their definitive Embeddedness or Pivot, usually referred to as 'God'. On the contrary, the sign, or rather: the *trace* — though subjected in the

Western logocentric paradigm to the so called 'thing in itself' — is 'pivotal'; the trace is pivotal in continually deferring *the* Pivot. All this is
pointed out in the following quotation. The passage at the same time
shows, however, a remarkable shift: a shift *from* a critique of 'God'-as-
Pivot *towards* a heterologous, more affirmative use of the name of
'God'.

> "The subordination of the trace to the full presence summed up in the
> logos, the humbling of writing beneath a speech dreaming its plenitude,
> such are the gestures required by an onto-theology determining the archeo-
> logical and eschatological meaning of being as presence, as parousia, as
> life without difference: another name for death, historical metonymy where
> God's name holds death in check. That is why, if this movement begins its
> era in the form of Platonism, it ends in infinitist metaphysics. Only infinite
> being can reduce the difference in presence. In that sense, the name of God,
> at least as it is pronounced within classical rationalism, is the name of
> indifference itself. Only a positive infinity can lift the trace, «sublimate» it
> [...]. [...] [T]he logos as the sublimation of the trace is *theological*. Infini-
> tist theologies are always logocentrisms, whether they are creationisms or
> not."[6]

This quotation is conspicuous. For, as we already noticed, not only does
Derrida repeat here that Western thought is prejudice-ridden (*i.e.* it is
prejudiced in maintaining at once the *spirituality* of truth, its *accessibility* to human thinking in virtue of their mutual commensurability, and
the *assurance* of truth's spirituality and accessibility by an infinite
being: 'God'), but he puts forward two definitions of 'God', that is: definitions of what 'the name of God' is able to express. The first definition
seems to be advocated by himself: God as deferral of difference (*différance*, from *différer*: 1) 'defer', 2) 'differ'), and, in the same breath, as
'death'. The second definition seems to be bound to the theological
metaphysics of infinity questioned by Derrida: God as 'indifference'.
We will see in a moment that both definitions are closely related to
another, or at least that the latter definition is self-contradictory and
finally comes down to the first one.

When taking a closer look at the immediate context of the quoted passage, one finds out unexpectedly that Derrida suddenly starts speaking
about 'the name of God' as more or less synonymous with *différance*:
deferral-or-difference, and so, with 'death' (finitude). But it is equally
striking that he does not limit himself (as for example Nietzsche does) to
just questioning the 'infinite being', which assures signs (traces) —

---

[6] *Ibid.*, p. 104 [*Ibid.*, p. 71].

which operate in virtue of their mutual differences — to join their meanings, and which — once taken away — leaves these signs to uncontrollable dissemination, unremittingly seeking after their infinitely *postponed* meanings. Derrida draws a conclusion from the implications of
the 'infinite being'. This infiniteness, being capable of reducing all differences (signs, traces) to the identity of a meaning, a signified or a
thing-itself, is itself without any difference. It is *non-* or *in*-difference in
itself. Would this not be the case, it would not be able to do what it does,
that is: assure and found meaning.

   Both definitions apparently contradict each other: God as Difference
and God as Non-Difference, as Indifference. This should not surprise,
for the first definition is suggested by Derrida himself, whereas the second one is implied by the same Western logocentric tradition — or at
least by 'the classical rationalisms' — he has repeatedly *put into question*. Nevertheless, this contradiction is only apparent. I shall try to
show, as I have already done by quoting the above passage, that Derrida
treats his own critique of ontotheological concepts of God — God as a
supreme being — as more or less conclusive, and that this conclusion
gives way to a *subsequent* affirmative *re-adoption* of the word or the
name 'God'. In this re-adoption, the notion of 'difference' plays an
essential role. Even indifference, supposed to be part and parcel of traditional (rationalistic) God concepts, appears to be capable of being
reduced to it; which would imply these traditional concepts to be self-
contradictory.

3. God and Violence

The way Derrida readopts the name of 'God' *affirmatively* is highly fascinating. Mysterious definitions which take the form of 'God is X' arise
throughout his work like a bolt from the blue. I will mention some of
them in what follows. What all these definitions have in common is that
they only shed light on one or another *aspect* and thus cannot be reduced
to each other. The very pretension to write an article on Derrida's conception of (the name of) 'God' would already be contrary to this 'conception' itself: 'God' cannot be conceived of, and that which is referred
to by the name 'God' cannot be reduced to some univocal concept. The
definitions Derrida uses always contain an element of surprise. So in this
article I will mainly 'treat' one of those aspects: the Derridean associa-
tion of God with *war* or with *violence*. If some common denominator of

all the different aspects *had* to be indicated, the (purely *formal*) notion of 'difference' might seem imperative. We have already, a moment ago, encountered this notion. In the final section of this article, I will try to interpret Derrida's affirmative use of the name 'God', with reference to the notion of 'correlation'.

In one of his earliest texts — the famous essay on Levinas from 1964, entitled *Violence and metaphysics (Violence et métaphysique)*[7] — Derrida explicitly equates God to 'difference'. He does so in a commentary on Levinas' philosophy of the otherness of the Other.

It is noteworthy that Levinas' philosophy, too, elaborates a notion of difference, a difference (in Levinas' own words) between the Other and the Same. The Other, according to Levinas, never wholly coincides with his appearance or with my perception; the 'difference' between the Other and his manifestation is irreducible. To be sure: the *word* 'difference' does not play such a big role in Levinas, and contrary to Derrida, Levinas seems less interested in (phenomenological) difficulties implying that things can only appear in a frame of reference or in a given context (Derrida: in difference). Nevertheless, Derrida appreciates Levinas' main urge to keep the Other outside the reach of our thinking: for Levinas, the Other keeps different from my thoughts or my conceptions. What Derrida effectively criticizes is the fact that Levinas at least seems to hedge his bets: (1) the bet of the Other as infinite alterity, as absolute difference, and (2) the bet of the Other as some instance accessible to thinking anyhow, that is, as some *kind* of presence. To explain the first bet (1), Derrida uses the metaphor of 'death': infinite alterity implies radical difference (with respect to anything thinkable, imaginable and presentable), implies *death*. The second one (2) is designated as 'positivity and presence'. Levinas, so Derrida argues, leaves his bets regarding the otherness of the Other ultimately undecided, these bets being mutually exclusive. Infinite otherness and positive infinity are incompatible.

> "Infinite alterity as death cannot be reconciled with infinite alterity as positivity and presence (God). Metaphysical transcendence cannot be at once transcendence toward the other as Death and transcendence towards the other as God."[8]

---

[7] J. Derrida, Violence et métaphysique. Essai sur la pensée d'Emmanuel Levinas. In: Idem, *l'Écriture et la différence*. Paris, Du Seuil, 1967 [J. Derrida, *Writing and Difference*. Chicago, University of Chicago Press, 1978]. Besides, what about the title of the entire volume, with respect to the definition of God: 'writing and *difference*'?

[8] *Ibid.*, p. 170 [*Ibid.*, p. 115].

Next, Derrida prepares his tentative nomination of God as Difference, as the other name of the difference *between* the infinite Other *and* that from which this Other differs (thinking, perception, world, etc.).

> "Unless God means Death, which after all has never been *excluded* by the entirety of the classical philosophy within which we understand God both as Life and as the Truth of Infinity, of positive Presence. But what does this *exclusion* mean if not the exclusion of every particular *determination*? And that God is *nothing* (determined), is not life, because he is *everything*? and therefore is at once All and Nothing, Life and Death. Which means that God is or appears, *is named*, within the difference between All and Nothing, Life and Death. Within difference, and at bottom as Difference itself. This difference is what is called *History*. God is *inscribed* in it."[9]

Whereas Levinas seems to adopt an indecisive attitude with regard to the infinite Other as radical alterity, on the one hand, and as positivity, form or presence (God as a person), on the other, Derrida cuts this knot for him. It may very well be, he says, that the name of 'God' is not capable of referring to a radical alterity (as this alterity would then again get within the reach of our comprehensive reflection or imagination). It may very well be that it is incapable of reaching beyond the border line of difference (of difference *as* border line) towards a person, figure or form that would be *both* thoroughly other *and* infinite. It is nonetheless capable of naming the border or difference itself, Derrida adds. 'God' would then be the name of the border, of difference, or even — using Derrida's own metaphor — of death. To be true, Derrida continues, this was already implied by our philosophical tradition. When this tradition called God 'Life', 'Truth', or 'Infinity', it did so in order to liberate him from all possible sorts of determinations and to indicate that God infinitely transcended those determinations. This means that as soon as such an utterly transcendent, entirely other God is not susceptible anymore to any specific determination whatsoever, calling him either *nothing* (i.e. total indeterminateness), or *anything* (i.e. comprehension of *all* determinations), would amount to the same. There would be no difference between calling him either Life (*full* Presence), or Death (*perfect* absence). Do not such designations remove themselves and phase themselves out into the pure indifference just mentioned?[10]

---

[9] *Loc. cit.*

[10] For 'God' as Death, see J. Derrida, *Apories. Mourir. S'attendre «aux limites de la vérité»*. Paris, Galilée, 1996, p. 49 [J. Derrida, *Aporias*. Stanford, Stanford University Press, 1993, p. 22].

It is not very difficult to grasp here Derrida's line of reasoning. For it figures both in Nicolas Cusanus, who called God the *coincidentia oppositorum* (coincidence of oppositions), and in Hegel, who as no other in the history of Western philosophy located difference within God himself. God himself, Hegel argued, does not coincide with himself from the outset, but consists precisely in a differing from himself. God or the Absolute is the unity of unity and opposition. Theologically speaking: it belongs to God to reveal himself in and as that which he is not and with which he does not coincide. But as Cusanus and Hegel finally reduce difference to ultimate unity (to an indifference that annihilates and sublates all differences), Derrida, on the contrary, maintains that we do not overcome difference. Let us return to the passage just quoted. For, what exactly does that mean: 'God' as Difference? We need to note here the distinction between the *name* 'God' and its *reference*: the X the name is supposed to refer to. This reference — conceived of in Western philosophical tradition, as it has been accomplished by Hegel, as an infinite being finally *devoid* of any determination or difference — is dissolved into itself by Derrida, as though it consisted of an inner contradiction. For infinite alterity excludes all positivity or determinability. What is left is only the name: 'God'. This name takes an *intermediary* position between the act of naming and the Named. It stops short at the border between language and its evoked beyond. As opposed to Thomas Aquinas, Derrida does not see how a perfect *res significata* (reference; 'signified object', i.e. God) could be denoted by the imperfect referentiality of our speech acts (*modus significandi*: '*mode* of signifying/referring'). Such a divine *res significata* is encapsulated in the *significatio*, that is: in the referring speech act itself. Language is incapable of escaping from itself. Precisely this is what the equivalent notion of 'death' — the Derridean metaphorical expression of difference — is saying, namely: the very incapacity of language to attain definitely its denoted meanings or signified objects, the very impotence of language to extend to a supposed non linguistic 'reality' that would be its significant foundation.

But at the very same time language is not wholly enclosed in itself, either. Were this true, then language or speech acts would not be possible at all. Our verbal signs (words) would not be able to set themselves free within our human communication, nor would they be fit to refer to anything else. An infinity of words or signs would then be indispensable to show the infiniteness of differences in 'reality' (one may recall here the complexity of Chinese scripture that, as compared to Western alphabets, needs a huge amount of characters to be ever 'complete'). A sign would not be a sign anymore, reference no reference, and language no language anymore. Language — 'reality' *as* language or *as* a frame of reference — refers to something outside itself, which it is at the same time unable to refer to directly, but which is evoked obliquely in the very *act* of referring. According to Derrida, the difference between language and its 'outside', the intermediary position between signs and that which these signs refer to, is 'God', that which is expressed by the name 'God'.

So God-as-Difference intends to express two things. First, it means — *ex negativo* — that this name ('God') can never immediately refer to some person or instance that would be both wholly-other and infinite. 'God' is not and cannot be the name of some supreme being, or of something that would in some way or another be susceptible of being thought or imagined as something infinitely transcending our reality. Second, it means — *ex positivo* — that 'God' is a relational 'concept'. Being an alternative name for difference, it refers to the poles of those elements that are effectively correlated, and only detach themselves of their interplay (their mutual differences) *after* first having been absorbed within it. So 'God' means: relation, interplay, interaction-between-inside-and-outside, or even *correlation*.[11] The name 'God' expresses the *entanglement* of, on the one hand, 'truth' or 'world' (as it manifests itself to) 'thinking' and 'perception' and on the other hand, of a radical alterity that cannot be thought apart from all this. The entanglement renders it impossible to clearly and distinctly dissociate these two *poles* and two treat them separately. On the contrary: it is primordial. Only *parting from* entanglement or difference polar, differential categories such as 'thinking' and 'alterity', or 'perception' and 'outside', not to say 'earth' and 'heaven', or even 'man' and 'God', loom up. The last two pairs of concepts are perhaps rather traditional or theological; *as* a pair at least, they do not dispose of an evident philosophical 'residence permit'. Still, *as* a pair, they attest the same dynamics as the others.

---

[11] One would do well here to call to mind the thesis of the famous Dutch 20th Century theologian K.H. Miskotte, according to which the 'essence of the Jewish religion' could be restated in terms of a doctrine of correlation: the *(cor)relation* between God and man is prior to their separate and independent existence. K.H. Miskotte, *Het wezen der joodsche religie. Bijdrage tot de kennis van het joodsche geestesleven in onze tijd.* Amsterdam, H.J. Paris, 1933. NB: the literal notion of *Korrelation* is to be found in Hermann Cohen (1842-1918), in his *Religion der Vernunft aus den Quellen des Judentums* (1919). Wiesbaden, Fourier Verlag, 1978 (1966) [H. Cohen, *Religion of Reason Out of the Sources of Judaism.* New York, F. Ungar Pub. Co., 1972 (Scholars Press 1995)].

3.1 War and Violence

The other associations of the name 'God' given by Derrida — Desert, Violence, Pubic Hair, Excrements — all fit in the scheme I have just tried to frame in a rather abstract way. In the following section I will delineate this with respect to closely interconnected notions such as 'war' and 'violence'.

Throughout Derrida's work we come across the vital, almost metaphysical or transcendental sense of 'violence' or 'war'. "War, therefore", as Derrida puts it in his essay on Levinas, "is congenital to phenomenality, it is the very emergence of speech [*parole*] and appearing."[12] And somewhat further: "Violence appears with *articulation*."[13] Should language, expression, phenomenon, appearing, perception etc., be possible at all, then *violence* is presupposed. Anything can only appear or reveal itself in a context or in a framework in which the phenomenon, the verbal expression etc., is *illuminated* — and this in a variety of ways, depending on the coincidental context or the fortuitous frame of reference. To give an example: I will only be 'myself' in the accidental context or framework I find myself in; only there, I will have 'significance': as a husband, as a father, as a university teacher, as a friend, as an acquaintance or a colleague, etc. But, as these contexts never entirely overlap, and as these contexts also alter or shift when taken separately, I can never really say that I am 'myself'. My real 'I' always seems to have been postponed. My 'true identity' always seems to have been violated, precisely by the very contextuality that first enables any 'I' or 'identity' to appear as such. My 'I' or my 'identity' is therefore only *an* I or *an* identity, never my real or definitive one. The violence encountering such a definitive identity or such a final *I* perpetually postpones them. But at the same time, this violence permits the *I* — *an* I — to appear on the scene: the 'violent' scene of a family, a lecture-hall, a meeting of relatives or a visiting of friends. There is no place I can really be said to be 'myself'; nevertheless, all those scenes offer opportunities to be *an* I or to be *a* self: irreducibly *opened up* to an ultimate I, coinciding with itself, an I that will not have been affected by any violence, but remains inescapably irretrievable.

Why in fact use such an extreme metaphor such as 'violence', whereas only the rather 'innocent' question of the possibility for

---

[12] J. Derrida, *l'Écriture et la différence*, p. 190 [J. Derrida, *Writing and Difference*, p. 129].

[13] *Ibid.*, p. 219 [*Ibid.*, pp. 149f.].

phenomena to appear (respectively for thoughts and ideas to be conceived of) is at stake? Why overload phenomenology — and philosophy
as such — with so heavy a term? And, in connection with this: what
exactly has this violence to do with God? I shall try to gradually develop
these questions further; yet, for now, I will draw attention to the particular perspective in which Derrida puts phenomenology and philosophy
as such, by using words like 'violence' and 'war' — and by even referring to them with the name 'God'. I am pointing here to the perspective
of a *theodicy*, that is: to the question of a possible *justification* of suffering (with respect to a good God who would admit it).

It is not wholly without reason that Derrida puts (phenomenological)
philosophy in the perspective of a theodicy. He is urged in this by the
question that Levinas had already asked about phenomenology: the
question whether — and if so: how? — an alterity can appear without
immediately being neutralized by a reflective or even an objectifying
consciousness. In his text on Levinas *(Violence and Metaphysics)* Derrida confronts us with the fact that the pure expression of the face of the
other, which finds itself in the trace of God, can only appear impurely.
To put it more concretely: God can only reveal himself in a non-divine
(i.e. human, phenomenal, phenomenological) way, which means: contaminated or affected by context, framework, background or perspectivism. It is evident that Derrida would forcefully reject Jean-Luc Marion's suggestion, some fifteen years later, according to which God
"plays [in Jesus Christ] a human role *in a divine manner*", without getting in touch with the ordinary being of things, people and phenomena
as such.[14]

It is striking how Derrida not only applies to God what in any case
also went for phenomena (viz. that they are subjected to the violence of
contextuality, which prevents anything from ever being itself, nor to be
either conceived or perceived purely). Derrida not only states that even
God — in order to be able to appear or to present ('reveal') himself —
is subjected to contamination by context, frame or referentiality, so as
being unable to present himself pure or undamaged. (This idea further
elaborates on Derrida's critique of ontotheology: the ontotheological
representation of God gets entangled within referential webs to such an

---

[14] Cf. J.-L. Marion, *L'Idole et la distance. Cinq études*. Paris, Grasset, 1977, p. 219
[J.-L. Marion, *The Idol and Distance*. New York, Fordham University Press, 2001,
p. 172]. Cf. also J.-L. Marion, *Dieu sans l'être*. Paris, Presses universitaires de France,
1991 (1982) [J.-L. Marion, *God without Being*. Chicago, University of Chicago Press,
1991].

extent that, to our thinking, God is unable to escape from them unambiguously or objectively). Derrida not only subjugates God to violence,
he even goes as far as *identifying* him with it and *applying* the name
'God' precisely *to* violence. In doing so, he puts phenomenology and
philosophy into the perspective of a theodicy. For, the name 'God', of
course, is not — any more than the word 'violence' — an arbitrary
word, suitable for noncommittal application to anything at all. It quite
definitely calls up associations that were also entailed by a more traditional use of the name. Derrida, as no other, seems to be very well aware
of this.[15] Now, when he, *on the one hand*, explains the opportunity for
phenomena to appear at all — and *a fortiori*, for concepts to be conceived of — in terms of *violence*, and, *on the other hand*, takes 'God'
to be a *name* for such violence, he then re-locates philosophy, phenomenology, epistemology etc., within the sphere of most people's
deeper (more proper?) questions: daily questions regarding the meaning
of existence, the reason for suffering, and God's presence or absence in
all this.

To be sure, Derrida does not give clear answers to these clearly stated
and well-known questions. But he opens a perspective that sheds a light
on those questions and that might be appropriate to disclose *possible*
answers, be they only initial or inaugural.

There is one outstanding place in which Derrida associates the name
'God' with violence and war; I am alluding to a reading of a passage of
James Joyce's bulky and almost impenetrable *Finnegans Wake*. This
reading can be found in *Two Words for Joyce (Ulysse gramophone.
Deux mots pour Joyce)* (1987). In Joyce's labyrinthine swan song, Derrida comes across something like a needle in a haystack. In the midst of
the never-ending and unreadable word craft of the great Irish author, we
suddenly find these two words: *he war*. Is this English? German? Or
both at the same time? Who is this *he*? What does or did he do? *Was* he
(German, cf. *er war*), was he warring, belligerently? Or all this simultaneously?

---

[15] As appears from his ascribing to Heidegger the use of the word *Kampf* ('struggle')
in times thoroughly impregnated by the words *Mein Kampf;* cf. J. Derrida, *Politiques de
l'amitié.* Paris, Galilée, 1994, p. 392. Or from his fastening to Jan Patočka, Czech
philosopher knowledgeable about Heidegger and his work, the very designation of God
by means of the words 'supreme being'; cf. J. Derrida, *Donner la mort.* Paris, Galilée,
1999, p. 52f. [J. Derrida, *The Gift of Death.* Chicago, University of Chicago Press,
1995].

As a second James Joyce[16], Derrida, with unflagging zeal, <u>explores all</u> <u>semantic nuances of the formula *he war*</u>. *He* is applied to God: God who, on the one hand, *is*, as he-who-is or as I-am-who-I-am (cf. Exodus, 3: 14) and who, on the other hand, wages war, 'wars' or, who *comes down* to war. Indeed, the passage's immediate context, in which the words *he war* figure, contain many Old Testament references; among them the story of the Tower of Babel, the construction of which was interrupted by God who delivered man to an irretrievable, 'Babel-like' confusion of tongues (Genesis, 11). I will quote here a fragment in which Derrida tries to translate, or to render, the words *he war* as scrupulously as possible:

> "I spell them out: HE WAR, and sketch a first translation: HE WARS — he wages war, he declares or makes war, he is war, which can also be pro-nounced by babelizing a bit (it is in a particularly Babelian scene of the book that these words rise up), by Germanizing, then, in Anglo-Saxon, he war: he was — he who was ('I am he who is or am', says YAHWEH). Where it was, he was, declaring war, and it is *true*. Pushing things a bit, taking the time to draw on the vowel and to lend an ear, it will have been true, *wahr*, that's what can be kept [*garder*] or looked at [*regarder*] in truth. God keeps himself to declare war."[17]

We have to read this passage in its vivacity and its playfulness. Derrida tries to read *he war* in such a way that all possible shades of meaning resonate *simultaneously*: he 'warred', 'he was', 'he (was) true/truth', 'he was *by* warring (belligerently)', 'it is *true* that he was there by warring', 'he *kept* himself to (wage) war', 'it is true that he kept himself to...', etc. In the quotation immediately following, Derrida insists on the *he*: who is this really? At the same time, he connects Babel with a 'Babel-like' confusion of tongues' (something which, in the immediate context, is also done by Joyce, however).

> "He, is 'He', the 'him', the one who says I in the masculine, 'He', war declared, he who was war declared, declaring war, by declaring war, was he who was, and he who was true, the truth, he who by declaring war ver-ified the truth that he was, he verified himself, he verified the truth of his truth by war declared, by the act of declaring, and declaring is an act of war, he declared war in language and on language and by language, which gave languages, that's the truth of Babel when YAHWEH pronounced its

---

[16] Derrida alludes to the similarity of their names, *James*, *Jacques*.

[17] J. Derrida, *Ulysse gramophone. Deux mots pour Joyce*. Paris, Galilée, 1987, p. 16f. [J. Derrida, Two Words for Joyce. In: D. Attridge and D. Ferrer (eds.), *Post-Structuralist Joyce. Essays from the French*. Cambridge, Cambridge University Press, 1985, p. 145 (trans. completed, RS). NB: the English translation is incomplete].

vocable, difficult to say if it was a name, a proper name or a common name that confuses."[18]

This complex but nonetheless playful and vivid Derridean meditation asks for a close reading and re-reading, if it is to be truly understood. Again, it is a scrupulous meditation on all polyglot semantic nuances of the formula *he war*. At the same time, Derrida tries to show the inner connections of all those semantic nuances and to let them resonate simultaneously. He-who-is is the truth, but this truth only *comes* true, is only 'verified', *in* and *throughout* this war. Truth is *in the* war, it is *at* war, in other words: it is not yet purely present nor is it unambiguously isolated *from* this war. Thus, war is irreducible and it makes us lose all our hold. Truth is *yet* to *come* true, it is *yet* to be verified; *as* yet, it is absorbed in the turmoil (of contextuality, phenomenality etc., but also *literally*: of physical violence, physical war, physical suffering!). Now, the Babel-like confusion of tongues caused by God himself, according to Genesis 11, has consequences for God himself. By declaring war upon (the one, uniform and univocal, transparent arch-)language he has also declared war upon *himself*, he has also waged war against and combated *himself*. Why? Because *post*-Babel renders *pre*-Babel inaccessible. As soon as the confusion of tongues — and that also means the phenomenological 'violence' of contextuality, see above — is an accomplished fact, then we cannot without any problem reach beyond it, towards a prior, primordial state of transparency, purity and non-violent peacefulness. Even more: from our point of view, everything *starts* with this primordial 'violence', with this 'war' of Babel-like confusion. The only horizon that seems to announce itself is the ('eschatological') horizon of a *future*: a future that will have been delayed from the very outset, but that nonetheless will already have been evoked also from the very outset. Violence, war etc., can only present themselves *as* violence, *as* war etc., in the *light* of a peace or a non-violence that does not (yet) exist, that only exists in its being-delayed (its being-deferred), but that looms up at the horizon (dividing line) *of* violence. The coming true of truth must originate with this unapproachable, irreducibly outstanding future.[19]

---

[18] *Ibid.*, p. 17 [*Ibid.*, pp. 145f. (trans. completed, RS)]

[19] In *Violence and Metaphysics* Derrida affirmed that "eschato*logy* is not possible, except *through violence*". J. Derrida, *L'Écriture et la différence*, p. 191 [J. Derrida, *Writing and Difference,* p. 130]. Previously, he had stated: "God, therefore, is implicated in war." *Ibid.*, p. 158 [*Ibid.,* p. 107]. Afterwards, in a text on Benjamin's critique of violence, Derrida puts it about the same way. By *pure* violence Derrida means here,

3.2 Theodicy?

There are other interesting passages in *Ulysse gramaphone* testifying to this 'theological' or 'theodicial' background of God-as-violence. In one of these passages, Derrida himself relates the untranslatable words *he war* to both the prohibition of images in the Ten Commandments (Exodus, 20: 1-3), and to the *fire* — that is, the *jealousy* of the (Jewish) God who does not tolerate idolatrous images (vs. 5) — and also, again, to God's self-introduction to Moses at the burning bush, saying 'I am who I am' (Exodus, 3: 14).

> "So that's war declared: before being, that is being a present, it was: was *he, fuit*, the late god of fire [*feu le Dieu de feu le dieu jaloux*]. And the call to translate rejects you: thou shalt not translate me. Which will also perhaps be translated in the banning of translation (as 'representation', 'image', 'statue', 'imitation', so many inadequate translations of 'temunah') which immediately follows the moment at which YHWH names himself ('Me, YHWH, your Elohim…')."[20]

In this quotation, Derrida treats the Exodus 20: 4 prohibition of images ("You shall not make for yourself a graven image") as a prohibition of translation; both these prohibitions root in a divine-violence-as-origin. The French word *feu* not only means 'fire', but also 'late' (i.e. 'deceased'). The second sense derives form the Latin perfect *fuit*: 'it' or 'he was' (from *esse*, 'being'). Again, Derrida tries to let several semantic nuances resonate *at the same time*, *relating* them subsequently, by means of the symbolic of the word 'fire' (= jealousy), to the prohibition of images and to its foundations: God, the unimaginable, *may* not be represented; his jealousy ('fire') does not bear any identifying shapes or translations.

---

as follows from the context, violence that takes place without any clear purpose or end; violence that takes place for its own sake; original violence, that is preceded by nothing that would explain it or that would give a good reason for it; a violence *prior* to any law or lawfulness that would be able to justify this violence. Cf. J. Derrida, *Force de loi. Le «fondement mystique de l'autorité»*. Paris, Galilée, 1994, p. 134 [J. Derrida, Force of Law: The Mystical Foundation of Authority. In: *Cardozo Law Review: Deconstruction and the Possibility of Justice*. 11 (1990) 5-6, pp. 920-1045.

[20] J. Derrida, *Ulysse gramophone*, pp. 40f. [J. Derrida, Two Words for Joyce, pp. 154f. (trans. completed, RS)]. Cf. "And God spoke all these words, saying: I am the LORD your God, who brought you out of the land of Egypt, out of the house of bondage. You shall have no other gods before me. You shall not make for yourself a graven image, or any likeness of anything that is in heaven above, or that is in the earth beneath, or that is in the water under the earth; you shall not bow down to them or serve them; for I the LORD your God am a jealous God." (Exodus, 20: 1-5).

Why is he not *susceptible* to being represented? Why is he unimaginable? Because he 'is' not, in the sense of being 'present', wholly coinciding with himself. By 'declaring war' — that is: by 'meddling in' the
world, the phenomena, etc. — he has abandoned such a being-present.
More to the point, if everything starts with this declaration of war, then
there has never been something like a divine presence or secure identity.
These have always been awaiting their fulfillment.

In the next passage, Derrida is still more specific: God cannot really
be discerned from 'war':

> "[The arch-event is war]. Not the God of war, but war in God, war for
> God, war *in the* name of God, just as one speaks about setting a forest
> *a*flame, war flaring up in the name of God. There is no war without the
> name of God and no God without war. That is, see above, without love.
> War can be translated with love, it is in the text."[21]

'God' and 'war', says Derrida, are not two different things: as if God
were to be distinguished from war. God *is* war, *is* combat or violence, *is*
relation or correlation with what he 'is' not (world, phenomena, thought,
experience, perception, etc.). Just as God cannot be isolated as a separate
identity that would first be present and *subsequently* would enter into
'combat', that *with which* he enters into 'combat' cannot be understood
separately, as though it were something *previous* to the 'combat itself'
(if one may still say so: the 'combat itself').

The fact that Derrida here even takes 'war' as 'love', shows (again)
that words like 'war', 'violence', 'combat' etc., adopt both literal and
metaphorical meanings. War equated with love, war of love: it might
remind us of the expressions 'to conquer' or 'to capture someone's
heart'. Lady Diana called herself a 'queen of hearts', because she wanted
to 'win her way into people's hearts'. War-as-love, is this not again a
discrete hint dropped by Derrida, situating talking about God as violence
or as war within the perspective of a theodicy?

So, the core question of any theodicy is, whether suffering (here:
'war') is meaningful. Can it be justified by God in the end? Are there
any good reasons for the suffering of humanity? Is there really a good
God who has good, just or lawful reasons to bring us evil, or at least not
to prevent it?

In the following lines, Derrida refers to this point; they are the last
ones I quote from his Joyce commentary.

---

[21] J. Derrida, *Ulysse gramophone*, p. 46 [J. Derrida, Two Words for Joyce, (my translation, RS)].

"*He war*, God's signature. In giving the law, and language, that is, languages, he has declared war. The establishment of the law, the institution of languages, *does not suppose any right* [...]."[22]

We notice here that Derrida's speaking about God-as-violence evokes the question of theodicy without really answering it: the question can only be *illuminated*, but definitely cannot be answered conclusively. There is no right or law (*dike*, cf. theo*dicy*) that was already there *prior* to the outburst of divine violence. This violence cannot be justified by any presumed pre-existent legal order.[23] Just as was the case with 'truth', a final justification — a theo*dicy* — is *still* ahead, irretrievably. To risk a comparison here, one might think of Franz Rosenzweig's thesis that truth *(Wahrheit)* still has to verify *(bewähren)* itself; it still has to come true, it still has to prove itself. Truth is not true *yet*.[24] Here and elsewhere, Derrida is greatly concerned with *not* insinuating that some justification (a theodicy) already secretly exists somewhere and only has to be revealed. A possible justification is only to be expected from the *future*. It does not exist in some (hidden) presence and, so, cannot (yet?) be delivered.

It becomes clear that Derrida in these passages and others like it does not just elaborate some interesting or provocative metonymy. By relating God to violence and war, he turns philosophy, phenomenology, ontology etc. into something like a 'live wire', a 'wire' charged with the 'life' of the theodicy-question, the question about suffering, the eternal question 'why?', in brief: the question of Job. In a footnote, anyway, Derrida refers to the book of *Job*, by means of a secondary source.[25] Job stands for suffering man, man who has been struck by the violence of illness or plague, man who asks: why all this upon me? A definite answer to this question *is* (still?) not available. The question is waiting for an answer that is *yet* to be given.

---

[22] *Ibid.*, p. 48 [*Ibid.*, (my translation and italics, RS)].

[23] Cf. J. Derrida, *Force de loi. Le «fondement mystique de l'autorité* [J. Derrida, Force of Law: The 'Mystical Foundation of Authority'].

[24] F. Rosenzweig, *Stern der Erlösung*, III, esp. pp. 437ff. [F. Rosenzweig, *The Star of Redemption*. South Bend, University of Notre Dame Press, 1990, p. 432]. Cf. also "God is the truth", truth itself being no *Allgemeinbegriff* (general concept), that would be capable of explaining God's essence in general terms.

[25] J. Derrida, *Ulysse gramophone*, p. 40f., note 1; not in English translation. In the book of *Job* it is God himself who inflicts violence or intrudes upon Job. Cf. Job 19: 6-7; 42: 7.8. Cf. also *Isaiah*, for example 42: 24-25; in 43: 10-11 God is even called 'enemy' (*'ojeev*). This word is etymologically related to the Hebrew name 'Job': *'Ijjoov*. 'Job' is a symbol for the one who has got meddled in a struggle or in a confrontation with divine violence.

4. Conclusion

Let us summarize in conclusion. By means of the name 'God', Derrida
refers to an 'original dynamism'. To develop this original dynamism, he
uses not only words such as 'trace', 'difference'/'deferral',
'writing'/'scripture', but also 'violence' or 'war', and finally even
'God'. The very name of 'God' is perhaps more than just an exchange-
able, merely contingent one, precisely because of its *current* onto-theological use. Derridean definitions, which take the form 'God is X' (for
example 'war', 'violence', 'difference', etc.), draw attention to an 'origin' or an 'all determining' process — be this a process that erases any
idea of an 'origin', 'beginning' or 'principle'.

   In repeatedly calling this process *God*, Derrida brings about interpretations that inadvertently fall back on (aspects of) the philosophical and
religious tradition, regardless of how many efforts he makes to eliminate
all 'onto-theological' remnants that pretend to make God accessible to
thinking. I think that Derrida aims at *renewing* traditional God talk
(within the philosophical-religious traditions) — and not, as for example
Sartre did, at abandoning it as if it were something obsolete. The inno-
vation in God talk Derrida realizes, applies this talk to a vivid *process*,
to something that *strikes* me and *affects* me — instead of applying it to
something that *is* or *exists*, as a neutral fact that would only *afterwards*
gain significance or meaning. Derrida's application of the name 'God',
his stimulating but frequently altering definitions seemingly try to prevent the process to grow set or to immobilize into something which I
would be capable of observing or reflecting upon *without* getting
involved 'myself'. Anselmian speaking about God as 'something above
which nothing can be conceived of', or Thomist hierarchies according to
which the question 'whether God is' comes prior to the question 'what
he is': they are miles away from, for example, that which is said about
God by expressions like God-as-violence. They come down to modes of
speaking that try to determine 'states of affairs' apart from any correla-
tive connection, *before* assessing their significance to us.

   The specific content the notion of 'violence' added to the name of
'God' — in this article I have mainly insisted on this — confronts us, as
we have showed, with the problem of *theodicy*: the question of suffering. This question is not solved by Derrida, it is touched upon, or better,
fanned (as we fan a fire). Throughout 'violence' looms an eschatology,
a future or a vista. But precisely because of the 'violence' at present
('violence' taken both phenomenologically and physically), eschatology,

according to Derrida, can never be treated as something assured. It is
threatened by violence itself, that is: it is disputed, deemed impossible
or improbable, suppressed, etc. But the 'essence' of violence itself, if we
may say so, in the very act of suppressing evokes that which is suppressed, that is: the idea of an end of violence.

The Dutch language contains the adage 'to live as God in France',
which means 'to live a life of Riley', 'to live in clover'. Well then,
would God, according to Derrida, feel at ease in France? I do not think
so. In conceiving of God as (original) violence, he dramatizes both God
'himself' — his 'essence' or his 'being' — and the use we make of this
name, 'God'. This name names something different from that which we
are used to naming with it.

Admittedly, in speaking about God-as-violence, Derrida does not
seem to pay much attention to any 'retribution' to those who have really
been ruined or molested by life's violence. In associating God with violence, he brings the theodicy-question to a head: the only consolation
left might then reside in the possible (non-violent, eschatological)
reserves the name 'God' still keeps back; these reserves would then be
meddled *in* violence and would only be capable of self-realization
throughout this violence. Derrida leaves this open, and does not develop
this possibility at all.

So, to Derrida, God has given up his 'French' life in clover from the
outset; he has never even lived it. Whether he will ever do so, remains
an open question: "he who was he in declaring war. He resounds, he
gives himself to be heard, he articulates himself and makes himself
heard right up to the end."[26]

[26] J. Derrida, *Ulysse gramophone*, p. 49 [J. Derrida, Two Words for Joyce, p. 157].

PHRASING GOD.
LYOTARD'S HIDDEN PHILOSOPHY OF RELIGION

CHRIS DOUDE VAN TROOSTWIJK

Introduction

If it is true that French philosophers need to be interpreted from the perspective of post-Heideggerian thought, then the title of this book might appear to be misleading. To think about 'God in France' might suggest that God is being regarded as the object of imaginative thought. However, this is precisely not the case with most of the philosophers dealt with herein. For example, the explicit question concerning God and the treatment of classical religious-philosophical (not to mention, theological) themes are almost entirely absent in the extremely wide-ranging and experimental work of Jean-Francois Lyotard. Yet, this doesn't mean that his work would be irrelevant to this volume, or to the question regarding the relationship to the absolute, the gods, the divine, or the holy in this late-modern — or if one wishes — post-modern era. Therefore, Lyotard's thought can be taken as an indirect answer to Derrida's intriguing question, 'how not to speak?' ('comment ne pas parler?') which is also the title of one of his articles. How not to speak about God? In his article, Derrida deconstructs the issue of negative theology as a problem of speech itself. The article echoes Heidegger's call to remain silent about God in this time of secularisation. But how to remain silent, if even the call for silence implies speaking about God? 'How not to speak?' implies the question, 'How to speak?'

As far as Lyotard is concerned, the question of God is primarily a question about how the absolute penetrates the discourse where it can only be present in a repressed way. How to think of the absolute, which has been targeting and spooking the discourse — while, at the same time, making it possible — since primordial times? This theme appears in explicit form first and foremost in his unfinished and posthumously

---

[1] J. Derrida, Comment ne pas parler? In: Idem, *Psyché. Inventions de l'autre*. Paris, Galilée, 1987, pp. 535-595.

published *La Confession d'Augustin*[2], as does the question of the encounter with the A/absolute, which is that of 'conversion'. Roughly speaking, three strategies can be found in Lyotard's work: speaking indirectly, speaking with a forked tongue, and ventriloquism. These three transformations (*Verstellungen* is the word Freud would use) of discourse can be taken as the inevitable effect of the encounter with the A/absolute. It is impossible to go beyond such a transformed and destabilized discursivity. Lyotard's deconstructive rewriting of Augustine's confessional discourse reveals the factual problems and the theoretical aporia of radical conversion, which is the total submission to the absolute Other. Confessing absolute experience would imply the utterance of the Absolute Phrase. The title of this article, 'Phrasing God' points to a double meaning: to speak about God (*phrasing God*) is only thinkable as the echo — *après coup* — of a '*godly phrasing*', a presumed *absolute phrase*.

1. The strategy of indirect speech

As far as Lyotard is concerned, it seems that the question of 'how (not) to speak about God' points in all three directions mentioned. Let us discuss first the indirect approach. Lyotard's religious-philosophical manner of speech is, above all, a speaking about other people's speaking. If the divine becomes an issue, it happens as a thinking-through and rethinking of a position which others took with regard to those (onto-) theological themes. Augustine is emblematic in this case because his entire life was devoted to the question of conversion and expression, which is to say, to the encounter with God and the discursive digestion of that encounter. Moreover, it appears that Augustine has accompanied Lyotard's wide-ranging oeuvre right from the beginning.

In order to illustrate Lyotard's indirect strategy, I will broadly sketch three distinct periods in this oeuvre, which could be labelled 'pagan', 'jewish', and 'christian', respectively. It should be noted, perhaps unnecessarily, that this classification doesn't mean to say that Lyotard has converted to any of those religions. 'Pagan', 'jewish', and 'christian' are put between inverted commas and are written without capitals.[3] They

---

[2] J.-F. Lyotard, *La confession d'Augustin*. Paris, Galilée, 1998 [J.-F. Lyotard, *Confession of Augustine*. Stanford, Stanford University Press, 2000].

[3] Lyotard used these in his work *Heidegger et les 'juifs'*. Paris, Galilée, 1988, in order to indicate the character of alterity of the 'Jews'. 'Pagan' would indicate the character of libidinism; 'Christian' that of 'passive conversion to the O/other' [J.-F. Lyotard, *Heidegger and "the jews"*. Minneapolis, University of Minnesota Press, 1990].

indicate traditions of thought which made him think himself. One could
even defend a quasi-dialectical development in Lyotard's thought here.
In a first phase, Lyotard was keenly interested in libidinal thought-
schemes ('pagan'). These are replaced by the introduction of ethics and
by a phraseological-pragmatic way of thinking ('jewish'). His later writings seem to be an attempt to connect 'pagan' and 'jewish' into a 'christian' pattern of thought, without presupposing, however, a reconciliation
between the two positions — as was the case in the Hegelian reconstruction of Christianity. This periodization itself gives an answer to the
strategic question of religious-philosophical importance: how (not) to
speak about the absolute?

1.a. Pagan ways of speaking about the absolute

At the time of *Economie libidinale* (1974), Lyotard formulated his
'libidinal' criticism, which touched already upon Augustine. One could
argue that he turned against one of the most well-known iconological
symbols: the burning heart with which the saint is often depicted in
images and statues. Augustine's famous quotation, "My heart is restless
in me, until it finds peace in You,"[4] forms the foundation of this symbol.
For Lyotard, this saintly heart knew all too well what it longed for. Its
flames reached for the contented life and for the witnessing knowledge
of God. Lyotard accuses Augustine of spuriously neutralizing desire in
this way and making it a teleological matter. The scorching *libido* is
turned into a neat, constrained *appetitio*, which Lyotard confronts with
his understanding of Freud.
   Libido is described in Freud's *Jenseits des Lustprinzips* (1920) in
terms of sexual energy which moves freely in the unconscious and
which, in consciousness, is bound to time, space, and meaning, which
are the constituent forms of reality. This split (*Entzweiung*) between the
conscious and the unconscious renders impossible the acquisition of
knowledge of the libido in its profligacy in a direct manner. After all,
knowledge presupposes consciousness and thus the connection of libidinal forces to 'images'. Everything we know about the libido is derived
from its indirect manifestations. It asserts itself in the dream, for
instance, by adjusting images from day to day life, by 'shifting' them, by
'inventing' them, but is ultimately independent. From this processing of
reality by the libidinal forces, which we witness in our dreams, something else follows as well. This processing causes images to align in new

---

[4] Augustinus, *Confessiones*, 1,i.

patterns and confuse or destroy existing patterns. From this we may
deduce, according to Freud, that two contradictory, yet always entangled, principles control the libido. We are dealing with the constructive
eros and the destructive *thanatos*.

Such a Janus-like libido is very important as far as Lyotard is concerned in his criticism of institutionalised religious discourse. Every representation is being threatened permanently by confusion and destruction. Stories, images, theories, and even the highest principle (the
Platonic idea, the God of Augustine) cannot escape this fate. Since
thought, too, is a form of representation threatened and founded by the
libidinal, the philosopher should adhere to two rules. Firstly, he should
be prepared to put his thought into perspective and to ridicule it. Secondly, he should try to think *affirmatively*. This means that he should be
receptive to the surprises and agility of the libido. In this way, the affirmative thinker affirms Being.

One doesn't have to read Freud in order to find these two modes of
thought. The so-called pagans of antiquity — with whom Lyotard identified himself regularly in this period of his working life — already
knew about it. "Every switch of energies carried the name of a God; for
every scream and intensity they had a small god or goddess, none of
whom served any purpose, that is to say, as long as one doesn't view
them with those sad, Platonic-Christian wide eyes. But after Augustine
had defected to the camp of the big Zero he did not want to understand
anything of this any longer."[5] Indeed, Augustine, in *The City of God*,
pokes fun at the pagans. They even analysed every detail of coitus and
invented a deity for every step of it.[6] In Augustine's view, folk paganism
stands for the reprehensible crumbling of the desire for unity.

Instead, Lyotard considers the submission of reality to some sort of
absolute principle as the truly objectionable act. After all, absolute (from
ab-solvo) means 'untied', relieved of this reality. The absolute transcends our comprehension, which is why Lyotard considers it, in this
period of his philosophical work, a purely phantasmatic construction.
The absolute is a 'figure de désir'. It is as a solid, immovable point,
invented by the intellect in order to canalize the confusing stream of
being. Augustine aims to control and guide desire from such an
absoluteness. That is why he believes in his compulsive 'point Zéro', his

---

[5] J.-F. Lyotard, *Économie libidinale*. Paris, Minuit, 1974, p. 17 [J.-F. Lyotard, *Libidinal Economy*. Indeanapolis, Indiana University Press, 1993, p. 8].

[6] Augustinus, *De civitate Dei*, VI, ii-vi; VII.

logos. He does not see that he is repressing the libidinal truth. He takes himself too seriously, the holy man. Instead of affirming existence in its singularity, he bows deferentially to 'his great Zero'. It is not Nietzsche, as many theologians would still hold, who is the great nihilist of the West, but Augustine.

Speaking about God in pagan terms means libidinal affirmation and destruction of metaphysical and philosophical discourses. Lyotard's rejection of Augustine in the *City of God* is strategic in a dual sense: Lyotard, himself, avoids having to speak about God, but opposes Augustine speaking about Him.

1.b. Phrasing the absolute in a 'jewish' way

Ever since *Au juste* (1979), a book in which he is questioned by Jean-Loup Thébaud about the political-ethical implications of such a libidinal approach, Lyotard turned to a philosophy of the *phrase*, a first sketch of which appeared in *La condition postmoderne* (1979), but which was only presented fully in his main work *Le Différend* (1983). His most important sources of inspiration are Kant, Wittgenstein, and Levinas, whilst Freud seems to have been forced into the background. In a certain way, this period of thinking may be characterized as 'jewish' given the accent laid on the ethical openness of discourse, as we will see below. The Kantian and Levinasian alertness to the 'natural fallacy', the irreducibility of the ethical law to the realm of nature, return in Lyotard's reflections on the way in which discourses are constituted in a infinite coupling of phrases ('enchaînement').

Yet, this does not contradict the reappearance of Augustine, an emblematic figure for Lyotard, on the scene of his thinking. As one of the first Christian metaphysical authors, Augustine set the trend for 'modernity'.[7] In *La condition postmoderne,* Lyotard criticised this using

---

[7] Both Augustine and Descartes are, as far as Lyotard is concerned (following Auerbach), the founders of modernity (see J.-F. Lyotard, *Le différend*. Paris, Minuit, 1983, p. 76; J.-F. Lyotard, *Tombeau de l'intellectuel*. Paris, Galilée, 1984, p. 77; J.-F. Lyotard, *Moralités postmodernes*. Paris, Galilée, 1993, p. 90). Descartes, however, does not adhere to the expropriation of the self by God, but is concerned about the effort of the self that wants to control all givens, including the self. (J.-F. Lyotard, *Le postmoderne expliqué aux enfants*. Paris, Galilée, 1988, p. 40 [J.-F. Lyotard, *Postmodern Explained. Correspondence 1982-1985*. Minneapolis, University of Minnesota Press, 1993, p. 20]). Later on, Lyotard became much more interested in the experience of submission of oneself to the absolute Other. Cf. J.-F. Lyotard, *Un trait d'union*. Grenoble/Sainte-Foy, 1993, p. 11 and 15.

arguments partially derived from Kant. Lyotard considers Augustine responsible for the modern habit of reconstructing factual history as a teleological development, using 'great stories' (*grands recits*). Modern thought utilises an all-embracing narrative to render reality intelligible. In this way, it makes us believe that time develops according to some eternal and lasting principle or other. Such a principle legitimises socio-political action and the sciences. Indeed, Augustine liked to quote from the gospel of John: "In the beginning was the Word, and the Word was with God, and the Word was God. [...] All things were made by him" (Joh.1:1-3). *Logos* serves here somewhat as the underlying principle of the creation. And since time is the product of creation, too, we can see through history by means of *logos*. *Logos* seems like a blueprint, a 'navel of time', out of which reality has been construed. It therefore follows that he who knows *logos* knows All.

The question is, however, how can a mortal human attain an insight in that eternal principle? For Augustine, the answer is clear: "And the Word was made flesh, and dwelt among us, and we beheld his glory" (Joh. 1:14). One gains access through faith. By means of faith one can arrive at a vision and will be able to comprehend the truth of being. Things (*res*) will become unambiguous signs (*signa*). As he describes it in his *Confessions*, the heavens, which are until now 'stretched like skin', — a book laid face down — will be read as a work of divine origin. The faithful who are in possession of *logos* will have received the all-seeing eye of the eagle (another symbol of Augustine).

However, ever since Kant taught us the essence of a 'transcendental illusion', we are acutely aware of the incredibility of great stories, according to Lyotard. Infinity has to be thought of in a horizontal way. Infinity, the idea of which is unrepresentable, reappears as an inevitable effect of discourse or, more precisely, of 'phrasing'. In its *articulated* form, a *phrase* (sentence, expression, even 'signal') is described as a 'universe' which is stretched out between four poles, four 'instances'.[8] First of all, by expressing a *phrase, a communicative situation is being created*. This implies, on the one hand, a pole by which the expression is uttered and, on the other hand, a pole which receives it. The sending agent (*destinateur*) and receiving agent (*destinataire*) both occupy their

---

[8] J.-F. Lyotard, *Le différend*, passim. See: "Articulation is what I call the totality of those minimal instances which make sure that a phrase attribute a *sentence* to a *referent* and that a phrase is provided with a *destinateur* and is aimed at a *destinataire*," J.-F. Lyotard, *Flora danica*. Paris, 1997, p. 63.

place on the communicative or pragmatic axis of the phrase-universe. Secondly, a *phrase* elucidates 'something' about 'something' else. In a *phrase,* a meaning (*signification*) is attributed to an object (*référent*). Referent and meaning are the two poles on the *semantic* axis. A 'régime de phrase' is defined by the specific relationship between these four instances. For instance, an imperative (you must!) does not permit the receiver to take the position of the sender. This would destroy the authority of the sender, which would cause the sentence to stop being an imperative. But — and this is how infinity is horizontalised — the way in which phrases are connected is not determined in any absolute way. For instance, the imperative of a sergeant at war — *Avanti!* — could possibly provoke laughter among the soldiers. That laughter determines *après coup* the uttered phrase and afflicts in this sense the regime in destroying its imperative character. It is in the *enchaînement* that signification and phrase-types are defined, always *après coup*, never predictable and therefore infinitely open. Like the commentaries in the Talmud, phrasing cannot come to an end. Every moment of connecting to a prior phrase is therefore a choice, is ethical in itself (However, at the end of this article we will see that this philosophy of the phrase refers to the question of the ' absolute phrase'.)

Again, direct speech about God is avoided. Moreover, Lyotard's phraseology is a systematic analysis of the reason why the idea of God cannot be articulated in any definitive way. In *Le Différend*, Lyotard explains that there is no legitimate linking between phrases about the absolute and phrases of empirical representation. No empirical knowledge exists of the object of an idea. The intellect is able to ponder ideas) but it is impossible to turn an empirical intuition thereof into a reality. It is irrational to boast about a scientific nature whilst referring to an idea. After all, one appeals, in this case, to an *'intellectus intuïtus'*, to a given, which is withdrawn from empirical judgement. That is why Augustine's perception of faith — if its ambition is to relate the encounter with the A/absolute in a discursive and rational way — finds itself confronted by many problems.[9]

---

[9] Although the *intellectus intuïtus* is Augustine's highest ideal, he does not consider himself as having reached that vision. "Intellectual understanding concerns the eternal vision, but faith feeds its infants with milk in the cradle of temporary existence. However, we now walk in faith, not in the vision. If we do not first walk in faith we will never arrive at the everlasting vision" (*De doctrina christiana* ll, xii).

1.c. Indirect speech: Lyotard's christian strategy

Probably the best example of Lyotard's indirect strategy is the unfinished *La confession d'Augustin*, which I will discuss now in more detail. We shall see how Lyotard combines elements from pagan libidinal philosophy and confronts them with phraseological insights. In this sense we could call this strategy 'christian': it combines insights from the 'pagan' and from the 'jewish' period of Lyotard's thinking. The book is a rereading of Augustine's celebrated *Confessions*, in which he speaks about his encounter with God or, more precisely, in which he searches for an expression of that unrecoverable experience.

Perhaps it only seems as if Freud disappeared during the period of *Le Différend*.[10] The libidinal motif shows up time and again in all kinds of writings of this period and later on (especially on the subject of art), for instance, in the very meaningful, in my view, yet in many regards unfinished (and perhaps impossible to finish) article *La phrase-affect* (1990), which he presented as a supplement to *Le Différend*. Being a supplement not neutral for deconstructive thought, the text influences retroactively the entire argument in *Le Différend* by inserting the theme of libidinality as an effect of the uncontrollable and, in that sense, traumatic encounter with 'something' (*La Chose*, God). Elsewhere Lyotard posits that the impressionable soul — the *anima* — is situated under the reasoning mind — the *animus* — with the *anima* being the necessary condition of thought which is not able to be absorbed into thought and conceptually reduced.[11] The majority of consciousness depends on the *infantia* of the unconsciousness; *logos* rests on *phone*, activity on passivity.[12] In this way, Lyotard re-enlists elements from the first, affirmative and libidinal period of his thinking, after the phraseological and pragmatic-analytical turn he took in *Le Différend*. The affirmative philosophy of the libido — substituted by the negative approach of phraseological pragmatism — returns in the philosophy of the *phrase-affect*, of the expression which makes itself felt noticeably *and* insusceptibly. In Lyotards' view, Augustine's encounter with his God has such a *phrase-affect* character.

---

[10] One could perceive phraseology as a 'translation' of Freud's metaphysical thought, as I have shown in C.H. Doude van Troostwijk, *Trouvaille: anamnèses de la critique*. Amsterdam/ Strasbourg, ASCA/Ianua, 2002.

[11] Cf. J.-F. Lyotard, Anima minima. In: Idem, *Moralités postmodernes*, pp. 199-210.

[12] Cf. J.-F. Lyotard, Voix: Freud. In: Idem, *Lectures d'Enfance*. Paris, Galilée, 1991, pp. 129-153.

2. Strategy of speaking with a forked tongue

The radical infinity of the *enchaînement des phrases* is stabilised in daily life by 'genres of discourse', which is to say by historically and culturally encoded habits to link up in a certain way with certain 'regimes de phrases'. Every *enchaînement* implies absorbing a phrase into a discursive regime that was not connected originally to the expression, but is often attended according to a specific 'genre of discourse' that coordinates the *enchaînement*.

This brings us to a second religious-philosophical strategy. Lyotard deliberately speaks with a forked tongue when speaking about the speaking of others about God. An original discourse is transferred to an unexpected 'genre of discourse', to another context of understanding (theoretical, practical, or artistic) and is thus rewritten. This religious-philosophical technique of *hermeneutical transposition* appears also in *La confession d'Augustin*. In line with the never-to-be-excluded open phraseological possibility, Lyotard applies strategically hermeneutical transpositions. In general, Augustine's *Confessions* is transposed to a Freudian horizon of understanding within which it speaks and makes one think. A more specific example of hermeneutical transposition can be found in a passage in which Lyotard 'explains' in mathematical terms Augustine's attempt at thinking and representing God's presence.

Augustine writes: "I made You out to be a being that surrounded Creation at all sides and permeated it, a being that was infinite on all sides, like a sea, a sea without end stretching immeasurably to all sides, and then as if that sea contained a sponge as large as a man would wish, but still of limited size, and then as if that sponge was entirely filled with water from that immeasurable sea."[13] God's complete presence cannot be grasped by any form of space or time, or by any concept. Nonetheless, Lyotard poses the question in his reflections on Augustine's *Confessions* of how man can have some idea about it. It is a question concerning ecstatic experience and religious trance.

In order to describe the experience, Lyotard brings Augustine's metaphor of the sponge up to date. He posits an analogy with conventional mathematics. According to the conventionalist, Poincaré, mathematics was not a matter of objective description and analysis. He considered mathematics to be a constructive occupation. To illustrate his

---

[13] Augustinus, *Confessiones*, VII, v.

point he put forward the *coupure-theory* of Dedekind. Euclidean space does not allow for definitive closure (*cloture*), contrary to what has often been thought. Starting from the lower and well-known one-, two-, and three-dimensional spatiality, it is possible to design a higher dimensionality. In all dimensions known to us there are geometrical shapes to be found which all have a cutting off point (*coupure*-function). A point breaks up a line, the line splits planes, and planes cut through volumes. What is remarkable is that by climbing the gradations, the coupure-function, too, shifts up a grade. And, what is more, the form that was initially characteristic loses its function the moment the level is raised. In theory, we can extrapolate to the still unknown fourth dimension if we adhere to this double principle of shifts. This will result in the plane loosing its coupure-function and passing it on to volume.[14]

In this analogy, Lyotard is concerned with two points. Firstly, the analogy deals with the insertion of a lower order into a higher one. Just as the three-dimensional order dissolves in the four-dimensional, the human soul in trance is absorbed — 'impregnated and preserved' — by divine plenitude. Secondly, the insertion implies the loss of representative functions. Just as there is a loss of a certain dividing function, according to the coupure-theory, the human subject in trance loses its power of discernment upon which representation is based. Lyotard calls this ability of representation spirit, *animus*. The *animus* denotes everything that makes the representation of things possible (intuitional forms of space and time, conceptual synthesis). Moreover, Lyotard ties the *animus* to the general function of representation of the negation. An object is not only defined by what it is in itself, but also by that from which it is distinct. The constitution of recognisable reality is rooted, therefore, in the power of discernment: in–out, all–nothing, man–woman, God–human being. In brief, *animus* is the name that indicates the *dual* ability of the constitution of reality within the subject. The encounter with the O/other, however, implies an explosion of this capacity, an opening up for the *anima*, the soul, a loss of subjective abilities or, as we will see below, a form of de-subjectivation.

[14] This mathematical vision had been discussed exhaustively by Lyotard in: J.-F. Lyotard, *Les TRANSformateurs Duchamp*. Paris, Galilée, 1977, pp. 79-82.

3. Strategy of ventriloquism

La Confession d'Augustin is a 're-reading' of Augustine's *Confessiones*.
The concept re-reading hides a third religious-philosophical strategy to
'avoid having to speak about God', which could be labelled a 'de-subjectivating strategy'. Firstly, it is clear how Lyotard's stylistic approach de-sub-
jectivises Augustine's speaking about God in the sense that it is a 'de-per-
sonalising'. He writes himself into the text of the *Confessiones*. Quotations
and fragments are inserted without the use of inverted commas in Lyotard's
own text. This has the effect of inter-textuality, which reminds one sometimes of ventriloquism. Lyotard speaks through the speech of another —
Augustine — who, in turn, speaks as if he has been addressed by Another.
Thus, a phraseological chain of speech ensues to which the reader has no
choice but to attach himself: the reading of the written text becomes ventriloquism; the text becomes an inner part. The endless sequence, which
gives meaning to a phrase only through a second phrase which is linked
to the first one, stems fundamentally from the fact that the *what* of
speech is, necessarily, too late when compared with the *that* of speech.

This puts the question of 'how (not) to speak?' in a new light again.
Every speech links up to what has been said and illuminates an original
opacity, which is never absorbed into that illumination. 'How (not) to
speak?' now becomes a task: how to speak in such a manner that justice
is done to the singular and unutterable fundament of speaking? Lyotard's
religious-philosophical speech is commemorative in this sense: a tribute to
something, which can never be expressed, because it accompanies, by definition, every expression as a necessary condition. His insertions of Augustine's text is not plagiarism, but a tribute to Augustine's own impression-
ability and an echo of his own insertions into a religious tradition.

De-subjectivation in trance-experience

Lyotard recognises ventriloquism in Augustine's experience of trance, in
his encounter with the absolute. In this de-subjectivating experience, control gives way to openness and passivity. It is a disclosure experience
(Ramsey), which captures a human being for a moment so completely that
it will later on design a specific language to be able to put it into words.[15]

---

[15] Joachim Track ties Lyotard's meaning for theology to this theme of 'disclosure'.
J. Track, Theologie am Ende — am ende Theologie? In: H. J. Luibl (hrsg.), *Spurensuche
im Grenzland.* Wien, 1996, pp. 15-64.

His encounter with the A/absolute in, for example, the famous Ostia-vision caused Augustine to write in sometimes swelteringly sensual and erotic-poetic prose.[16] In *La confession d'Augustin*, Lyotard notes that a visit by the A/absolute means 'touch', 'penetration', 'lifting of sexual inhibitions', in short, the *incarnation* in the most literal sense of the word. The trance results in a transubstantiation, which may be compared to the Roman Catholic Eucharist. The body (*corps*) of one in ecstasy, by which Lyotard means the voluminous body of the representative experi-ence, changes into 'flesh' (*chair*) or even into 'flesh of the soul' (*âme-chair*).[17] The *animus,* which is distinct from the body to the extent that it controls its constituent preconditions for being, loses its distance. With-out the framework of representation, however, the body crumples and changes into an indifferent mass. The body becomes flesh. A second effect is that something emerges from the *animus* which had been put out of action, something which Lyotard, as we have seen, coins the *anima* (soul).

   Prior to the entry of impressions into the representative registers of the *animus*, there is *anima*, the sensitivity to naked existence. The *ani-mus* takes care of the objective constitution of reality: sense impressions acquire form and meaning and are localised in a recognisable world. But not only is ability required for *what* the things are, the openness for the fact *that* they are is also necessary. Impressions presuppose impression-ability. The 'being' — the *that* of things — is not derived from or stored in frameworks of imagination. It only makes itself felt, here and now, like an actual occurrence. This primary presence is noted by an ability which can be distinguished from the representative *animus*, yet is not an entirely separate entity. The *anima* is nothing more than the feeling (*affectus*) which exists only in the actuality of the impression (*affectio*).

   I have called the trance an explosion because the preconditions of rep-resentation are exploded in a trance. But it is an implosion, too, since it confuses the constituent contrasts and makes them dissolve in one another. Therefore, Lyotard writes that trance is a 'plosum'. This is more than a simple pun. In the trance, the role played by contrasts is over. The distinction between *in* and *ex* is no longer applicable. 'To be elevated'

---

[16] Augustine has experienced many ecstasies. "And so now and then You lead me into a very unusual affliction (*affectum*), a strange bliss inside me: should it find fulfilment within me, it would be something unspeakable, which is no longer part of this worldly life" (Augustinus, *Confessiones*, X, xl).

[17] The neologism *âme-chair* (flesh of the soul) is possibly a reference to J. Lacan, *Télévision*. Paris, 1974, p. 16.

into the fullness of God can no longer be distinguished from the downward descent of His absolute presence. The trance is the descent of the absolute into body and spirit in such a way that they lose themselves in that absolute. It is a *coupure*-experience. It is *primal*.

According to Lyotard, Augustine was thinking of this 'primality' when he wrote: "You were more inner than my deepest inner being and higher than my highest height."[18]

The encounter with God is withdrawn from the representative contrasts, and thus also from the contrast of an *inner* versus a *outer*. "Augustine," Lyotard wrote in his *Postmodern fables*, "was, together with St Paul, the first to reveal the overlap between the self and the Other, who is deeper in him than he himself. Deeper, in the sense that the self cannot understand it."[19] The term 'inner' has been used improperly by Augustine. It serves only as an indication of the incomprehensible secret of religious experience because, in actual fact, the innermost is at the same time the outermost. The absolute which settles in me is, at the same time, the absolute in which I am settled: "Where did I get to know You, eternal Being, who transcends my comprehension. Where else but in You, who is above me?"[20] God is deeper in man than his innermost self, and higher than his highest point. The religious language which results from the trance experience cannot help but resort to the *oxymoronic*, to expressions in which the two extremes meet: the most intimate Other, the fartherestmost proximity, the most general singularity, the lasting transience, and the absent presence.

To conclude, one could maintain that the strategy of ventriloquism was adopted by Augustine himself. As such, the *Confessions* is a de-subjectivating way of writing and, as a result, the work of *anima*. Augustine's *Confessions* is something entirely different from endorsing some article of faith or other. "The saint," according to Lyotard, "wishes to confess *himself (se confesser)*." This does not mean that he presents his God with just any old sin. 'Se confesser' means the total submission of the self, absolute de-subjectivation, the sacrifice of the so-called personal life story to its author, the creator, who has always been the true owner of life. To the French ear, the verb 'se confesser' has a connotation of passivity. Passivity lurks under the activity of confessional writing. One

---

[18] Augustinus, *Confessiones*, III, vi.
[19] J.-F. Lyotard, Intime est la terreur. In: Idem, *Moralités postmodernes*, p. 182.
[20] Augustinus, *Confessiones*, X, xxvi.

has already been created and written up by the other. The purpose of
the confession is to transform the writing subject into the object of
divine scripture. Final expropriation is the future of the autobiographical
re-appropriation of the past which takes place in the confession. That
is what is meant by a *radical* conversion. But is such a conversion
possible?

4. Resistance to conversion

Meanwhile, the life that lives throws up many roadblocks on the way to
this surrender of the self. In *La confession d'Augustin* Lyotard shows
this in two motifs related to sexuality and in a third motif related to
semiotics. The first motif concerns the fundamental *inability* of conversion and relates to *distentio*. The second motif concerns the principal
unwillingness to convert. This is the motif of *consuetudo*, the 'force of
habit' and 'laziness'. Although Lyotard attempts to treat both these
motifs independently, *distentio* and *consuetudo* are intimately related. If
what is in a state of *distentio* has crumbled, *consuetudo*, from the Latin
suo, 'to join' or 'to sew', is offered as a cure. This duo *distentio-con-
suetudo* hinders the absolute conversion is three ways. Firstly, writing is
an activity which inevitably takes place in chronological time. One word
follows the next, and the meaning of a sentence or text is only established at the end, *après coup*. Moreover, those little scribbles on the
countless 'tablets' on which the 'old prelate from Hippo' used to write
his confessions still need to be read all over again, that is to say, need to
be given a voice, before they can acquire meaning. The writing remains
in concreto subjected to the chronological *distentio*, the temporal spread
which resulted from *distentio* understood as radical self-alienation. If
Augustine, through his confessions, aims to claw back at time lost due to
idleness, he will face a Sisyphean task. The time it takes to write creates
a never-ending spiral: he writes in order to write away the past, which
thus includes the past of his writing, through which he attempts to write
away the past.

In so doing, time and again, Augustine falls back on his old rhetorical habits (and 'genres of discourse') to embellish and pepper his texts
with clever remarks. Time and again, he bows his head for the 'devil'
of rhetoric and aesthetics. He can do nothing — and does not wish differently — but rely on that 'which has already been written', the *fatum*,
the 'discourse of the other'. After all, an author can only survive the

distentio of writing by means of the conventions of style and grammar and the 'genres of discourse'. Without such a literary *consuetude,* every step to the next phrase would evoke, again and again, the merciless torment of 'how to link-up now?' the torment of reflexive contemplation without rule or regulation.

The second type of resistance relates directly to the libido, the desire for the actual. This desire is not of itself aimed at God. This *sexual* passion is a fierce competitor of religious pathos. Most likely, the sexual passion is the stronger of the two because it manifests itself far more easily. In daylight, the subject takes a neutral stance towards images and thoughts, which arouse him at night and give him pleasure. Moreover, the sexual gets mixed up with the religious. The dream — which was seen as a conduit for the gods in antiquity — is shaky ground for Augustine. He never knows for sure whether it comes to him from God or from the sexual.

But why would Augustine want to deliver himself to religious ecstasy, which is hard to experience? Orgasmic pleasure offers itself almost daily. Deep in his human, all-too-human, flesh he feels disgust (*aversion*) for the 'change' (*conversion*). Day after day the sexual libido surprises him with yet another trick. Day after day he is offered yet another easy and tasty dish. He gets used to it: "Because my will was wrong (*perversa*), she turned into passion (*libido*), and while I served this passion she turned into a habit (*consuetudo*)."[21] Sexual pleasure is a persistent form of *consuetudo.* It makes the subject find peace in itself. The burning heart which believes to be seeking God delivers itself in the sleep of lust to sexual pleasure. Why seek for peace in God if it can be found in the self? The peace of the sexual habit takes on the peace of the conversion, and has a good chance of winning.

The third motif of resistance concerns the indistinguishable signs of the dream. Just as in Lyotard's interpretation the entanglement of the sexual and religious desires postpones the conversion indefinitely, so is it hindered by a *semiotic* entanglement as well. "The absolute is the empty name for that which transcends all forms and objects, whilst it is situated nowhere else but in those."[22] Indeed, the absolute explodes the structures of representation, yet there is no other place where it can make its presence felt than in representations. The fact that we have a notion of what *cannot* be represented is only possible due to the fact that

---

[21] *Ibid.,* VIII, v.
[22] J.-F. Lyotard, *Moralités postmodernes,* p. 34.

manifests itself somehow in what *can* be represented. Precisely because it stands apart from representation, the absolute cannot be grasped separately. That is why one *cannot* distinguish the signs through which it represents itself from run-of-the-mill, well-known signs. At least, not at first sight. Their absolute character may show up later, *après-coup*, in *distentio*.

For instance, when Augustine's depression over questions of meaning takes hold of him and he turns to the life he lived to seek indications of a divine nature, it turns out that the voice of a drunk, Ambrosius, who sits around reading quietly, and the children's song *tolle lege* have had appellative value. Only then does he recognise the guiding hand of God in his life, which, without realising it, put him in touch with Ambrosius.[23] Only then does he hear Creation cheer and rejoice because it has been made by God.[24] The absolute keeps itself 'discreetly' hidden, remains modestly and separately detached, and, thus, can only be discerned (*discernere*) at second sight.

But how strong are these signs? How strong is Augustine's *will* to decipher them and to listen to their calling? Or is it the force of habit (*consuetudo*) again which disturbs it all? The saint has plenty of philosophies and views of the world which make reality liveable to him. And is it not the case, all things considered, that there is nothing which does not bear the signature of the Creator? If God is everything in everyone, if he has created everything, if, therefore, all reality is 'ready-made', a readily available sign of God, is it not, then, rather arrogant to isolate just a few examples of the absolute? Everyone who professes to praise God for His guiding hand in life still has not given up his own authorship.

Distentio and *consuetudo* are in cahoots in preventing conversion. But the final blow they can deliver makes itself felt when the issue of the inevitable *forgetting* comes to the fore. The meeting with the A/absolute creates a hole in the memory, and confuses the coordinates of representation of time and space.[25] Therefore, it has to be forgotten. It has always been forgotten. It is nothing but the big *forgetting*, the 'primal trauma'. I cannot say *what* happened; I cannot even say *that* something happened; and, still, I have this indefinable and eerie (*unheimlich*) feeling

---

[23] Augustinus, *Confessiones,* V, xiii.

[24] *Ibid.,* XI, iii.

[25] I have discussed the disturbing effect of conversion in C.H. Doude van Troostwijk, La confusion d'Augustin ou la conversion inachevable. In: *Labyrinth* (vol. 2), 2000 (http://labyrinth.iaf.ac.at/2000/troostwijk.html).

that I have forgotten 'something'. I am haunted by the impossible memory of a necessary forgetting.

This 'primal forgetting' can be compared to the experience of one's own back. I can neither get rid of it nor can I look at it, and, in this sense, it is 'forgotten'. This forgetting is following me around, haunts me, and the torment only gets more unbearable the more I resolve, like Augustine does in his confessions, to submit my entire life to the absolute Other. How to avow something which has been forgotten from the outset? The temptation to invent strategies of forgetting, in order to shut up the memory of the big forgetting, is all too present. *Chronos* — the well-ordered *distentio* of 'before' and 'after' — and the *consuetudo* want to register everything in that temporal sequence. In short, *chronology* as such, is a strategy to forget the big forgetting. It is an attempt to 'anaesthetise' the existential pain of *distentio*. How could someone who professes faith ever be able to liberate himself from this? In what language?

5. The aporia of phrasing the absolute

According to Lyotard, Augustine's desire to submit his entire being to something he calls the creator is the result of his 'childlike nature', his *in-fantia*. There is something immemorial in every human being. His life had already started well before his mind could grasp it. He is born out of the unknown. His screams as a baby, his jealousy, sadness — he cannot remember any of this the moment he gains consciousness. Only older and other people can tell us who and what we were, before we knew we existed. Our childhood only gains form and meaning through 'discourse'. A human is the product of the discourse and the writings (*écriture*) of the other. He is the result of alterity.

This discourse, which is not originally ours, becomes our own along the way. It is draped like a cloth over the immemorial. It thereby threatens to cover up the original, big forgetting. It 'threatens' because no human will ever succeed completely in forgetting forever; nobody will achieve the 'Endlösung', not even with the help of a 'grand narrative'. Now that Augustine has taken the path of the 'effect of alterity', he is able to follow it back even further. Where was he before he was even a child? What language was spoken when not a single person spoke? "There is nobody who can tell me that: neither my father nor my mother were able to do that, nor the experience with others, nor my own memory. [...] From where does a living creature originate but from you, oh Lord? Or does anyone exist who is so capable, that he can create himself?"[26] Augustine discovers through his reflections on his childhood that he is the effect of the absolute Other. He invents or discovers (who are we to discern?) God as the great Writer. Augustine is a child not only in his own life but even in his reflections, which causes him to follow the path of his God.

One would think that Augustine's discovery provides the incentive to conversion for which we were looking. However, nothing could be further from the truth. By writing it down as a moment in his life to be professed, he simultaneously erases it:

> "As the subject of the work of profession, the author in the first person himself forgets that he himself is the work of the writing. He is the product of time: he counts on himself, he believes to act, to have control over himself, but he is repeatedly betrayed by the deception which the sexual has arranged — especially with regard to the writing — by postponing the moment of presence in all forms of time."[27]

The conversion to the everlasting is annulled at the moment a mortal author takes the seat of the Eternal. The saying 'he who writes, will live' does not apply in the case of the absolute. Could it be otherwise? Can one imagine a 'type of sentence' — a *régime de phrase* — which could convey the absolute? How would the phrase-instances relate to one another in the phrase which poses the absolute?

Let us first call this phrase the 'absolute phrase' and let us then try to define it by joining Augustine on the road along which he discovered his God. Augustine wondered about his own childhood of which he had no recollection whatsoever. That puzzlement is a first phrase. Its referent is 'my own childhood'. Augustine knew of the existence of this *référent* because he once had been told: 'You have been a child, too'. The moment he was addressed, i.e., was a *destinataire*, he was, at the same time, the *référent* of that address. He was the subject of it. Moreover, in that phrase, the expression of him being a child gave *meaning*. He discovered that he was not the author of his own being. Augustine became the subject in the etymological sense of the word. The fact that he used the word 'I' was due to the fact that he had been subjected (*subjectus*) to sentences which were attached to him by others right from the start.

[26] Augustinus, *Confessiones,* I, vi.
[27] J.-F. Lyotard, *La Confession d'Augustin*, p. 56.

But now he goes even further back and arrives at the point where there are no witnesses anymore. This point is situated at the other side of human phrasing. It is *absolute*. However, together with John the Evangelist, it tells us that *logos* is situated here, in that *primal phrase* which created being. It is the phrase which made human language possible, the absolute prerequisite for phrasing, the instigating moment of the phrase-universe. Augustine does not want to leave even the smallest piece behind in his confession. If his confession wants to express the 'absolute phrase', he will have to utter the 'primal phrase'. He should, at least, phrase in such a manner that the primal phrase always can be heard. That is why, according to Lyotard, Augustine keeps addressing the Creator with 'thou' (*toi*). This way, a permanent shadow of the 'primal phrase' is cast over his text, clearly visible to the reader.

But Augustine also invokes (*invocatio*) him in order to guide his hand and live in his expressions, since he is the only author of creation and, thus, of the creation of the *Confessions*. By this invocation he aims directly for the *aporia* of the confessional phrase. When the creator and his 'primal phrase' is invited to join the phrase of the one who confesses in order to turn it into the 'absolute phrase', it will lead to the 'collapse' of the phrase-universe. Because, after all, this 'thou' to which Augustine turns, is the original and real sender. The contrast between the communicative instance of *destinateur* and *destinataire* explodes. Their difference implodes into something indistinguishable. The creator to whom I turn is the same person who turns to himself through me. The absolute phrase has no direction on the axis of communication: points of departure and arrival overlap. On the *semantic* axis, too, we see signs of confusion. The total life — even that which was there before I knew it — needs to be sacrificed. My childhood, my permanent absence from myself, the other part of the self which cannot be represented, the 'being', are all objects, the *referent* of the absolute phrase. But what is that absolute 'being' other than the full presence of the 'thou' who is 'everything in everyone', as Saint Paul says? The referent of the absolute phrase is therefore the same as its *destinatiare*, which we found to be identical to the *destinateur*.

And, finally, in order to complete the explosion and implosion — i.e., into a 'plosion' — we ask the question about the 'contents', the *meaning*, of the absolute. The absolute is not related to anything by definition. It, therefore, cannot mean anything else but itself. *Voila*, the aporia. The four poles of the phrase-universe blend together in the absolute phrase into some sort of '*Indifferenzpunkt*'. The two axes no longer stretch out. It is the end of the *distentio*, the end of the articulated phrase.

Augustine and Lyotard: do they share the same obsession with the Absolute Phrase? Do they share the same destiny? Where would the subject be without the constituent ability of articulated phrasing? It cannot be a reference-pole or meaning-pole of the absolute phrase. This means that if the confession were to succeed entirely, if the conversion were to be absolute, the self would disappear just like that. The 'author' would have to become — to use a pun by a Lacanian biographer of Augustine — the perfect 'ôteur', the one 'who takes away' every representation, and, therefore, the remover of his own self.[28] The self is pushed aside by the absolute. Or is that going too far? The absolute has no place. It dissolves in the all-embracing sea of full presence. By inviting the absolute into the little hole of its representing and constituent phrase, the self has disappeared. He who digs a pit for the absolute shall, himself, fall in.

6. Conclusion

Phrasing God: the God of phrasing and the phrasing of God. Lyotard's indirect philosophy of religion is mostly concerned with the question of discourse. In fact, as we have showed, there is no independent philosophy of religion. God cannot be a metaphysical 'object' for Lyotard, which does not mean that he blindly rejects the use of the notion of 'God' as being meaningless. 'God' is, in a certain genre of discourse, the name for the absolute singularity. When Lyotard, himself, speaks about theological 'objects', it is, however, mostly in an indirect way. Nonetheless, it is fascinating to find this indirect approach throughout his philosophical development, which we have divided into three periods ('pagan', 'jewish', 'christian'), certainly in a much more global manner.

Fascinating, too, is the never-disappearing interest of Lyotard in the figure and thought of Augustine, which, biographically speaking, could be related to his youthful ambitions to become a Dominican monk or historian.[29] When we follow the trajectory of this interest in the father of the church, which culminated in the unfinished and posthumous booklet *La Confession d'Augustin*, we discover three strategies of speaking

---

[28] Cl. Lorin, *Pour saint Augustin*. Paris, 1988, p. 35.
[29] J.-F. Lyotard, *Pérégrinations*. Paris, Galilée, 1990, p. 15.

about God in a philosophical way. We baptized them respectively: speaking indirectly, speaking with a forked tongue, and ventriloquism. And, it is especially this last strategy that merits the most attention of the philosopher of religiosity. Augustine's desire to be converted in a radical way leads him to write his *Confessiones* in such a way that this writing process itself opens the space for grace or rebirth. Being converted implies that the Absolute subject reshapes my existence entirely. It is not me who speaks, but God himself speaks in my speaking. My *phrasing of God* has to be considered as being, at the same time, *God's phrasing of me*. It is this impossible desire for the A/absolute phrase that seems to have haunted Jean-François Lyotard. In this sense, he shares, with Augustine, the same fate of being an '*ôteur*' the one who takes away

Translation: Maarten Doude van Troostwijk (Oxford)

THE PARADOX OF GOD'S APPEARANCE ON JEAN-LUC MARION

RUUD WELTEN

1. Introduction

Twentieth century philosophy may well be labelled the philosophy of *'Godforsakenness' ('Gottvergessenheit')*. In the wake of Nietzsche, who found God dead, last century's philosophy was preoccupied with fortifying a people, bereft of their God. First and foremost, the remains of divinity had to be dismantled. The German philosopher Martin Heidegger accused both philosophy and theology of shamefully fixing the divine, of having God play the part of the ultimate *being* and, therefore, appointing Him, metaphysically speaking, as the ultimate cause of everything.

This accusation is called *'onto*-theology'. In onto-theology, God is the foundation of human understanding, keeping our ignorance in check. But the idea of God involves a human understanding that is limited, finite, and a God who is infinite. The aim of onto-theology is to soothe our disquieted incomprehension of His *being*. Some have taken Heidegger's onto-theological argument as a justification for silencing any thought on or of God. But, is it possible to speak about God without falling into onto-theology?

Heidegger's fierce criticism has been an inspiration to philosophy as well as theology. In France especially, Heidegger's views were given a warm welcome. Recently, however, in France, voices may be heard breaking the silence on God. Some French thinkers in the tradition of Husserl's phenomenology and Heidegger's philosophy are of the opinion that an ineffable God cannot be of any consequence to humanity. Emmanuel Levinas is, perhaps, the most influential representative of this attitude. In *Of God who comes to mind (De Dieu qui vient à l'idée)*, he says: "If God has a meaning, philosophical discourse must be able to comprehend God of whom the bible speaks." Here, Levinas recognises the difficulties of expression, of *not* reducing God to an object of desires, be they individual desires or those of philosophy and theology. Is it possible to speak of God without becoming an onto-theologist, without finding yourself speaking about a golden calf and not about God at all? The French philosopher Jean-Luc Marion (1946), fascinated and moved by Heidegger's appeal, observes that silence on God does not do justice to sincere belief in Him. But how does one, after post-modernism, speak of God? And, to complicate matters even further, how can one speak about a God who gives Himself, a God who is not the result of theoretical constructions or psychological desires? It is my aim to describe Marion's efforts to answer these questions. Similar to Levinas and Henry, Marion has phenomenology and, more specifically, its reformation playing a key role.

In 1982, Marion's much discussed *God without Being (Dieu sans l'être)* caused a commotion in theology and philosophy. At the *École Normale Superieure,* Marion had been taught by, among others, Jacques Derrida. Ferdinand Alquié, an expert on Descartes, had supervised his thesis on Aristotle and Descartes. Currently, Marion lectures at the Sorbonne in Paris and at the University of Chicago where he is successor to Paul Ricoeur. He is also the general editor of the prestigious *Épiméthée*-series published by the *Presses Universitaires de France,* as well as leader of Sorbonne's *Centre d'Études Cartésiennes.* His work covers a range of philosophical and theological issues. His work on Descartes has amended the French conception of the history of philosophy. He has three extensive studies on the structure of modern French philosophy: the 1975 *On Descartes's grey ontology (Sur l'ontologie grise de Descartes),* the 1981 *On Descartes's white theology (Sur la théologie blanche de Descartes)* and the 1986 *On Descartes' s Metaphysical Prism (Sur le prisme métaphysique),* as well as many articles mostly published in *Cartesian questions I and II (Questions cartesiénnes I and II).* Since the late 1980s, though still interested in Descartes, he has increasingly focused his attentions on phenomenology, Husserl, and Heidegger, publishing, in 1989, *Reduction and Givenness: Investigations of Husserl, Heidegger, and Phenomenology (Réduction et donation, recherches sur Husserl, Heidegger et la phenomenology).* Still another area of his thought focuses on theological matters. He made a name for himself with the 1977 publication *The Idol and Distance (L'idole et la distance),* the 1982 *God without Being* and the 1991 *The Crossing of the Visible (La croisée du visible).* On several occasions he has explored the theme of Christian love, charity.[1] Recently, he has

---

[1] J. L. Marion, *Prolégomènes à la charité.* Paris, 1986 [J.-L. Marion, *Prolegomena to Charity.* New York, Fordham University Press, 2002].

published a book on eroticism, *The Erotic Phenomenon (Le phénomène érotique)*. His heterogeneous areas of interest in both philosophy and theology might lead one to suspect a dispersion of Marion's scientific attention. However, in his 1997 *Being Given: Towards a Phenomenology of Givenness (Étant donné. Essai d'une phénoménologie de la donation)*, we see the various disciplines of his thought merge. His 2002 *In Excess: Studies of Saturated Phenomena (De surcroît: Etudes sur les phénomènes saturés)* contains further explorations into themes first addressed in *Being Given*. Dedicated to his tutors, Ferdinand Alquié and Jean Beaufret, who was co-responsible for launching Heidegger's philosophy in France, Marion's thesis in *In Excess* already gives a clue to the traces he will be following in the years to come. In it, two previously separated but decidedly French traditions meet, which serve as the standing *Leitmotiv* throughout his entire oeuvre.

It is not Marion's goal to restore the once self-evident God, or a metaphysics that proves His verity. Marion affirms the loss, which is not just a construction of the mind: we have, indeed, slain God. Nietzsche's claim is correct and Heidegger's onto-theological argument is all-important. This, however, is not to God's detriment; instead, it is in His favour. Paradoxically, this line of thought is actually not unusual in Christianity. For instance, mystics such as Eckhart and John of the Cross proposed the idea that any novice of mystical experience should leave God in order to find Him. To become receptive of God, one should renounce all images of Him that may be produced by human desire. Marion hears Nietzsche's madman bellowing out for this destruction, which necessarily precedes revelation. In this day and age, revelation does not stand a chance unless we uncompromisingly appreciate this point of view. But how can the emptiness in our agnostic culture be experienced as part of God's revelation without a relapse into theological nostalgia or metaphysical restoration? The death of our old, idolised God has not automatically led us to the disinclination or inability to believe, as philosophy has shown over the last couple of decades. Indeed, some even speak of a theological revolution in philosophy: a tempting premise, but as it turns out, premature and unable to help us pin down the actual philosophical importance of God. If there is a God, it is not because I feel the urge to speak about Him, but because He speaks to me. This is the key to Marion's work as I see it. He applies this one key to two formerly separated traditions. Marion uses both religion and phenomenology to set up conditions that will allow us to openly receive God's precious gift. Some philosophers blame the structure and inertia of the Catholic Church for the present general *'Godforsakenness'* and idolatry. But Marion is not a theological reformer: he calls attention to idolatry within philosophy and theology themselves, just like Heidegger. Thought, according to Marion, is indeed capable of opening up to God. This prospect of a non-fixed image of God is what Marion holds out to us: he calls it the 'icon'.

2. Idol and icon.

In *God without Being*, Marion develops a pair of concepts for the phenomenological interpretation of long-standing theological themes. 'Idol' and 'icon' refer to two different ways of divine appearance. An 'idol' may literally be a statue, made of bronze or marble, but may also refer to an image or concept of God. According to Marion, we can think about God without the help of a fixed image or concept. In order to prove this, however, he must appeal to those same theologies and philosophies that once incorporated God into their conceptual systems. Marion must re-read the relevant theology and philosophy and create an atmosphere in which God, once again, may be mentioned in earnest and not just quoted. In this way, God can be freed of conceptuality and idolatry once and for all. This non-conceptual, non-idolized 'appearance' of God is what Marion calls the 'icon'. Here, the word does not refer to beautifully painted wooden panels depicting holy scenes. The difference between idol and icon stems from the difference in their phenomenological structure. The distinction between them lies in not *what* they refer to but the *way* they refer. Their difference is not about veracity, but simply about different ways of looking.

2a. The idol.

The idol is the image of God or the divine, adjusted to human, finite standards. It is a "human experience of the divine."[2] Marion is mainly interested in the image or concept of God. 'Idol' refers to the structure of thought on God within human limits. Although its etymological background casts a cloud over the term 'idol' in so far as it usually conveys a negative connotation, still, this negative connotation must to be

[2] J.-L. Marion, *L'idole et la distance*. Paris, Grasset, 1977 (quotation from 'Le livre de poche', 1991), p. 20 [J.-L. Marion, *The Idol and Distance. Five Studies*. New York, Fordham U.P., 2001, p. 6].

suspended long enough to examine the mechanisms initiated while the divine is conceptualised. The idol represents just one way to relate to the divine. Marion does not question the idol's capability to represent God. 'There is no doubt that the idol is an effective image, shaping the divine into a God," says Marion.[3] The idol is no less authentic than the icon. But its representation of the sacred is limited; its beauty lies solely in the human eye. "The idol consigns the divine to the measure of a human gaze."[4] As a result, the gaze creates the idol.[5] Without a centred gaze, there is no idol. 'Idol' (*eidolon*) means 'image', denoting 'that which is seen'. It is entirely fixed by visibility. Therefore, the difference between idol and icon may also be explained in terms of visibility and invisibility. The idol represents the visible; the icon represents the invisible. 'Vision' is central to this explanation: the idol is 'that which is seen' and no more. The idol fulfils the gaze, so Marion calls it "the prime visible."[6] The onlooker is fully satisfied by what he sees. This type of perception is called idolatry and, characteristically, it is fixed. Fixedness therefore, may well be the idol's most important characteristic.[7] The idol is created by the desire to see and fixes what is seen. In other words, the idol *is* exactly there where the gaze halts. Like eyes scanning the horizon: when I am at the beach looking at the horizon, my eyes are in constant motion and I can only actually see its hazy contours. But when suddenly a ship appears, my eyes, now with an anchor point, will clearly fix on the horizon and settle down to do their job: looking. Eyes need to be anchored in the same way consciousness requires a fixed point; consciousness is at a loss when faced by an incomprehensible, infinite, and invisible God. In this respect, fixedness is a necessary condition for vision. Consequently, it is the gaze that creates the idol.[8] In other words, the idol represents a way of looking *at*. We can think of this in terms of infatuation, which is a phenomenon that has similar characteristics. When falling in love, I cannot see the subject of my infatuation objectively: through my hazy eyes of love, I see heavenly eyes, the

[3] *Ibid.*, p. 21.

[4] J.-L. Marion, *Dieu sans l'être*. Paris, Presses Universitaires de France, 1991[2], p. 24 [J.-L. Marion, *God without Being*. Chicago and London, University of Chicago Press, 1991, p. 14].

[5] J.-L. Marion, *Dieu sans l'être,* p. 19 [J.-L. Marion, *God without Being,* p. 10].

[6] J.-L. Marion, *Dieu sans l'être*, pp. 18 f. [J.-L. Marion, *God without Being,* p. 9].

[7] J.-L. Marion, *L'idole et la distance*, p. 20 [J.-L. Marion, *The Idol and Distance*, p. 6].

[8] J.-L. Marion, *Dieu sans l'être*, p. 19 [J.-L. Marion, *God without Being,* p. 10].

purest skin, etc. I create my own image and am in love with this image. Subsequently, I want my subject, made by me, to live up to this image. The idol is like a mirror; it is merely reflecting my desires. The mirror itself is invisible; only the reflected image is visible. That which is reflected is the gaze itself.[9] The metaphor of the mirror implies that looking is fulfilling the intention of the gaze and, as such, makes transcendence impossible. The gaze is obsessed by itself. I see nothing but my own gaze. Marion quotes the nineteenth century philosopher Ludwig Feuerbach who, like Nietzsche and Marx, understood 'idolatry' to mean 'idolisation of the self'. Feuerbach reduced God to 'the mirror of man'.

The idol is the image of God cut to the size of human imagination. The image comes in different shapes. It is philosophically important that the idol may take the shape of an idea or concept. The concept of God is neither infinite nor incomprehensible; conceptualisation means assimilation by human imagination. God, the concept, is given its rightful place within a logical order. Philosophy has a history of conceptualising God in this way. In fact, 'onto-theology' is nothing other than a metaphysical name for the conceptualisation of God.

2b. The icon

Describing the icon seems not to be overly complicated. The icon is God, Himself, appearing free of individual desires. But it is not that easy. First, God does not appear in the visible world. When I see Him, who is to say He is not just a figment of my imagination? How easily we relapse into idolatry, seeing only the God we want to see! Remember, the icon cannot be fixed, since fixedness is characteristic of idolatry. I can never say, 'Now I have pinned down the icon, devoid of any idolatry', for such pinning down implies fixing and therefore lapses, again, into idolatry. Now, Marion has not written a manual on seeing God. His commitment is not to psychology but to philosophy. He wants to understand why philosophy has never been able to reach the icon. He wants to develop a breakthrough philosophy that does not fix God. As I wrote earlier, Marion is interested in the different phenomenological structures of idol and icon, but his early work deals mainly with the theology of the icon.

---

[9] J.-L. Marion, *Dieu sans l'être*, p. 21 [J.-L. Marion, *God without Being*, p 12]; J.-L. Marion, *La croisée du visible*. Paris, La Différence, 1991, 1996² (quotation from the edition, published by Presses Universitaires de France, 1996), p. 121.

As is the case in the Eastern Orthodox Church, the standard for this 'theology of the icon' is found in Colossians 1:15[10]: "He is the image of the invisible God...." The Greek word for image is *eikoon*. The mediaeval iconoclastic controversy has positioned the terms idol and icon in diametrical opposition to each other and, in this respect, they differ as a result of historic factors.[11] The iconoclasts rejected any image of God (a radical ban on images found today only in traditional Judaism and Islam). The iconodules, on the other hand, retired the icon from the imputative public eye in order to preserve it, thus originating an opposition.[12]

As a result, the Orthodox Church has been developing a theology of the icon for many centuries.[13] The icon is the image of God, secured against the threats of the iconoclasts. Still, that is not saying much about the intrinsic implications. The icon thwarts that which applies to the idol. The icon is not apparent, not analysable, not visible, not comprehensible. Representing a non-idolatrous attitude, the icon is the counterpart of the idol. The icon overcomes the invisible mirror, the fixing, and the intentional gaze, which applies to the idol. The icon itself claims the gaze of the onlooker. The gaze no longer belongs to the onlooker but to the icon itself.[14] The lure of the Orthodox Church's icons of Christ, facing the onlooker, is based on a similar experience. "In the idol, the gaze of man is frozen in its mirror; in the icon, the gaze of man is lost in the invisible gaze that visibly envisages him."[15] The icon does not fix; it "unbalances human sight in order to engulf it in infinite depth."[16] The idol is cut to the size of human imagination, but the icon recognises no standards but its own infinite transgression.[17] In short, it must first be acknowledged that the icon is not an idol and, therefore, it can never become the subject of idolatry.

---

[10] Cf. J.-L. Marion, *Dieu sans l'être,* p. 28 [J.-L. Marion, *God without Being,* p. 17]; J.-L. Marion, *La croisée du visible,* pp. 102, 135; J.-L. Marion, *L'idole et la distance,* pp. 22, 215 [J.-L. Marion, *The Idol and Distance,* pp. 7, 175-6].

[11] J.-L. Marion, *Dieu sans l'être,* p. 15 [J.-L. Marion, *God without Being,* p. 7].

[12] J.-L. Marion, *L'idole et la distance,* p. 22 [J.-L. Marion, *The Idol and Distance,* p. 7]; cf. J.-L. Marion, *Dieu sans l'être,* p. 15 [J.-L. Marion, *God without Being,* p. 7].

[13] E.g., John of Damascene, *De sacris imaginibus orationes*; Theodore the Studite, *Antirhetica* (*Antirrethics*); Among others, Leonid Ouspensky and Wladimir Lossky on the theology of the icon in the twentieth century, W. Lossky, *Der Sinn der Ikonen.* Bern, 1952; L. Ouspensky, *Theology of the Icon.* New York, 1978.

[14] J.-L. Marion, *Dieu sans l'être,* p. 31 [J.-L. Marion, *God without Being,* p. 19].

[15] *Ibid.,* p. 32 [*Ibid.,* p. 20].

[16] *Ibid.,* p. 37 [*Ibid.,* p. 24].

[17] *Ibid.,* p. 33 [*Ibid.,* pp. 20-22].

The icon is about the existence or "presence of a non-object," says Marion.[18] It seems an object does not necessarily have to be simultaneously present. The object of Marion's phenomenology is not an object like the intentional object of traditional phenomenology. An intentional object is the focus of a gaze, an object that appears because of this orientation. This intentionality is characteristic to the traditional phenomenology as expressed by Husserl and Heidegger. But the icon is a non-object since it cannot be objectified. I do not focus upon it, rather, it focuses on me. The icon is not an object, no *spectacle*.[19] "The idol does not result from a vision but provokes one,"[20] says Marion. This implies a reversal of orientation: the idol refers to the God my gaze creates. The icon, on the other hand, focuses its gaze on me.[21] The icon, we learn, refers to a "perfect reversal" of intentionality.[22] Invisible, the icon gazes at us. But reversal cannot be the *only* issue here, for phenomenology is always solely about that which appears to consciousness! What is important is not just that the intentionality of the icon is orientated towards me instead of the reverse, but the consciousness experiencing this as a gift that is given. The icon is the intentional gaze of the other in me. The icon approaches me, gives itself. The point is this gift to consciousness. Proceeding from an egotistical intentionality, this gift cannot be received. So, how do I experience the icon gazing at me? How do I receive it?

3. God and onto-theology

As we have said, the notions 'idol' and 'icon' are used to develop a phenomenology about a God who gives Himself and who is not the result of theoretical constructions or psychological desires. This phenomenology, however, is not fully detached from ontology. In Western philosophy, ontology has been the deciding factor in all thought on God. In metaphysics, God is thought of as a *being*. In straightforward terms, this means that we speak of God as if he *is*, in the same way all things, such as humans and animals, around us *are*. A being is something of which we can say that it *is*, like me, you, my cat, the tree, a word, a thought.

[18] J.-L. Marion, *La croisée du visible*, p. 43.
[19] *Ibid.*, p. 45.
[20] J.-L. Marion, *Dieu sans l'être*, p. 28 [J.-L. Marion, *God without Being*, p. 17].
[21] J.-L. Marion, *La croisée du visible*, p. 148.
[22] J.-L. Marion, *Dieu sans l'être*, p. 31 [J.-L. Marion, *God without Being*, p. 19].

But can we say God is? For Marion, idolatry is primarily the objectification of God as a being. He comes up with what we might call a reversal of onto-theology. This does not imply criticising theology or any religious line of thought. Again, Marion is not out to restore the God that
once was or a metaphysics to prove Him real. The reversal lies in Marion's theological, not ontological, analysis of Heidegger's onto-theological accusation. But what does this imply? According to onto-theological standards, God is, has beingness. Scholastic theology, quite aware of
a problem here, developed the doctrine of analogy. I may call my neighbour a good man and I may call God good, but I cannot possibly mean
the same thing by 'good' in these cases. Terms such as 'good' are equivocal (ambiguous, not univocal or identical). But this does not solve the
ontological problem. Even saying, in an analogous context, that God is
the prime or the highest form of being does not solve the problem, for
He is nevertheless thought of as *being*. Marion opposes and wants to dis-
mantle such thought on God. Heidegger, in contrast, does not aim his
criticism of onto-theology against idolisation and does not elaborate on
strictly theological matters.. For him, the problem is how to avoid thinking being in terms of God. Without exaggeration, one might say that the
main theme running through all of Heidegger's works after *Being and
Time (Sein und Zeit)* is an effort to think the *being* of what *is*, which,
according to him, is an issue that Western philosophy has overlooked
throughout the ages. The *being* of that which *is* has always been understood to *be* just like me, you, my cat, the tree, a word, a thought, which
is to say that even the 'highest' form of being, or the 'ultimate cause',
can still be *reduced.* According to Heidegger, philosophy has to
renounce the God that *is* and, more specifically, renounce the ultimate
cause (*causa sui*).[23] Marion, on the other hand, wishes to free all thought
on God from ontological predicates. In this sense, 'onto-theology'
becomes a swearword denoting philosophies that speak of a God that *is*.
In *God without Being*, Marion uses the notion of onto-theology on
behalf of theology, trying to shield God's divinity. Heidegger uses the
term on behalf of the Being, trying to prove that it is not open to objectification. Onto-theology floats between philosophy and theology, which
is where Marion's thought finds its home. As far as Marion is concerned,
onto-theology has served to greatly benefit idolatry: the idol is an image

---

[23] M. Heidegger, Die onto-theo-logische Verfassung der Metaphysik. In: Idem, *Identität und Differenz*. Pfüllingen, Neske, 1957, pp. 70-1 [M. Heidegger, The onto-theo-logical constitution of metaphysics. In: Idem, *Identity and difference*. New York, Harper,
1969, pp. 71-2].

of a God who is functionally the prime being or ultimate cause. Its counterpart, the icon, marks a philosophy that shirks onto-theological issues
in order to enable thought on God. Such a philosophy has, as shown by
both Heidegger and Marion, intentional thought getting in the way.
From onto-theology Marion extracts a demand on both theological and
philosophical thought on God, a demand that must be met before one
can think the icon and forget about the idol.[24]

4. Gift and givenness

Since the late 1980s, Marion has increasingly focused on the phenomenological development of the concept of 'appearance'. In *God without
Being*, he freed God of ontological determinations, but kept quiet about
the phenomenological implications of doing so. Obviously, Husserl's
traditional phenomenology does not enable us to think the 'gift of God'
or, rather, 'God's givenness'. In *Being Given*, Marion develops a phenomenology based on the christological description in *God without
Being*. He studies the appearance, the *original gift*. Phenomenology
replaces a critical onto-theology. Marion withdraws from the theological
arena, from the debate on God; he leaves behind that place between philosophy and theology and moves instead, toward an undiluted phenomenology. And, indeed, he must make this move. If he wants to show how
God gives Himself, how the phenomenon 'God' appears to us, a closer
look at what it means to *appear* is necessary. He cannot use the paradigm of God's existence as a starting point — a paradigm is a hypothesis, and whether provisional or otherwise, it is not based on appearances.
Marion's subject is no longer God, but the non-ontological way in which
God appears. As we recall, God does not appear *because* I focus on
Him. Or better, it is not God's way of appearing (as an idol or an icon)
that is at issue, but the origin of His appearance and, more specifically,
how this appearing differs from what is given in intentional phenomenology. What does a phenomenology of the original gift have to say
about God's appearance? Marion wants to develop a phenomenology
that specifies the antagonism between the idol and the icon, something
he did not get around to doing in *God without Being*. He focuses not on
how God is thought, but whether or not our cognition and intuition are

[24] J.-L. Marion, *L'idole et la distance*, p. 34 [J.-L. Marion, *The Idol and Distance*,
p. 19].

capable of receiving that which does not spring from us, of contemplating that which *gives itself*. So, paradoxically, Marion cannot presuppose any kind of divine phenomenality (like God's invisibility, for instance). But for Marion, this is no philosophical flaw; rather, it is essential to the phenomenology of God.

The issue of givenness, central to all phenomenology,[25] needs to be rephrased. Marion's approach is very detailed and often highly technical. This is unavoidable, anticipating ready criticism about cutting phenomenology to the size of God. However, delving into an account of these technicalities is not necessary here. Rather, we must confine ourselves to the main issue at hand, namely, what is givenness, or, rephrased in Marion's terms, what is donation? Therefore I will confine myself to the main issue: what is givenness (*donation*)?

Phenomenologically speaking, what does this question mean? What I perceive is *given* to me. It is a gift. All that arises in my consciousness is given to me. Husserl uses the term '*givenness*' (*Gegebenheit*). Marion uses *donation*. I use 'givenness' or, even more apt, '*giving*'. The French term *donation* is difficult to translate univocally: it may mean '*present*', '*gift*', 'donation', 'giving', or 'givenness'. In all cases, it is derived from the verb '*to give*'. But Marion does not adopt Husserl's point of view. He has no intention of reducing the gift to yet another principle. What *is* 'giving' or a 'gift' when, for instance, I say in everyday language, 'I am giving my friend a gift'? Strange as it may seem, it does not refer to the one who gives, to the recipient, or to the gift. The act of giving a gift cannot be reduced to any of these three factors. It does not refer to a 'what'; it refers to a 'that' — what matters is not *what* I give, but *that* I give. 'Donation' refers to a given *that* solely gives itself. This is the *phenomenon*. Donation shows itself, but can only do so during the act of giving. *Donation* is showing us the ultimate gift. Of course, Husserl has already pointed out that 'phenomenon' is equivocal, denoting both the act of appearing and the appearance itself,[26] a distinction which is rather

[25] Cf. E. Husserl, *Ideen zu einer reinen Phänomenologie und phänomenologischen Philosophie. Erstes Buch, Allgemeine Einführung in die Phänomenologie*. HUA III-1, §1 [E. Husserl, *Ideas Pertaining to a Pure Phenomenology and to a Phenomenological Philosophy*, First Book. *General Introduction to a Pure Phenomenology*. Dordrecht/Boston/London, Kluwer, 1982, §1].

[26] J.-L. Marion, *Étant donné. Essai d'une phénoménologie de la donation*. Revised second edition, Paris, Presses Universitaires de France, 1997, p. 101 [J.-L. Marion, *Being Given. Toward a Phenomenology of Givenness*. Stanford, Stanford University Press, 2002, p. 69]; J.-L. Marion, Le phénomène saturé. In: J.-F. Courtine (ed.), *Phénoménologie et théologie*. Paris, Criterion, 1992, p. 90.

crucial for Marion. Therefore, Marion says when *donation* as givenness (or appearing) equals the rise (or appearance) of that which gives itself, we can speak of a *fold* of *donation*.[27] Again, the point is not that the phenomenon is a representation of an (appearing) object. The ultimate gift is layered; it has multiplicity instead of the singularity characterising representation where one thing simply represents another thing. 'Appearing' needs to free itself of the 'imperialist a priori conditions of understanding' otherwise intentionality remains involved; it is simply perceiving as we already understand it, which neglects the *thing itself.* The thing itself, for Marion, is *donation.*

Typically, a gift is *received*, not *understood*. For Marion, this implies a crucial difference between science and theology. Science treats its subjects as objects. The animal is to the biologist what the chemical reaction is to the chemist or what human behaviour is to the sociologist: all objects of science. The object is studied and understood. Heidegger once said that theology is a science amongst other sciences, with its object being religion and not so much God.[28] This is essentially mistaken, according to Marion. Theology is not about objectified subjects; rather, it adopts *a receptive openness* towards that which is given. The criticism that science reduces the world to its object has been long-standing in the tradition of phenomenology, which is based on what is given and, as such, renders all scientific knowledge incidental. Marion's view reveals similarities to the view of Michel Henry. Although divergent in details, both approach theology phenomenologically, not dogmatically. In Marion's work, *donation* takes on many theological shapes and forms. Clearly, Marion replaces the aforementioned 'object' with the 'idol'. Science has its own idols (an observation dating back to Bacon), while theology maintains the iconical core of the gift, as crystallised in the gospel of Jesus Christ in which the 'good news' is received unobjectified. *Charité,* Christian love and charity, also refers to a gift that cannot be objectified. This gift is represented in the celebration of the Eucharist. Thus, Christianity manages to receive the gift without reverting to idolatry. *Being Given* is entirely focussed on the gift. The big difference between *Being Given* and the earlier text *God without Being* is that the former shows Marion committing (to) undiluted phenomenology. As

---

[27] J.-L. Marion, *Étant donné,* p. 31 [J.-L. Marion, *Being Given,* p. 19].
[28] M. Heidegger, Phänomenologie und Theologie. In: Idem, *Wegmarken.* Frankfurt am Main, Klostermann, 1978[7], pp. 45-78 [M. Heidegger, Phenomenology and Theology. In: Idem, *Pathmarks.* Cambridge, Cambridge University Press, 1998, pp. 39-62].

inevitably follows from his surrender to phenomenology since *God without Being*, his methods are no longer semi-theological and semi-phenomenological. When God is not an idol, not an object of science, when Christ gives Himself, the phenomenological structure of this gift must be studied and explained without the help of theological and christological paradigms. The Eucharist, for instance, is taking a Christian experience for granted, so theologians have gone out of their way trying to show its seminality for centuries. Phenomenologically speaking, such 'theological remains' land Marion in trouble in *God without Being*. A phenomenology cannot be based upon an intrinsic principle or desideratum. Again: God does not appear because I focus on Him, and certainly not because I desire to establish an alluring new school of metaphysical or theological thought. The 'itself' in 'giving itself' immediately renders such a school of thought incidental. We turn now to Marion's main 'givenness': the saturated phenomenon.

5. The saturated phenomenon.

Previously, we saw Marion reassessing phenomenology, assuming the original gift. The gift appears, but not like an object, not like an idol. Asking, 'Does God appear?' or 'Does Christ appear?' would make Marion a crypto-theologian, a theologian in the guise of a phenomenologist. So the question must be: 'Is it *possible* to describe an appearing that is *not* subject to my orientation, my *intentionality*?' If this is possible, God's appearance is *possible*. In *Being Given*, Marion develops a phenomenality that is 'saturated', or fulfilled. Within the saturated phenomenon lies the answer to Marion's question.

What is this 'saturated phenomenon'? First, let us look at the latter half of the term: phenomenon. A phenomenon is something I perceive, either inwards or outwards. Phenomenology describes the appearing of phenomena. Husserl has specified how the phenomenon appears as I am oriented towards it. Orientation, or intentionality, is a prerequisite for appearing. But what I behold rarely coincides with what I physically see. My consciousness fills the gaps in my perception. Looking at a cube, for instance, I will never see more than three sides at the same time. Still, I see a cube, in full. The phenomenon 'cube' as perceived by my consciousness does not coincide with my physical perception, my *intuition* of it. The thing I am looking at, Husserl explains, is an intentional object to me. This means it exists as an object towards which I am oriented.

I see something, but only my intentionality, or orientation, enables me to perceive a cube. I do not intuitively see a cube. Intentionality refers to the search for coincidence or consistency between the actual materiality of something and my thoughts and qualifications about it. Attaining this consistency, Husserl says, equals the fulfilment of the intention. So consciousness is always pursuing the fulfilment of its intentions.

Now, this consistency between intuition and intention actually remains untenable, indemonstrable, for it is not immediately given. In other words, intuition is always accompanied by a surplus of meaning.[29] When I call a piece of paper 'white', according to Husserl, the intentionality of the word 'white' is only partly fulfilled.[30] The intuition of 'a piece of white paper' certainly does not fulfil the intention of the meaning of 'white paper'. The meaning of 'white paper' does not depend on my intuition of a particular piece of white paper, but refers to all possible pieces of white paper.[31] Intuition needs to be filled by intentionality. Therefore, intuition is always lacking, indigent. Marion concludes that Husserlian phenomenology is characterised by the determination of a phenomenon constituted by a *deficiency*: that which gives falls short.[32] This deficiency is not incidental or accidental, but a necessary condition of phenomenality itself. This seems remarkable. The main aim of Husserl's phenomenological efforts is a return to the thing itself (*Sache selbst*), and his own analysis renders this impossible! How can I return to the *Sache selbst* if my intuition is inadequate to do so? Is phenomenology bringing itself to ruin here? Because of the way consciousness is structured, the phenomenon needs filling as much as intuition does. By definition, the subject always interprets what is given.

After observing this apparent unattainability of the *Sache selbst*, Marion nevertheless continues to ask whether a phenomenon characterised not by deficiency but by a surplus of intuition might be possible.[33] Undoubtedly, such a phenomenon is not and cannot be thought by Husserl. For him, the fulfilment of the intention poses the outer limit. To him, Marion's idea of a surplus of fulfilment would be no more than a

---

[29] E. Husserl, *Logische Untersuchungen. Zweiter Band, Zweiter Teil Untersuchungen zur Phänomenologie und Theorie der Erkenntnis.* Husserliana XIX/2, 1984, p. 660 [E. Husserl, *Logical Investigations. Volume 2.* London and New York, Routledge, 2001, *Fifth Logical Investigation*].

[30] Marion is quoting Husserl; J.-L. Marion, Le phénomène saturé, p. 93.

[31] E. Husserl, *Logische Untersuchungen, Zweiter Teil* [Edmund Husserl, *Logical Investigations, Volume 2*].

[32] J.-L. Marion, *Étant donné*, p. 272 [J.-L. Marion, *Being Given*, p. 194].

[33] *Ibid.*, p. 276 [*Ibid.*, p. 197].

figure of speech, which could only be understood phenomenologically in terms of fulfilment. The phenomenon Marion has in mind is not reticent, not inadequate, not deficient. It is *le phénomène saturé*: the fulfilled or abundant phenomenon. Marion calls it saturated (*saturé*) because it does not need to be filled by intentionality. It is not lacking and needy; it is rich and saturated. 'Saturation' refers to abundance, but there is more to it than that. The saturated phenomenon abundantly shows itself *while* retiring from phenomenality. It blinds me, overriding my intentionality. This means it does not depend on my orientation or on my interpretation of it. According to Husserl, such a surplus is unthinkable.

Let me try to elucidate things. I am standing on the porch, dusk is falling and, slowly, I am becoming aware of a shape off in the distance. My imagination is supplementing the vague contours — I see an angry man — until I see things clearly: 'Oh, it is the garden hose, left out there by someone! Intuition failed me for a moment, unable to perceive the shape clearly and outright. Only partly comprised of intuition, the phenomenon 'hose' showed itself inadequately. 'Phenomenon' refers to the overall picture my mind ends up with. This implies fallibility: I see a man standing in the dark! (Actually, it is a garden gnome sitting on a mound). Another example: What about the phenomenality of the sun? Trying to look at it, my eyes inadvertently close and my hand comes up to cover my eyes; I turn away. But, in this case, intuition does not fail me. The phenomenon does not show itself inadequately. On the contrary, the phenomenality of the sun is characterised by a *surplus*: it blinds me; there is *too much* light. My intuition is not inadequate but is saturated. Examples such as these explain phenomenality in terms of light and visibility. However, a burning passion, for instance, might also show itself as a saturated phenomenon. In this case, the phenomenality is not about light or visibility but about love, attention, or affection itself. We can imagine that saturation is the complete fulfilment of my senses to the point of overflowing, like a river overflowing after heavy rains. Saturation, in this respect, exceeds limits and involves extravagance, excess. This excess is not only found in single phenomena, like the sun. A phenomenality that cannot be reduced to a purely intentional structure but is tributary to a non-phenomenal origin is, nonetheless, called 'saturated' by Marion. Phenomenological ideas such as Merleau-Ponty's Flesh (*La chair*), Michel Henry's Life (*La Vie*), or Levinas' *alterity* all have to do with saturated phenomenality. Derrida's difference (*différance*) is also saturated in so far as it refers to effects of textuality that cannot be reduced to subjectivity.

Obviously, the saturated phenomenon is not just an alternative to Husserl's 'deficient' phenomenon. Instead, the saturated phenomenon offers phenomenology its sole chance of survival. Marion has demonstrated that the deficient phenomenon renders phenomenology impossible. So the opposing question — whether a phenomenon characterised not by inadequacy but by a surplus of intuition might be possible — will have to be answered in the affirmative if phenomenology is to stand a chance. More significantly, the saturated phenomenon paves the way for a phenomenality that is capable of thinking the phenomenon of 'divine revelation'.

So far, a religious phenomenon can also be understood as a saturated phenomenon. As invisible, it overwhelms me like the sun I cannot, strictly speaking, see. This is why the three monotheistic religions have, to a large extent, rejected any representation of the divine ("Thou shalt not make images....") and banned all images of the holy. As recent as 2001, Cairo's influential Al-Azhar University would only allow the distribution of an animated cartoon about the life of the prophet Mohammed if the strict rules on religious representation were obeyed. As a result, the final script provided for a blinding light, playing the part of Mohammed. To the worshipper, Mohammed is a saturated phenomenon. But Marion does more than just describe the phenomenality of the saturated phenomenon. For him, *Christ* is the ultimate potential of, the limit to, the saturated phenomenon. What does he mean?

We recall that in *God without Being* Marion referred to Christ in accordance with Colossians 1:15 as the image of the invisible God. In contrast, the phenomenological methodology of *Being Given* cannot be based on such a christological *assumption*. In this text, Marion speaks on behalf of phenomenology. A phenomenological exposé, unlike a christological one, does not allow for Jesus Christ to be an indisputable theoretic paradigm. If Marion wants to commit (to) undiluted phenomenology, which is limited to what is given, he can presuppose neither God nor Christ. Phenomenology can only be based upon the givenness of the phenomenon itself. Simply claiming that the phenomenology of the divine 'is quite different' from the phenomenology of the rest of the world will not do. If the phenomenology of the divine 'is quite different', this is because, in intensity, the saturated phenomenon transcends other phenomena. For Marion, Christ is not the paradigm of a theology, but the paradigm of the phenomenon *'revelation'*.[34] How does Marion

[34] *Ibid.*, p. 329 [*Ibid.*, p. 237].

describe the revelation of Christ (which is not the revelation of theology but the revelation of *phenomenology*? The saturated phenomenon actually becomes manifest *in this revelation*. The saturated phenomenon is a *possibility* of phenomenology. Without this possibility, Marion's phenomenology would not be phenomenology at all but empirical science with God as its object. Without the saturated phenomenon, the phenomenological status of Marion's philosophy would wane. Therefore, Marion will not say that Christ shows himself to mankind; rather, Marion outlines a phenomenology with room for revelation. According to Husserl and Sartre, such phenomenality is *a priori* impossible. As a result, Marion will not claim that Christ is the *only* possible saturated phenomenon: Christ is the *ultimate* saturated phenomenon, the possibility that is itself saturated by the possibilities of saturation. The saturated phenomenon is not to be fixed, however, its phenomenological *possibility* needs to be demonstrated. The saturated phenomenon does not represent Christ, but it shows us the structure of God's appearance.

So, the 'saturated phenomenon' and the 'religious phenomenon' are not automatically the same. The saturated phenomenon is not exclusive to one single object or idea, as though God, alone, would naturally appear as a saturated phenomenon. The 'sublime', as formulated by Kant, for instance, also represents a saturated phenomenon. Instead of having the saturated phenomenon and the religious phenomenon coincide, in *Being Given* Marion seems to maintain that the ultimate in religious phenomena is the saturated phenomenon. If he is right, Marion has reached his goal. The phenomenon 'Christ' appears wholly phenomenologically without the help of all sorts of theological constructions. 'Christ' is a possible saturated phenomenon, not an intentional construction. Even better: the phenomenon 'Christ' is saturated with all possible saturation and is, therefore, the ultimate saturated phenomenon.

To get to this point, Marion has used a somewhat complicated metaphysical schedule borrowed from Kant who claimed such a schedule would befit all human knowledge (for the insiders: quantity-quality-relation-modality). Marion chooses this schedule, all-important in the history of modern thought, because he wants to show how the saturated phenomenon transcends it every time. Philosophically, the saturated phenomenon transcends Kant's painstaking demarcations. Therefore, neither metaphysics nor epistemology can capture the phenomenon that Marion is trying to describe. Kant's metaphysics offers four kinds of saturation. Taking Marion's phenomenology as a starting point, I will now proceed to describe two of these saturated phenomena: the 'idol' and the 'icon', and compare them with Marion's earlier definitions.

5a. The idol

Strikingly, the idol as a saturated phenomenon no longer directly opposes the icon, as it did in *God without Being*. Still, its actual characteristics have not changed. The idol carries a distinctive feature of the saturated phenomenon: it is fully visible, exceeds abundance, and, so, is fully saturated. The idol fulfils my intentionality (to the brim) and reflects a blinding light: intentionality brought to a head. 'Idol' is now only being used because of its phenomenological characteristics. In *Being Given*, its onto-theological connotation is dropped.

What do the phenomena 'Christ' and the 'idol' have in common in terms of saturation? They are both unbearable. Marion quotes Mark 9:2-3: "There he was transfigured before them. His clothes became dazzling white, whiter than anyone in the world could bleach them." Brought to a head, the visible is so intense that it blinds, becomes unbearable. The phenomenon 'Christ' is characterised by a phenomenological surplus. He is unbearable to us.

5b The icon

According to Marion, the saturated phenomenon is *irregardable*: it 'cannot be looked at'. From the description of the icon in *God without Being*, we understand that the icon, as a saturated phenomenon, looks at me, not the other way around. The phenomenon manifests itself independently. It cannot be objectified. Specifically, the saturated phenomenon invalidates the subjective conditions of experience and therefore cannot be constituted as an object. As a non-phenomenon, it does not disappear (as Kant would have it), but gives the *irregardable* part of itself. (Remember the sun: the fact that I cannot look straight at it does not mean that it is not there, that it does not give itself.) 'The saturated phenomenon' matches 'the phenomenon that will *not be reduced to our self*'. Again: it looks at me, not the other way around. It is the other, facing me, obscured, and invisible. Not surprisingly, Marion refers to Emmanuel Levinas here who has based his phenomenology on the face of the other. For Marion, this is the way Christ appears: He gazes at me, not the other way around. Recall the beautifully painted wooden panels depicting the holy, the lure of Christ facing the onlooker, the human gaze lost in the icon. In Western art, it was Dürer who first used this inverted gaze in painting his self-portraits.

But here, the icon refers to even more. All possible saturation, not just one or two modi, converges in the iconical Christ.

6. The paradox

Unlike *God without Being*, which mainly contains a description of onto-theology in both philosophy and theology, *Being Given* is undiluted phenomenology. The ultimate in saturated phenomena is Christ. But this does not prove that the saturated phenomenon 'Christ' is more than fulfilled intentionality, more than just an idol. But, again, Marion is not after such proof (unlike religion seeking the proof for the existence of God); he only wants to establish a possibility. It is possible for Christ to appear through the idol, beyond idolatry. Methodologically, Marion is no longer caught *between* philosophy and theology. The fact that the philosopher's God is 'quite different' from the God of the doctrine of divine revelation is no longer relevant. In fact, phenomenology's aim has become 'describing the phenomenality of the revelation'. The 'saturated phenomenon' has not been taken from theology in order to be, abruptly or gradually, inserted into phenomenology. It has become a figure of phenomenology itself.[35]

In *In Excess: Studies of Saturated Phenomena*, which follows *Being Given*, Marion develops his views on the four Kantian categories that inspired the notions of idol and icon. The title '*Du sucroît*' is equivocal. It not only means 'in excess' but also 'needless to say'. In these respects, it refers to the abundance of the saturated phenomenon, but the book also refutes some ignorant (according to Marion) commentary on *Being Given*. It comprises four separate papers, each treating a Kantian category, and two additional papers. The matter of Christ as possibly being the ultimate saturated phenomenon is approached aesthetically. For instance, the similarity between Dürer, Descartes, Rothko, and Levinas (apart from the fact that, to some degree, they keep turning up in Marion's work) is that their creations do justice to the human experience of God.

Marion constructs his philosophy by continually interrogating other philosophers. Despite the academic weight of his writings, theology is sensitive to his philosophies. Increasingly, Marion is considered to be an

---

[35] *Ibid.*, p. 326 [*Ibid.*, p. 234].

influential philosopher, especially because of his efforts to put ancient, theological views on the idol and the icon in a philosophical perspective, and because of his religious orientation towards phenomenology. But his thought and his work are also considered paradoxical. On the one hand, he ceaselessly demonstrates the inadequacy of Western philosophy, and even theology, to understand the self-willed appearance of God. On the other hand, he proves the possibility of such an appearance through that same philosophy and theology. Atheism's proposition that God's appearance is no more than a mirror image of human desires should not be opposed but explored in order for a phenomenology of the untainted gift to be feasible. However, even phenomenology cannot actually touch the ultimate appearance of God: another paradox. After all, phenomenology is about the structures of appearances; it is not a science about an object, *about that which appears*. Having God appear is not Marion's ultimate goal. Phenomenology offers a helping hand, but is not capable of solving the theological problems that accompany God's appearance. Again and again, methodical phenomenology forces itself to postpone theology in order to remain undiluted. Marion is not asking whether God is a phenomenon. He just wants to demonstrate a possibility of perception, untainted by the intentions of consciousness. His work, as fundamental phenomenology, shows a lasting affinity with Husserl.

There is still some more to be said about the paradoxical nature of Marion's thought. Unless willing to join his tête-à-tête with theology, philosophers familiar with the work of great twentieth-century phenomenologists like Husserl, Heidegger, Sartre, and Merleau-Ponty might find Marion quite annoying.

He meticulously develops a phenomenology of the saturated phenomenon, postponing the possibility of God's appearance and, yet, he obviously anticipates such a possibility: he *wants* the phenomenon 'Christ' to be possible. What is left, then, of Husserl's methodological atheism which was once so evident? What need is there, apart from the longing to face God, to have phenomenology renounce its methodological footing in intentionality and the phenomenological reduction? Perhaps Christ, the ultimate saturated phenomenon, is a result of thinking in bad faith (*mauvaise foi*). Absolutely nothing about the philosophy of the saturated phenomenon points directly and inevitably to the phenomenon 'Christ' (hence, Marion's emphasis on the possibility). Marion has first built his phenomenology and, only consequently, noticed its applicability to the phenomenon 'Christ'. Are we looking at a hidden Christian agenda? Are appearances deceptive after all? Does Marion conform to phenomenology's methodical atheism, *only* to gaze at the ultimate in saturated phenomena, Christ? Moreover, does this highly Christian *leit-motiv* also imply his giving up on the all-essential inter-religious debate? Does Christianity have exclusive rights here?

Any theologian that tries crossing the abyss that separates us from the gift of God using Marion's philosophy as a stepping stone will tumble down at the sight of Him and inadvertently destroy all that is *phenome-nological* about that philosophy. Why? Because by *idolising*, by fixing, our theologian has *completed the possibility*, turned it into an actuality. In my opinion, Marion's phenomenology of possibility is a phenome-nology of *hope* rather than crypto-theology. If theology is addressed at all, it is only in the context of a theology of hope. Marion will not show us God; he just makes sure there is room for God to show *Himself*! Thus, Marion emphasises the difference between appearance and per-ception. Something appearing does not *a priori* urge me to perceive it! There is a structural difference between *appearing* and *perceiving*.[36]

The saturated phenomenon is a paradox. The ambition of Marion's thought lies in his attempt to examine the paradox instead of avoid it. The paradox is structural and not to be shunned. The saturated phenom-enon does not appear univocally (*doxa*), but deviously (*para*). The satu-rated phenomenon does not result solely from the activity of my con-sciousness but has its own intentionality, oriented towards me. Like the idol and the icon, the saturated phenomenon is unlike the worldly phe-nomena my consciousness conjures up. The relation between self and phenomenon is reversed: a paradox. I am listening to some music. I may know the piece, I may have heard it before. When it touches me, it exe-cutes itself, unexpected, unanticipated. Listening to music, I think I am fully receptive, susceptible. I, listening, do not make the music but the music makes me.[37] I am not a subject but a witness (*témoin*). I testify to, but do not create, truth. This witness observes, approaches, and is sus-ceptible like no ordinary observer: a paradox. For Marion, only a phe-nomenology capable of reflecting on this paradox can be a prolegomena to a theo-phenomenology, doing justice to the self-willed appearance of God. Phenomenology itself, damaged, limited as it is by Marion's argu-ments on idolatry, will never be able to truly recognise God. Such is the paradox of God's appearance.

---

[36] *Ibid.*, p. 13ff [*Ibid.*, 7ff].; J.-L. Marion, *De sucroît. Etudes sur les phénomènes saturés*. Paris, Presses Universitaires de France, 2001, p. 35.

[37] J.-L. Marion, *Étant donné*, p. 302 [J.-L. Marion, *Being Given*, p. 216].

PHENOMENOLOGY, LITURGY, AND METAPHYSICS. THE THOUGHT OF JEAN-YVES LACOSTE

JOERI SCHRIJVERS

Jean-Yves Lacoste, a Parisian theologian and philosopher, has taught in Chicago, Tübingen and Cambridge, where he is permanent fellow of Clare Hall. His own works focus explicitly on phenomenological issues. His first book, *Note About Time. Essay on the Reasons of Memory and Hope (Note sur le temps. Essai sur les raisons de la mémoire et de l'espérance)* (1990), discusses the aporias one is confronted with when (absolute) signification or meaning derives from contingent historical conditions. *Experience and the Absolute (Expérience et Absolu)* (1994), his second book, engages in a thorough discussion with Heidegger. For Lacoste, between the Heideggerian 'world' and 'earth', there might be another possibility open to human beings: the possibility of faith, and of the liturgical experience. In his latest book, *The World and the Absence of the Work of Art (Le monde et l'absence d'œuvre)* (2000), a collection of articles written between 1994 and 1997, Lacoste explores this third possibility from the perspective of the experience of the work of art and the experience of resting.[1]

In this article I present Lacoste's *phenomenology of liturgy* — where liturgy is defined not only as the celebration of the Mass but, more generally, as the relation of men and women to God. Secondly, Lacoste's account of the work of art is developed. Thirdly, Lacoste's phenomenological analysis will be criticised by returning to Heidegger's understanding of being-in-the-world. This serves as an occasion to engage in a philosophical critique of Lacoste's description of the liturgical experience. This critique will open onto the question to what

---

[1] J.-Y. Lacoste, *Expérience et Absolu. Questions disputées sur l'humanité de l'homme.* Paris, Presses Universitaires de France, 1994. Abbreviated, in the text, as *EA*. The concluding section of this book is translated in: G. Ward (ed.), *The Postmodern God. A Theological Reader.* Oxford, Oxford University Press, 1997, pp. 249-264; J.-Y. Lacoste, *Le monde et l'absence d'œuvre et autres études.* Paris, Presses Universitaires de France, 2000 (Hereafter *MO*); J.-Y. Lacoste, *Note sur le temps. Essai sur les raisons de la mémoire et de l'espérance.* Paris, Presses Universitaires de France, 1990 (Hereafter *NT*). All translations are, unless otherwise noted, mine.

extent the liturgical experience is still determined by metaphysical views. Indeed, the suggestion is that 'the theological turn of French phenomenology'[2] might very well be yet another *ontotheological* turn. Broadly speaking, ontotheology is the enterprise that confuses finitude and infinity.[3] However, this confusion has its roots on the part of the finite, not on the side of the infinite itself. It is a finite being that proclaims to have found God. As Heidegger pointed out, ontotheology only surfaces within philosophy when thinking tries to think what it cannot think. 'God' will serve as a 'God of the gaps'. His name enters into the philosophical textbooks every time that thought is confronted with its limits. God is an instrument, *used* to save the system from its own contingency and incoherency. At the end of the chain of beings, there is 'God', as a beacon, a supreme being that liberates our attempts from futility. God ought to do what finitude cannot: He *must* be a foundation; He *must* be invoked to conceal the limits of thought — and yes, 'this is what we all call God'.

1. Lacoste, Heidegger and the Liturgical Experience.

As a phenomenologist, Lacoste inquires into humanity's *aptitude for experience*. In our modern age of nihilism with its virulent will to power and autonomous subjectivities, we have somehow lost a sense of wonder and found ourselves incapsulated within our world. In short, the modern subject values whatever he or she wills, whereas wonder only arises out of the recognition that our being, in one way or another, is open to a donation (of signification) from elsewhere.

This immanent worldview is precisely what Lacoste perceives in Heidegger. Heidegger, according to Lacoste, outlined the two basic experiences of human beings at the end of the millenium: on the one hand, the atheistic world, in which angst, death and care prevail, on the other, we experience serenity while dwelling upon the earth (*EA*, 7-27).

Experience, according to Lacoste, is founded upon our embodiment or, in his terms, our 'situatedness' or 'placedness' (*EA*, 7-9, 'localité'; 'avoir lieu'). Being human necessarily involves, because of our corporeality,

---

[2] Reference is to the title of Janicaud's critical work, *Le tournant théologique de la phénoménologie française*. Combas, Editions de l'éclat, 1991 [D. Janicaud, *Phenomenology and the "Theological Turn". The French Debate*. New York, Fordham University Press, 2000].

[3] For a more elaborate view on this, see the Introduction to this volume.

some kind of place. In this way, the 'world' and the 'earth' are possibilities that appear to our placedness. Inquiring into our aptitude for experience, Lacoste asks whether this aptitude is restricted to only these two transcendental experiences of world and earth. In fact, it is broader. Heidegger himself, in his analytic of *Dasein*, never judged experiences of friendship, for instance, to be inexistent. In and through care, we can be involved with others, albeit in an existentiel way. However, Lacoste wonders whether Heidegger overlooked the (ontological) importance of these existentiel experiences (*MO*, 82-83). According to Lacoste, human beings are not condemned to passively undergo the presence of the world and the earth. There is a certain freedom towards this transcendental constitution. Lacoste labels this freedom: *project* (*NT*, 27-30). Whereas the Heideggerian *care (Sorge)* is the existential (transcendental) relation towards the future, the *project*, for Lacoste, aims at the appropriation of this future. Take for example the preparation of a meal for some friends. If I want to invite some guests and welcome them to my dinner table, I will have to buy the necessary ingredients today. 'Today', the present, thus becomes an area of meaning, and the future, in a certain sense, is already now. 'My' future consists in preparing a meal for my friends tomorrow. The Heideggerian care prevents, precisely because of its inherent openness towards the future, the present from becoming the locus of meaning. But Lacoste makes the project consist in nothing other than this joyful present. In and through the projective appropriation of the future, that future becomes *mine* and, in this way, another genuine human possibility.

The liturgical experience is just such a project. In the same way that I can decide to prepare a meal for my friends, I can decide to direct my attention to God in prayer or in the Eucharist. However, for Lacoste, as a project, distinct from the Heideggerian care, liturgy involves a *transgression* of our being-in-the-world. Liturgy is a desire to see and experience God and to anticipate the future already prepared for us; liturgy is thus an anticipation of the Kingdom of God. Just as the project of preparing a meal is, here and now, experienced as a 'realised anticipation' of that future, liturgy anticipates our absolute future: it is *as if* God is present in prayer. Indeed, in a first moment, the liturgical experience conflates God's presence and God's proximity (*EA*, 75). How? Because

[4] Although Lacoste only considers the 'project' in *Note sur le temps*, it isn't difficult to notice the structure of the project in the liturgical experience of *Expérience et absolu*. Moreover, in *Expérience et absolu*, Lacoste explicitly denotes the liturgical experience as a project. See pp. 41, 194, 196 and 227.

liturgy can only be understood eschatologically, that is, it can only be understood from an absolute point of view. Lacoste points to the possibility of the (Hegelian) master and slave praying together. Indeed, my foes are never refused entrance to the church where I am praying. It is in this sense that the liturgy must be understood as a fragile realisation of the eschatological good (e.g. *EA*, 62).

However, we know that our projects are not always realised. Dinner can be postponed and my supposed mastery over the future is again confronted with its limits. The project, according to Lacoste, tends to forget that the future, in whatever way I may comport towards it, is always uncontrollable. That is why our projects are a kind of *divertissement*: the project tends to confuse its anticipation of the future with the future as such. In this way, the future is, from this moment forward, mistakenly understood as a project (*NT*, 39).

We don't pray if we don't believe God to be near. Therefore, the desire to see God risks some sort of impatience, even to the extent that one interprets the liturgy solely as a project — as if God is present whenever I want God to be present. Indeed, the *non-place* (e.g. *EA*, 34) evoked by liturgy, opens up a space wherein that which keeps us at a distance from God's coming — the 'world', the 'earth' and history — is placed between brackets. Not only does Lacoste remind us of the fact that the master and the slave praying together can only be understood eschatologically, he also points to the figures of the pilgrim and the hermit to make this liturgical non-place phenomenologically plausible (*EA*, 28-40). However, the liturgical non-time (*EA*, 101) and non-place of prayer is threatened by the weal and the woe of every project. Faith and prayer risk to interrupt being-in-the world to lose itself completely in the enthusiastic vision of God's kingdom.

Lacoste claims, however, that the liturgical experience is prevented from being merely a distraction, since the fact that people present themselves to God does not mean that God 'presents' himself to them. I present myself to God in prayer, and confess to be at God's disposal, but God does not present himself as the pages of this text present themselves. Therefore, the liturgy has to reckon with a *non-experience* (*EA*, 49-66). This non-experience has to be understood phenomenologically with reference to the logic of the sacraments and the church. While the believer desires to dwell in the kingdom, (s)he prays in Church. While he or she is eager to experience God, God is in the Church, absent to both perception and to affectivity. While faith relies on the eternity of the kingdom of God, the believer finds him- or herself in the *kairos* of .

the Church — every Sunday in Mass. Thus, between the believer and God always already stands the materiality and the historicity of worldly realities, for instance, in the *bread* that is broken and the *wine* that is shed. The plenitude of the eschatological enters this world in a fragile tension with a worldly phenomenon (*NT*, 198; *EA*, 112). The consequences of such a non-experience are twofold. On the one hand, the desire to see and 'experience' God, in other words the desire for an other-than-being, is sobered by this worldly appearance of the Absolute, by God's appearing *in* being. It is this that, according to Lacoste, appeals to the believer's *patience*: God will come, but not *because* you and I are praying (Cf. Mt. 24, 36). On the other hand, this non-experience summons the believer, precisely because of this worldly appearance, not to ignore his or her worldly *responsibilities*. The liturgical experience therefore takes on an ethical form as well. Liturgy is prevented from being a distraction, not only because of the appeal to the believer's patience, but also because of the fact that this logic of the church and of the non-experience is essentially a "reminder of our historiality" (*EA*, 112).[5] The believer's desire to experience God and the corresponding risk of losing oneself in enthusiastic contemplation of the kingdom is countered by the reference to the neighbour and to our historical responsibilities towards him or her: "No one can participate in the logic [of the liturgy], without being instructed that our neighbour too possesses a sacramental dignity" (*NT*, 213). However, this ethical element need not necessarily be restricted to the human other. Since the logic of the liturgy is not only a relation between God and humankind, but also the relation of God to the world and to the cosmos, one can easily imagine how the liturgical experience instructs us of our ecological responsibilities as well (*EA*, 224-225)![6]

Thus, the non-experience is, according to Lacoste, best conceived of as a *kairos* that allows the liturgy to be, instead of a distraction, a *conversion*. Indeed, it takes *faith* to recognize, in these worldly realities, the presence of God. The believer's conversion consists in the confession that, whatever his or her eagerness to experience God may be, this eagerness does not oblige God to present himself. Once again, the enthusiastic desire to be near God needs to be brought to crisis and summoned

[5] Compare J.-Y. Lacoste, *Note sur le temps*, p. 193.

[6] The translation in *The Postmodern God. A Theological Reader* reads: "And because the reconciliation of God and humankind is also the reconciliation of God with the cosmos, the liturgical relation of humanity and God cannot annul the links of knowledge, mastery, or transfiguration that humankind maintains with the cosmos", p. 257.

to patience. It is precisely this discrepancy between men's intention to experience God and the non-experience or God's refusal to satisfy that desire, that alerts the liturgical project to its limits. The project, be it liturgical or otherwise, resembles modern, autonomous subjectivity. As divertissement, it refuses to open itself to that which gives itself, it is no longer aware of its precarious nature and understands itself as an autonomous affair. The project of modern subjectivity consists in the refusal to see signification as a gift or as given. This subjectivity, Lacoste contends in *Experience and the Absolute*, undergoes a *decentering* only in the liturgy, since only in the encounter with the Ab-solute the autonomy of the subject is interrupted. The ethical aspect of the liturgical experience illustrates this well. According to Lacoste, the ethical endeavour *does* encounter, in this world, an absolute imperative — the appeal to do good everywhere and always (*NT*, 49-51; *EA*, 80-85). However, this appeal, discovered in and through being-in-the-world, needs the interruption of the liturgical experience with the world to interpret the ethical exigencies correctly. One could object, of course, that one need not be liturgical in order to be ethical. But, according to Lacoste, this would miss the point of the decentering of the subject intended by the liturgical experience. Left to itself, ethics can only respond to the absolute appeal in its own way. In its claim to know how one should respond to the absolute appeal, it would construct the signification of this appeal as it construes its projects: autonomous, and reluctant to integrate other points of view. In this way, the door is open for totalitarianism and ethics would, accordingly, dissolve into terror. On a more personal level, the interruption of the liturgical experience would distinguish between an ethics that serves my own interests and an ethics that is truly a 'being for the other' in which the sacramentality of the neighbour can be respected. Ethics thereby becomes a 'second liturgy' (*EA*, 90). However, the relation between ethics and liturgy remains somewhat ambiguous. For we all know that the subordination of ethics to a liturgical experience can amount to a terror of the religious itself. In Lacoste's words, the believer always already must counter the suspicion that he or she "is unable to exist in the world in a humane manner" (*EA*, 83). Therefore, ethics is not only a second liturgy, but also its first critic (a.o. *EA*, 68)

How, then, is modern subjectivity interrupted? Over and against the autonomy and the activity of the modern project Lacoste posits the *radical passivity* of the liturgical experience. Modern subjectivity undergoes a crisis (*NT*, 194) and is exhausted (*EA*, 226) by the fact that what it wills and desires, i.e. the absolute future of the kingdom of God, does not present itself. The liturgy is a transgression of every aptitude for experience where consciousness disposes of (*EA*, 183). The non-experience is, therefore, a crisis of intentionality—if intentionality is defined as consciousness *of*, then it is this 'of' that is placed between brackets when people expose themselves to God in prayer. Thus the believer lives in an empty present and a dead time (*EA*, 178). Liturgy manifests the margins of being-in-the-world. *Dasein* relates to the liturgical beingthere, as acting relates to non-acting, sensing to non-sensing, experience to non-experience. If one would want to speak of intentionality in the case of the liturgical experience one should say that the believer in this experience becomes the object of God's intention: whereas people understand themselves as aiming at God intentionally, they stand before God as a *soul*. This concept of the soul must not be confused with its medieval counterpart: the liturgy contaminates the transcendental constitution of subjectivity by suggesting that, for both the intersubjective relations and for the relation *coram Deo*, our embodiment serves as a more appropriate paradigm (*EA*, 187). We are exposed to God and the other in our corporeality and not primarily as a 'thinking thing'. This is the essence of the liturgical experience: liturgy is putting oneself at the disposal of God (*EA*, 182), a consenting to deliver my being into God's hands (*EA*, 188). Lacoste conceives of the being of the religious person as a being that neither desires nor acts and thereby is forced into a 'position' where (s)he can only receive. What is given, in prayer and in the Eucharist, is the *confirmation* of my project to be at God's disposal. Recall that the liturgical experience is a non-experience: it is an abandoning of my desiring, projecting and experiencing self that eventually can amount to boredom (*EA*, 179). It is exactly this abandoning of self, which is confirmed by the Word of God that one hears in the Eucharist. Indeed, in praying and celebrating the believer embodies a passivity that precedes every conscious act; liturgy is the recognition of our status as *creatures.* The liturgical confrontation with God obliges one to acknowledge that being always is being given, whether we direct ourselves towards being in a projective manner or not. This confirmation and incarnation is, in Lacoste's opinion, the *eschatological* truth of our being-there (*EA*, 208-210). The truth of our being is our kenotic emptying of ourselves for an other. Only an other can speak words of confirmation over our being. In this way, the liturgy is a conversion, an *imitatio Christi*.

Since the Eucharist and prayer are not only instances that remind the believer of creation, but also recall Christ's words and deeds, they are at the same time the *kairos* within which the believer contemplates the Resurrection as the accomplishment of earthly life. It is Christ who offers us the eschatological mode of our being-there: Christ's obedience towards the will of His Father eventually led him to the Cross.[7] It is this abandoning of self that, in the Eucharist, is proposed as the accomplishment of earthly life. Correspondingly, the believer is invited to live his or her life according to a will to power-lessness (*EA*, 197-201). Liturgical experience is essentially that experience in which human beings renounce their status as *Dasein* or (modern) subject to gain a total passivity in which the manner of our being-there is revealed or given to us. Again, what is given to the believer in the Eucharist, is a way of being-there faithful to a vocation. In the Eucharist, the believer is given to him- or herself as that being that has to be its vocation: he or she is revealed to him- or herself as the being that is called and promised to a being as (the being of) Christ.

Lacoste's description of this liturgical and ethical passivity deserves special attention. There are two instances in which he elaborates on this decentering of modern subjectivity. The first, already cited, states that the liturgical experience suggests that, for the relation 'coram Deo', our embodiment serves as a more appropriate paradigm (*EA*, 187; 45-48). However, Lacoste goes on to say that of this liturgical passivity, "it is not totally wrong to affirm that the objective dimension of [this] being-before-God is more radical still than that of the carnal presence before God, an objectivity, moreover, that is akin to that of the thing — one can say that the believer is in the hands of God as the clay [...] is in the hands of the potter" (*EA*, 188).[8]

   Thus, far from being a genuine decentering of modern subjectivity, the liturgical experience turns out to be a simple inversion of the terms that constitute this subjectivity. Instead of encountering and exercising my power over objects, I discover myself as a powerless object in relation to God, conceived of as (supreme?) Subject. This inversion will be criticised more in detail below, but first I will present Lacoste's more recent works.

[7] On Christ's status as a servant, see J.-Y. Lacoste, *Note sur le temps*, pp. 169-183, pp. 202-207.

[8] Compare J.-Y. Lacoste, *Expérience et Absolu*, p. 182 and Idem, *Note sur le temps*, p. 171.

2. Lacoste's Later Works: Liturgy and the Work of Art.

The reader, perhaps, is wondering whether the liturgy is the only experience that grants access to the truth of our being. The truth of our being is, theologically speaking, that kenotic emptying of ourselves that lays no claim whatsoever upon either being or God and that involves passively awaiting donation of signification from elsewhere.[9] Philosophically, it means the recognition that being, no matter what projects we are involved in, is always already being-given. Indeed, the way of life proposed by liturgical experience is *ascesis,* a voluntary choice for poverty. Lacoste asserts that only such a poverty is faithful to our ontological condition, in which death will, in any case, dispossess us of all property (*EA,* 207-213). However, to this philosophical truth of our being we are granted access, the reader will recall, when we distance ourself from the (Heideggerian) being-in-the-world. At the time of *Experience and the Absolute,* Lacoste was convinced that the liturgical experience was the only experience capable of subverting our being-in-the world. However, that changed when *The World and the Absence of the Work of Art* was published.

In this book Lacoste points to two experiences that are, in one way or another, similar to the liturgical experience: the experience of the work of art and the experience of resting.[10] The *work of art* liberates human beings from their involvement with world and earth because it puts the appearance of every phenomenon other than itself between brackets. The work of art calls for our undivided attention and its appearance is to be understood with reference to the joy and the rest that it produces. Art promises and delivers an unconcerned present. Over and against the care for the future, the work of art offers a joyful constitution of the present.

---

[9] 'From elsewhere' means, of course, that I do not conceive of myself as the source of meaning, as would do modern subjectivity. In my *Jean Yves Lacoste: A Phenomenology of Liturgy,* which will be published in *Heythrop Journal* (July, 2005), I take this to be the occasion to speak of a correlational theology in Lacoste: the liturgical poverty, a poverty towards God, co-relates to an ontological poverty, in which I confess myself to be powerless towards my finitude.

[10] For the experience of resting, one can consult: J.-Y. Lacoste, En marge du monde et de la terre: l'aise. In: Idem, *Le monde et l'absence d'œuvre,* pp. 3-22. In this paragraph an interpretation is given of two texts of Lacoste, which can best be read together: J.-Y. Lacoste, Le monde et l'absence d'œuvre. In: Idem, *Le monde et l'absence d'œuvre,* pp. 55-106, and J.-Y. Lacoste, The Work and Complement of Appearing. In: J. Bloechl (ed.), *Religious Experience and the End of Metaphysics.* Indianapolis, Indiana University Press, 2003, pp. 68-93.

The experience of *resting* is similar: take, for instance, the pause we take from our work. This interruption, however, does not mean that I am no longer 'there'. It does mean, on the other hand, that my 'being there' is no longer determined by the Heideggerian world and earth, even though I rest in the world and on the earth. Instead, a certain calmness and joy determine my 'being there', which Lacoste calls the 'being-well-there' (*MO*, 19). I know that this pause cannot last forever and that I soon will have to be concerned with my work once again. During such interruption, Lacoste states, I am content but in no means satisfied (*ibid*). I still have to *care* about my work or my life but these concerns are temporarily put between brackets. Pause is neither more nor less than the quiet enjoyment of a between (world and earth). What is at stake in 'resting' is the real, albeit fragile, unconcerned-ness wherein world and earth are kept at a distance. My place of resting is the place where I dwell. Thus, *Dasein's not-being-at-home (Unzu-hause)* is not relevant to understand this experience. But neither does my resting place remind me of my roots in the Heideggerian 'earth'. The experience of resting must be conceived of as an excess and transgression of the transcendental expressions of our being human, *Dasein* and *mortals*. Lacoste concludes that the experience of resting must be conceived of as a *sabbathic experience* (*MO*, 21). Resting reminds one of the rest of creation and finds, as its theological equivalent, the pause that God took after creation. Hence, one is thankful for this resting, a time in which everything was 'good, very good'.

It is through his analysis of the experience of the work of art that Lacoste develops his *ontology of affectivity*, through which, in turn, his criticism of Heidegger gains significance. Let us start with Lacoste's conclusion: the appearance of the work of art confronts one with the mere *possibility* of the 'world' and the 'earth'. Why? Lacoste's question is: how do we *know* the existence of the world and earth? It is not perception that instructs us of their existence. In *Being and Time*, Heidegger pointed to angst as that occasion where our being-in-the-world can be noticed. Neither is the 'earth' an object of perception. For instance, Heidegger introduced the earth, using Van Gogh's painting of a peasant's pair of shoes as an example. However, it is not what the work of art shows, i.e. the 'shoes' as such, but what the work of art makes appear, i.e. the 'earth', that is important. Thus, 'world' and 'earth' are horizons without which we wouldn't perceive or undertake anything whatsoever. This is the reason why Lacoste proposes that, to understand Heidegger's lecture on art correctly, one must return to Heidegger's

earlier insight that it is only through affectivity that we know what it
is to be.[11]

This, however, raises another problem: is it *necessary* that we feel the
presence of the 'earth' whenever we contemplate, for instance, Van
Gogh's painting? Surely not. Consider two theses. Affectivity is passive.
No matter how eagerly one wants to see the painting of Van Gogh after
reading Heidegger, for example, there is no guarantee that one will
effectively *see* the painting as a work of art. One cannot control one's
affective life: it is possible that one wanders through a museum unatten-
tively and uninterested. Moreover, according to a thesis which Lacoste
takes from Derrida, the latter being inspired by the art historian Shapiro,
the shoes on the painting of Van Gogh were not the shoes of a peasant,
as Heidegger argued, but, on the contrary those of a city-dweller.[12]

All this, according to Lacoste, leads to the following conclusion: to
see the work of art *as* a work of art, implies that, at the very least, one
has *seen* the work of art. Inevitably, therefore, a certain subject is
involved in the interpretation of the work of art. Thus, although Heidegger in his tract took great pains to avoid the return of aesthetics, and the
corresponding distinction between a subject that stands over and against
an object of art, one cannot deny that a certain subject enters into his
interpretation. A simple syllogism illustrates this: a) to perceive the
work of art as a work of art, it has to exercise a certain power over us;
b) that power does not always occur. Conclusion: to give an interpretation of the work of art as a work of art, or even to speak of it, presupposes that at least one *saw* the work of art and that one was *affected
by it*.

Derrida's comment on Van Gogh's painting leads Lacoste to a second
conclusion: Heidegger's rather rural interpretation of the earth does not
necessarily arise from the perception of this particular work of art. On

---

[11] Of course, Lacoste is conscious of the fact that Heidegger, in *Der Ursprung des
Kunstwerkes*, is not concerned with the question of affectivity and that what he, Lacoste,
is proposing is absent from the letter of the text. However, there are hints of it in Heidegger's text that make Lacoste's proposal not so awkward altogether. Cf. M. Heidegger,
The Origin of the Work of Art. In: Idem, *Basic Writings*. London, Routledge, 1994,
pp. 139-212, p. 151: "Perhaps, however, what we call feeling or mood, here and in similar instances, is more reasonable — that is, more intelligently perceptive — because
more open to Being than all that reason which, having meanwhile become *ratio*, was mis-
interpreted as being rational". In the German text, see M. Heidegger, *Der Ursprung des
Kunstwerkes*. Stuttgart, Reclam, 1970, p. 18.

[12] Cf. J. Derrida, Restitutions. On the Truth in Painting. In: Idem, *The Truth in Painting*. Chicago, Chicago University Press, 1987, pp. 255f.

the contrary, one has to take into account a diversity of affective answers to the work of art. Indeed, other determinations of my affective answer to the work of art are equally possible: contemplating the shoes on Van Gogh's painting, I could be reminded of my finitude, or, using Lacoste's formula, of "the pathetic fate of the mortal of whom there remains for us only a pair of shoes".[13]

If this is the case, then the question must be asked to what sort of a realm or horizon the work of art draws us. According to Lacoste, determining the affective answer to the work of art as an experience of the 'earth' is and *can* only be a partial determination of the excessive presence that overwhelms us when perceiving a work of art. However, if that presence instructs us about what it means to be, then a return to those Heideggerian concepts that think that which is real for human beings is inevitable. Indeed, the all too apparent finitude of our being-in-the-world cannot be ignored and, of course, we all are in some way rooted in the earth. However, these concepts have their origin in one's affective life and this affectivity always suffers from a partiality towards just that which it tries to determine conceptually. Hence Lacoste's hypothesis: the rupture of the work of art makes one enter into a realm where one is confronted with the mere possibility of the appearance of the world and the earth. From this, one must conclude that, in one way or another, affectivity is *older* than, or, at least "richer than the constitutions in which it takes its form" (*MO*, 101). The attraction of the artwork interrupts the Heideggerian being-in-the-world and delivers us into "the moving outline of a field"[14] (of which) and in which free, but always partial, affective constitutions, deconstitutions and reconstitutions succeed one another without deciding which constitution is the most original (Cf. *MO*, 97; 101). The experience of the work of art is an experience of "the limits of the world and forces one to admit that our aptitude for experience in fact exceeds our aptitude for experiencing the world" (*MO*, 101).

Thus, in his later works, Lacoste acknowledges that the liturgical experience is not the only experience that can manifest a rupture with being-in-the-world. The rupture of the work of art shows that an interruption of being-in-the-world does not necessarily coincide with an experience of the earth. In the encounter with the work of art human beings discover an affective freedom towards their transcendental make-up. One

---

[13] J. Y. Lacoste, The Work and the Complement of Appearing, p. 84.
[14] Ibid., p. 84.

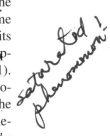

can see just how experiences such as friendship or love which, like the work of art, presuppose a joyful constitution of the present, become ontologically significant. Equally, the liturgical experience, with its inherent possibility of the master and the slave praying together, presupposes such an interruption amounting to a joyful present (e.g. *EA*, 71). From the fact that such an interruption is now considered to be philosophically legitimate, one can infer that the liturgical experience, at the *margins* of the world, also receives ontological significance) The somewhat Barthian depiction of this experience in *Experience and the Absolute* is corrected and can now be co-related to the experience of the work of art and to that of resting.

3. How (not) to Interrupt Being-in-the-World? Heidegger.

What can we make of all this? The reader familiar with Heidegger's works surely will wonder whether Lacoste's endeavour is not, from the outset, condemned by Heidegger in *Being and Time*. Indeed, we need to examine whether an interruption of being-in-the-world, for Heidegger, is possible at all. What precisely is 'being-in-the-world'? First of all, it is *not*, as Lacoste tells us, the thinking of our placedness (*EA*, 7-11). The reader should note that speaking of a place as the primordial fact of being human immediately refers to a place *in* the world, which is the same as saying that people conceive of themselves as over and against a world. Lacoste thus seems to understand *Dasein* not as a 'being-in', as Heidegger would, but as a 'being-in something', which Heidegger reserves for the being of entities at hand, as water is in a glass.[15] Such an opposition of humankind and world is precisely what Heidegger wanted to overcome with his analytic of *Dasein*, since "there is no such thing as the 'side-by-side-ness' of an entity called 'Dasein' with another entity called 'world'".[16]

As *Dasein*, men and women do not conceive of themselves as subjects wandering about in a world. It is as *Dasein* that we work in our house and, for instance, wound us with a hammer.[17] This is what Heidegger calls *concern* (*Besorgen*). This ontological and non-ethical *Besorgen* does not notice 'objects' in the world. The subject-object distinction

---

[15] Cf. M. Heidegger, *Being and Time*. Oxford, Basil Blackwell, 1967, p. 79-80
[16] Ibid., p. 81.
[17] For the famous example of the hammer, see Ibid., p. 98-99.

arises on a wholly other level. Take, for example, playing the guitar. While playing the guitar, i.e. care involved with things which are ready-to-hand, one doesn't reflect on the chords and on the corresponding finger settings. The guitar only becomes an object (present-at-hand) for a thinking, reflecting, subject when one, while playing, starts reflecting on these settings. But, and this is Heidegger's point, then one is not playing anymore — in fact, one can no longer play —: the (retreat of the) world and our *Besorgen* appears.

By now, it should be clear: *according to Heidegger an interruption of our being-in-the-world is impossible.* Even the (priest celebrating mass) would, for him, fundamentally, be involved in a caring relation with his world. Thus, *Dasein* is his world; it is not in the world. Again, my contention is that Lacoste's neglect of this prevents him from thinking a decentering of the subject in the liturgical experience. The liturgical experience, whether or not one calls it a 'non-place' (*EA*, 34), presupposes our place as a place over and against a world. That is why the liturgical experience cannot escape the language that opposes a subject to an object. We have already seen that modern subjectivity is reversed into its opposite: instead of being a subject-before-God, the liturgical experience turns the believer into an object before God. However, should not an attempt to think such a 'decentering' try to overcome the subject-object opposition? Perhaps there needs to be thought an openness and relation to God that does not neglect Heidegger's accomplishments in phenomenology.

4. Otherwise-than-Being or Being, but Otherwise?

One could wonder, of course, if such a phenomenology of liturgy is still phenomenology or, rather, whether one must sweep away attempts like these, since they entail a 'theological turn of French phenomenology'. According to this latter statement, phenomenology of the kind Lacoste proposes is, in one way or another, unfaithful to the basic atheistic presuppositions of the phenomenology Husserl envisioned. (Phenomenology and theology should not be confused.) In a recent commentary on Lacoste's work, Jean Greisch expresses a similar reluctance.[18] Is a phenomenology of the liturgy capable of describing what happens when

---

[18] J. Greisch, *Le buisson ardent et les lumières de la raison. L'invention de la philosophie de la religion. Tome 2: Les approches phénoménologiques et analytiques.* Paris, Cerf, 2002, pp. 266-291, pp. 283-284.

consciousness is stripped of its basic characteristic? Can one still speak of phenomenology when the decentering of the subject amounts to a consciousness that can no longer be depicted as 'consciousness of'?

But should one not take an attempt as that of Lacoste at face value, i.e. as a theologian who elaborates on faith in a phenomenological manner. The non-experience of the liturgy could then be understood by philosophers as well: one needs neither faith nor theology to see that in Church nothing happens. The faithful leave the church unchanged.[19] Furthermore, Lacoste would admit that, from a philosophical point of view, this non-experience is an atheistic experience (*EA*, 177; 181). A phenomenology of liturgy results from the confrontation of the phenomenological gaze with the being-there of the believer. It is in this sense that a phenomenology of liturgy does not markedly differ from a phenomenology of labour. The phenomenological method can be applied to whatever region of human activity one wills.

However, Lacoste does not only envisage this non-experience from a philosophical point of view. To interpret this non-experience as an *imitatio Christi*, surely invokes theological reasons. But is all theological reasoning, from the outset, excluded from philosophical rationality? If one takes the phenomenology of liturgy at face value, i. e. as the confrontation of the phenomenological gaze with the life of the believer, are we not in a better position to evaluate the phenomenological accomplishments of Lacoste's endeavour? After all, one should pay close attention to the relation between the world, which can be approached phenomenologically, and the liturgical experience, which is, according to its critics, theological and therefore not accessible in a phenomenological manner. The liturgical experience, according to Lacoste, is not a flight into otherworldliness, it is, on the other hand, an experience in which the presence of the world is felt more vividly than ever (*EA*, 88; 175). The liturgical experience is affected by the condition in which it arises: "Even the eucharistic gift, in which the Absolute takes place here and now, is conditioned by the interposition of the world. To say that this presence is 'real', does not make it diaphanic or theophanic. This interposition is obvious in an ontic manner: it must be detected in the materiality of bread and wine. But these ontic realities carry with them the ontological density of the world" (*EA*, 112). This is neither an 'otherwise than being' (Levinas) nor a 'god without being' (Marion);

---

[19] J.-Y. Lacoste, Sacrements, Ethique, Eucharistie. In: *Revue Thomiste* 84 (1984) pp. 212-242, esp. pp. 227-228.

this is being 'but otherwise'. The relation of men and women to God is, according to Lacoste, always already contaminated by being. Believers celebrate in the world and the liturgical experience never stops reminding them precisely of this world. This is the reason why this liturgical experience can be depicted phenomenologically. It is the description of that what happens when I bless myself with the holy water when entering the church[20]: "it is as men of flesh and blood that we approach the Absolute. As men of flesh and blood, it is our body, praying with the hands crossed, kneeled down or with the palms of the hand wide open to receive the *sancta*, that phenomenalises the relation coram".[21] What happens in Church and in the liturgical experience is, as Greisch correctly argues, "the projection of a different light on the phenomena of the world, an invitation to envisage them differently".[22] Such a change of perspective need not be irrational. On the contrary, it is an 'other thinking' ('pensée autre') that attempts to explain its attachment to and its embeddedness in a tradition in a rational way.[23]

It is this explanation that severs from phenomenology, not the liturgical experience as such. Faith, in the liturgical experience, amounts to just such a change of perspective. Lacoste's works, certainly his most recent one's, all aim to describe just how such a change of horizon can be effectuated. Heidegger's being-in-the-world may not be interrupted, it must, on the other hand, not be understood as depicting the totality of human existence, the totality of our 'aptitude for experience'.[24] Lacoste points to a freedom towards our transcendental constitution. Heidegger's 'world' and 'earth', finitude and sacrality, may be always present, knowledge thereof is affective. Therefore, according to Lacoste, the human exceeds *Dasein*.[25] Lacoste's inquiry into our affective life aims at understanding how such a change of horizons can be achieved. Faith involves a change of horizons: instead of perceiving and existing in an immanent world and earth, faith is the endeavour to

[20] The point is taken from Greisch, *Le buisson ardent,* p. 269.

[21] J.-Y. Lacoste, La connaissance silencieuse. Des évidences antéprédicatives à une critique de l'apophase. In: *Laval théologique et philosophiques* 58 (2002) pp. 137-153, p. 147.

[22] J. Greisch, *Le buisson ardent*, p. 269. My translation.

[23] *Ibid.,* p. 269 and 274.

[24] The reader is reminded that Heidegger, throughout his life, regretted that *Being and Time* was interpreted anthropologically.

[25] Just as Lacoste wonders why the work of art is absent from *Being and Time*, he wonders why the book never speaks of 'man' ('l'homme') but only of *Dasein*, cf. J.-Y. Lacoste, *Le monde et l'absence d'oeuvre*, p. 74.

see world and earth within the horizon of the absolute future of God's promise.

It is within this horizon of faith that believers discover their ineradicable attachment to being. And it is here that opinions differ. According to Lacoste, this embeddedness causes one to wonder to what extent the change of horizons effected in faith hints at a truth prior to the decision to believe. Indeed, theologically, faith must be considered as a gift or as a grace — it is a transgression of the transcendental conditions of being human that, therefore, cannot be reduced to these conditions (e.g. *EA*, 24-27) and the recognition that my auto-conversion (my decision to believe) might point to a hetero-conversion (faith as gift of God). This, one could say, is the temporal mode of procedure of faith: it is through faith that the subject comes to believe in a God who first gave me to be, in God as Creator.[26] This insight only subsequently throws a different light upon being. Only now being appears to be, in Lacoste's words, "pre-eschatological" (*EA*, 168). The term already indicates that it awaits its fulfilment: being and its projects are *only* sketches of signification. They do not know that of which they are a sketch (*NT*, 84). This presupposes, of course, both that the attachment to being can be overcome and that theology knows how this is to be done. The liturgical experience, therefore, remains trapped in what it wanted to reject: the desire to see and experience God. Indeed, this desire for a full-presence of God is never left altogether, it is only postponed: *patience* is the liturgical virtue par excellence (*EA*, 111). Thus, there seems to be in the works of Lacoste a certain metaphysical nostalgia towards God's full-presence and an immediate experience thereof. According to deconstructionists, on the other hand, the attachment to being cannot be subordinated to a time or a place in which this attachment (to being, to materiality, to the body) would be undone. They would undoubtedly object to Lacoste both that it is not at all sure whether our projects are to be conceived of as *sketches* of a signification that will reveal, give and present itself more fully and that it is uncertain whether these sketches are sketches of a *signification* at all. The first objection would correspond to Derrida's line of reasoning[27], the second would follow Heidegger in pointing to people's 'thrownness' (*Geworfenheit*): behind every signification stands the mute fact of being-thrown into the world.

---

[26] The point is taken from L.P. Hemming, *Heidegger's Atheism. The Refusal of a Theological Voice*. Indianapolis, Indiana University Press, 2002, p. 50.

[27] Cf. R. Sneller's article on Derrida in this volume.

5. Conclusion.

One might wonder whether this metaphysical nostalgia lies at the origin
of the already indicated recurrence of the subject-object distinction.
Indeed, the liturgical experience throws a different light upon being. The
question, of course, is what such a different perspective on the phenomena of the world amounts to. Within the horizon of a longing for God's
full-presence, being is almost automatically understood as a hindrance
and an obstacle for people's relation to God. According to Lacoste,
being — being-in-the-world — stands between God and humankind
(e.g. *EA*, 50). It is, therefore, *in* the liturgical experience that being is
conceived of negatively: only if one assumes that an eschatological
presence of God will liberate the liturgical experience from its (worldly)
constraints, being as such appears as a sketch or even as "a facticity that
cannot interpret itself" (*NT*, 84). One could object that this is the point
where a phenomenology of liturgy leaps into metaphysics: it is no
longer the description of the life of the believer, celebrating in a world,
that matters, it is its overcoming that ought to be the ultimate goal of this
relation to God. Whilst it need not be problematic to believe in God's
coming, it remains to be considered whether this coming can and must
be inscribed as the 'telos' of the relationship between humankind and
God. Surely, if this goal is defined as that which, ultimately, surpasses
the worldly conditions of faith, then, of course, such a goal could only
be achieved at the expense of precisely those conditions. Thus, within
the liturgical experience a metaphysical move must be detected: in re-
inscribing an otherworldliness as the *telos* of faith professed in a world.
This move, as already indicated, returns in the description of the liturgical experience. Whereas, at first, it is suggested that for the liturgical
experience our embodiment serves as the appropriate paradigm, Lacoste
immediately goes on to say that this liturgical passivity resembles the
passivity of an object towards a subject (*EA*, 188). Thus, the negative
light thrown upon being, suspected to be a hindrance for the relation to
God, finds its pendant in a negative light thrown upon our embodiment:
the body must be detached of itself to become an object.

 In *Experience and the Absolute*, the decentering of modern subjectivity amounts to a simple inversion of the terms. This inversion of, for
instance, intentionality, of course, remains trapped in that which it tried
to overcome; whereas the project's divertissement consisted in the
refusal to see signification as given, a refusal that results in seeing the
future as the (controllable) object of my intention, the solution Lacoste

proposes still adheres to the problem it wanted to resolve: God's gaze upon human beings is equivalent to the projective gaze of human beings towards objects. It may be no longer people that exercise power and control over objects, it is God who, *like* a modern subject, encounters nothing other than objectivity.

Could the relation between men and women to God be described otherwise? Is it possible to think the relation of men and women to God as an encounter between *singularities*, i.e. as free and embodied agents? Should we, perhaps, not turn to Levinas, to undertake such an endeavour? After all, it is Levinas who seems to be well aware of the problem we tried to describe throughout this article. According to Levinas, the signification that arises in the encounter with otherness, is not a signification by relation to another term.[28] The face of the other signifies of itself. This otherness, therefore, cannot and must not be described as, to use Lacoste's words, a sketch of signification relating to a full-presence of that signification. If relationality is depicted in this way, 'relationship', according to Levinas, is conceived of theoretically, i. e. logically or dialectically, and thought remains in the onto(theo)logical and metaphysical "objectivity characteristic of relations".[29] To Levinas' mind, such a relationality always strips at least one of the terms of the relationship of its singularity. Hence Levinas' attempt to think the other as other by means of a "defense of subjectivity".[30] Thus, Levinas' conception of a 'relation without relation' seems to counter the problems one can perceive in the works of Lacoste, wherein God's subjectivity is conceived of in relation to the objectivity of the believer's body.

Therefore, with regard to Lacoste, the question is not whether God feels at home in France, but whether men and women are at ease with this 'French' God.[31] After all, is not this 'God' that turns me into an object in the face of God, once again the Sartrean God/other who *cannot* do anything other than objectivise me?

---

[28] E. Levinas, *Totalité et Infini. Essai sur l'extériorité.* La Haye, Martinus Nijhoff, 1974⁴ [E. Levinas, *Totality and Infinity. An Essay on Exteriority.* Pittsburgh, Duquesne University Press, 2002, 1979, p. 261].

[29] E. Levinas, *Autrement qu'être ou au-delà de l'essence.* La Haye, Martinus Nijhoff, 1974, [E. Levinas, *Otherwise Than Being or Beyond Essence.* Pittsburgh, Duquesne University Press, 2002, 1981, p. 82].

[30] E. Levinas, *Totality and Infinity*, p. 26.

[31] See the Introduction to this volume.

Theodore de Boer (1932) studied classical philology, philosophy, and theology at the Free University of Amsterdam and the Catholic University of Louvain. He received a PhD in Philosophy at the University of Utrecht in 1966. From 1968 until 1992 he was professor of philosophical anthropology at the University of Amsterdam; from 1992 until 1997 he was professor of systematic philosophy at the Free University of Amsterdam. He is a member of the Institut International de Philosophie, Paris. Among his numerous publications are: *The Development of Husserl's Thought* (1978); *Foundations of a Critical Psychology* (1983); *The Rationality of Transcendence. Studies in the Philosophy of Emmanuel Levinas* (1997).

Johan F. Goud (1950) is Remonstrant minister in The Hague, and lecturer of cross-cultural theology at the Theological University Kampen. He holds a special chair in philosophical theology from the Perspective of Liberal Christianity at Utrecht University. His publications include: *Levinas en Barth: een Godsdienstwijsgerige en Ethische Vergelijking* (1984 diss. Leiden; German translation 1992); *God als Raadsel. Peilingen in het Spoor van Levinas* (1992); *Een Kamer in de Wereld: Religieus Eclecticisme en de Theologie* (2000, inaugural lecture at Utrecht).

Peter Jonkers (1954) studied philosophy at the Catholic University of Louvain. His doctoral dissertation was on Hegel's philosophy (1982). Currently, he is professor of philosophy at the Catholic Theological University at Utrecht. He publishes on German Idealism, contemporary metaphysics, and philosophy of religion. His recent publications are: "Crying in the Desert? Speaking About God in Our Time" (2000); "The Importance of the Pantheism-Controversy for the Development of Hegel's Thinking" (2002); "Illusory Imagination versus Nihilistic Reason: A Historical-Philosophical Case Study of the Role of Imagination in Religion" (2003).

Joeri Schrijvers (1977) works as a Research Assistant of the Fund for Scientific Research — Flanders (Belgium) (FWO-Vlaanderen) in the Research Group "Theology in a Postmodern Context" (Faculty of Theology, Catholic University of Louvain). He is completing his dissertation at Louvain on the decentering of the (modern) subject in the so-called theological turn of French phenomenology.

Rico Sneller (1967) is assistant professor of moral philosophy at the Theological Faculty of Leiden University. His main topics of research include questions pertaining to the idea of an absolute Good (as opposed to contextualizing tendencies in contemporary moral philosophy), political theology, modernity's religious heritage, ethics and metaphysics, etc. His dissertation topic was on Derrida and his relationship to negative theology (1997). He also published a book on the idea of an absolute Good.

Chris Doude van Troostwijk (1962) studied theology and theatre studies at the universities of Utrecht, Amsterdam, and Leiden. He holds a PhD in philosophy from the University of Amsterdam (ASCA). He has taught philosophy at the

Faculty of Education in Theology and at the Faculty of Humanities at ASCA, and works as a philosopher and media-advisor for IANUA, philosophie et culture in Strasbourg. He co-translated *La Confession d'Augustin* into Dutch. Some of his recent publications are: *Trouvaille, Anamneses de la Critique* (Kant, Freud, Lyotard) (2002); *The Sixth Sense (philosophers and poets speaking on death / zesde zintuig. Denkers en dichters over de dood)* (2003); *Une Phrase de Rien* (2004).

Guido Vanheeswijck (1955) is currently full professor of philosophy at the University of Antwerp and part-time professor at the Catholic University of Louvain. His recent publications include: *Voorbij het Onbehagen* (2002); *The End of Metaphysics as a Transformation of Culture* (co-author) (2003).

Ruud Welten (1962) studied music at the Rotterdam Conservatory and philosophy at the Erasmus University at Rotterdam. He is lecturer of philosophy at the Catholic Theological University at Utrecht and lecturer of philosophy, aesthetics, and ethics at several Dutch universities. His field of research is contemporary phenomenology, with special attention to the phenomenology of religion. His doctoral dissertation treated the phenomenological structure of the religious prohibition of images (2001). His publications include two books on Levinas, and articles on Husserl, Jean-Luc Marion, Michel Henry, Merleau-Ponty and Sartre.

PRINTED ON PERMANENT PAPER • IMPRIME SUR PAPIER PERMANENT • GEDRUKT OP DUURZAAM PAPIER - ISO 9706

N.V. PEETERS S.A., WAROTSTRAAT 50, B-3020 HERENT